John B Eis

The Jesuits

A Eulogy of the Society of Jesus against Dr. Rev. Bennett

John B Eis

The Jesuits
A Eulogy of the Society of Jesus against Dr. Rev. Bennett

ISBN/EAN: 9783744659284

Printed in Europe, USA, Canada, Australia, Japan

Cover: Foto ©Lupo / pixelio.de

More available books at **www.hansebooks.com**

THE JESUITS:

A Eulogy of the Society of Jesus,

AGAINST

Rev. Dr. BENNETT,

PASTOR OF WESLEY CHAPEL, COLUMBUS, OHIO.

BY

REV. JOHN B. EIS,

RECTOR OF SACRED HEART CHURCH, COLUMBUS.

COLUMBUS, OHIO:
THE COLUMBIAN PRINTING COMPANY.
1889.

PREFACE.

The occasion of this lecture on "The Jesuits" was the following: Dr. Bennett, a minister of the Methodist Church, preaching in Wesley Chapel, Columbus, O., attacked the Rector of Sacred Heart Church, and stated in his little weekly, "Our Methodist Paper," that he wondered "to what depth the Romish Priest would descend next." Then he assaulted the memory of the hero-leper, Father Damien, of Molokai; next he delivered several lectures against the Catholic Church. His crowning effort was a violent outburst, entitled, "The Jesuits." In this essay he told his astonished audience, among a number of old calumnies, that the Society of Jesus had a hand in murdering President Lincoln.

After the crusade was over, the Rector of Sacred Heart Church announced that on the feast of St. Ignatius, the founder of the Order, he also would deliver a lecture on "The Jesuits." He viewed the subject from such a standpoint as to refute all the lectures of Dr. Bennett at one and the same time.

Still it was impossible to crowd into his refutation a correction of every error committed by the lecturer. One ludicrous mistake may be mentioned here, because it could not be touched in the defense of the Society of Jesus.

The Doctor heard somewhere, that there are but three main reasons for which the Catholic Church grants separations to married persons—commonly called divorces from bed and board. He procured some book on Catholic theology and discovered there, so he thought, eighteen such reasons. Then he triumphantly proclaimed his discovery to the Patriotic Sons of America in a public lecture. But unfortunately for him, although he is a Doctor of Divinity, he made a great blunder in mixing up the impediments to marriage with the reasons for divorce. There is an infinite distance between preventing an improper marriage from taking place and destroying a valid marriage after it has been consummated, which can never be done. Dr. Bennett's ideas about the Catholic religion are just as confounded as are those of the Devil in the book of Job on cursing, which he calls "blessing" in the following passage: "Stretch forth thy hand a little and touch all that he has and see if *he blesseth* thee not to thy face." (Job I, 11). But the Devil has this advantage over the Doctor, that he "who rules the realms below," like the Greek, calls evil things good, while the Doctor calls good things evil.

In one of his lectures Dr. Bennett claimed to be "internally moved"—by what spirit he did not say—to fight the Catholic Church. Now it is a question who that spirit was. If it was the Devil, this old liar must have changed his tactics of late and left his former traditions, because heretofore he used to disguise himself as an angel of light, but now he seems to descend to a depth which he never explored before.

In the opinion of the author of this lecture, Dr. Bennett is not worthy of any notice whatever. It is not to him that this reply to his slanderous talk is addressed. But the people who listened to him are worthy of great attention. They belong to the most refined elements of society in the Capital City of Ohio. The Catholics want to live in peace with them and enjoy their esteem.

LECTURE.

INTRODUCTION.

My Brethren:—You are gathered here this evening to hear a defense of one of the greatest orders of the Catholic Church. It is the Society of Jesus. The matter is of importance to the people of Sacred Heart congregation, for the Society of Jesus makes its influence felt in this place. Your Pastor was educated in a seminary of the Order; he acknowledges no theology but theirs, and teaches the same principles as they do. Here are the teachers in our schools; they instruct your children; they are imbued with the same principles as the Jesuits are. For they have their novitiate in a congregation presided over by members of the Order who teach and guide the Sisters in their spiritual life.

Now, if the principles which we teach and which you profess and according to which you act, are as evil as they are represented to be, my dear brethren, what is Sacred Heart congregation? It is a brood of vipers and no more. But "By their fruits ye shall know them," says our Divine Savior. You may look, but in vain, through the poor-houses and inspect the penitentiaries and prisons, you will not find a single one of these people who have professed and practiced the principles and teachings in question; they cannot be found there. You may go around within the limits of this congregation, but you will not find there the unprotected widow nor the forsaken orphan. Wherever the hand of these people can reach, there the widows and the fatherless are supported. If anything, my dear brethren, proves that principles are good, it must be the life which people, who profess them, lead; for "By their fruits ye shall know them." How would you fare, you, who are living outside of the Catholic Church, if we did profess those evil principles that are falsely imputed to the Jesuits, and if we acted according to them? For instance, if we acted according to the principle, as we are accused of doing to-day, that "the end justifies the means," what would become of you? How would your property fare? How would your lives fare? How would the peace and happiness of the whole community fare? Very badly indeed! For such are the principles of highwaymen and cut-throats, and you would find no worse enemies than the people who worship in this place. But you know well how peaceful they are; you know well how steadily and quietly they go to their work, and how little they trouble you. On the contrary, they assist you everywhere in all good undertakings.

PROPOSITION.

In order to understand the position of the Jesuits, I have to give you a short synopsis of church history. For the Society of Jesus occupies a providential place in history, and its influence has been beneficial in every direction. We believe that this great Order has been raised by God Almighty, by Divine Providence, as one of the greatest helps of civilization, for spreading the Christian religion and establishing the Catholic Church among all the nations.

I.

PROVIDENTIAL PLACE IN HISTORY.

The Church has two elements, one Divine, the other human. The Divine element can never be improved in itself; it was as perfect in the beginning as it will be at the end of days, as, for instance, the number and the nature of the Sacraments. There are seven of them and there never will be more nor less. But the human element in the Church is subject to development and change, as, for instance, the ceremonies of the Sacraments. Like a human being developing from year to year, from childhood to manhood and to hoary age, so the Church develops and grows more beautiful every day. When we were children, we were the same persons we now are, but we did not look then as we do now. If you take a photograph of yourself, made when you were young, and compare it with what you are at present, you do not recognize both as representing the same person, although you are the same person, having the same characteristics and the same individuality.

There are people who pretend that the Church should have no growth, no development. On the contrary, according to them, we ought to throw off all those human institutions which have arisen in the Church—Rites, Orders, Rosaries, Hoods and Cowls, and let the "wind blow them transverse ten thousand leagues awry." Then we should return to the simplicity of the days of the Apostles. This is just as impossible as for a lady to wear the dresses of her childhood, or for a man to wear the shoes which he wore when he was a boy. The Church has grown immensely from the small beginning which it had; it never can retrace its steps, but it can only advance. This doctrine is that of Christ when he compares his Church to a mustard-seed: "The kingdom of heaven is like to a grain of mustard-seed, which a man took and sowed in his field. Which indeed is the least of all seeds; but when it is grown up, it is greater than any herbs, and becometh a tree, so that the birds of the air come and dwell in the branches thereof." (St. Matt. XIII., 31, 32).

So much about the growth of the human element in the Church. Although its Divine element cannot be improved in itself, as stated before, still it can be brought forth to better advantage in our knowledge of Divine truth and its application to our moral life. Thus what is truth to-day has been truth from all beginning, but it may not have been always known or acknowledged as such. For instance, it is true that the Blessed Virgin Mary was preserved from original sin, but that truth was not always clearly understood, and it took time to show this doctrine in its proper light. In this sense the Divine element of the Church is also susceptible of development and growth.

This applies particularly to the marks of the Church. When Christ founded it, it had all the marks which it has to-day, and always will have, but they did not shine in such wonderful light as they now do. For instance, how could the Catholicity of the Church fully appear while it was still confined to Jerusalem and Palestine? We can follow the development of these marks of the Church in the pages of history. We see there how one after another received its due attention at the hand of Providence, and the Church of God was unmistakably stamped and sealed with them.

The mark of the Church which first of all had to be fully

established before the eyes of the world was its Apostolicity. It was to be shown above all other things, that the kingdom of Christ was not a Jewish concern ; that it was not built on Moses ; that it was not the continuation of the old law. It is a new institution, founded by Christ, and built on the Apostles. Unless this point was clearly understood from the start, the Church could not prosper—she could not make her appearance among the nations of the world and claim their attention.

St. Paul is the champion of the Apostolicity of the Church. In his epistles and in all his life as reported in the Acts of the Apostles, two ideas master all the rest : they are the distinction of the works of the old law from the faith of the new and the right of the Greek as well as of the Jew to belong to the Church of Christ. He knows no privileged class in the house of God. The crowning conclusion of this Apostolicity of the Church was the destruction of the temple of Jerusalem. Within eight months from this catastrophe of the downfall of Judaism, the main sanctuary of the gentile world, the temple of Jupiter on the Capitoline hill in Rome, also fell a smoking ruin. From that time it was to be known, to Jew and Gentile, that they had no longer separate places of worship: "For now you are no more strangers and foreigners, but you are fellow-citizens with the saints and the domestics of God: built upon the foundations of the Apostles and Prophets ; Jesus Christ being the chief corner-stone : in whom all the building framed together groweth into a holy temple in the Lord : in whom you also are built together into a habitation of God in the Spirit." (St. Paul, Eph. ch. II., 19, 20, 21, 22).

The second mark of the Church, my brethren, which had

to be developed historically, was the Holiness of the Church.

This Holiness implies that the Church is not a kingdom of this world, but of a higher one; a realm of truth and virtue, whose aim, and whose means to obtain that aim, and the life of whose subjects, are of a higher order than the common life of nations. They are supernatural.

In the kingdoms of this world they build streets, they conduct wars, they protect life and property, they promote trade, they accumulate wealth; they do all those things which belong to the material existence of man. But above this there is a higher region, a broader and grander field, a field of truth and a field of virtue. This realm of truth and virtue is that of Christ. "My kingdom," says He, "is not of this world." It is not like that of the Babylonians or the Greeks; it is not like yours, the Roman Empire; my reign penetrates into regions whither yours cannot enter whither yours cannot reach; my kingdom is a holy one: its aim is in heaven. Nor is it by flesh and blood that this kingdom shall be conquered: the lives of its members are different from the daily life of this world; it is a life of purity, it is a life of humility, it is a life of charity. Such is the Holiness of the Church. It establishes the fact that between the kingdom of Christ and the governments of this world, there is no cause for strife, but that they can live in perfect harmony and peace together, each having its own sphere of action, distinct from the other.

The legion of martyrs showed that this earth is not our home. We, with them, give up willingly everything, property, friends and life itself, in order to gain an everlasting dwelling in the house of the Father in heaven.

The means to gain that home were shown to be supernatural beyond a doubt by the Doctors of the Church, particularly by St. Augustine, who demonstrated, against the heretics of his time, the absolute necessity of Divine grace to perform the acts of Christian virtue.

Then came that host of Holy Hermits who turned to the solitude of the desert, and, in cloisters, lead a life of self-denial and mortification ; a life which people of this world would despise, and would call those who practice it "fools," while the Lord calls them "blessed." "Blessed are the poor in spirit, for theirs is the kingdom of heaven." (St. Matt., ch. V., 8).

When the world was fully convinced of the supernatural character of the Church, it was time to show that the kingdom of Christ was One. It shall not be divided among the Greeks and the Romans, among the French and the Germans, among the English and the Americans, but there shall be One shepherd and One fold over the whole earth, having only One head—Peter and his successors, the Popes of Rome. "Thou art Peter and upon this rock I will build my church and the gates of hell shall not prevail against it." That is the text.

Therefore Divine Providence raised the Papacy in the middle ages to the exalted position which, as every body knows, it then occupied. "They shall," so says the Prophet about the kings and queens, " worship thee with their faces towards the earth, and they shall lick up the dust of thy feet." (Is. XLIX., 23).

It was not without contest that the Popes occupied this position above the princes of this world. In Constantinople they found their antagonists. The patriarchs of that imperial city aspired to the same height ; they dared to call themselves ecumenical patriarchs. The German emperors, in their fight against the papal power, raised anti-pope after anti-pope against the lawful Popes ; the French king, Philip the Fair, tried to create a French Pope on French soil.

All these endeavors had but one principal aim, namely, to split the Church and thereby destroy its Unity. At one time, indeed, after the disastrous period of the residence of the Popes in Avignon, a more perilous one followed, and it seemed that the Church was torn to pieces, while two and even three popes ruled it at once. Then a new and fiercer enemy than kings and emperors had proved to be at times, arose against the Unity of the Church. It was the clerical democracy at the council of Basle, which tried to reduce the Pope to the inferior position of a president of a republic, having nothing else to do but to nominate candidates for offices and sign the decrees of a council declared in permanancy, like the congress of a republican state. The Church had never seen more dangerous times than those ; its whole organization as framed by Christ, was to be changed from a monarchy as it is, into a republic with a thousand heads.

But the Church came out victorious as it always does ; its final victory for its Unity being won at the council of Florence during the rule of Pope Eugene IV. Then the union between the East and the West was established, the clerical democracy was destroyed, and since that time the Church has never seen two Popes ruling Christendom at once. Never since has an attempt been made to split it. Thus there is one Shepherd and one fold, as there is but "one body and one spirit, as you are called in one hope of your vocation, one Lord, one faith, one baptism, one God and

Father of all, who is above all, and through all, and in us all." (St. Paul Ephes. IV., 4, 5, 6).

Now, my dear brethren, we arrive at the time of the Jesuits. We come to the last and most conspicuous mark or character of the Church; that is its Catholicity, its character of universality. From it the Church draws its name, although Apostolic, Holy and One, it is pre-eminently Catholic, and therefore friend and enemy call it by that name. It was the Catholicity of the Lord's doctrine which was so distasteful to the Pharisees and provoked their hatred to such an extent that they delivered Him up to be crucified. For according to Him, His kingdom was to be not for the Jews alone, but for the Greeks and the Romans as well. It is a kingdom for all the nations of the earth. It shall spread from the rising of the sun to the going down thereof. There shall be no hill and there shall be no valley where the praises of God, through Catholic tongues, shall not ring. "Ask of me, and I will give thee the gentiles for thy inheritance and the utmost parts of the earth for thy possession." (Ps. II., 8). So sang the holy king David of the future reign of Christ. Here the Church stands ready in battle array for the conquest of all nations; she will shrink from no danger or hardship, when called to plant the glorious cross on every shore; her sons are as brave as they were at the time of the martyrs. No power on earth will rout her armies, yea, all hell aroused will see its black battalions "Sent howling to the realms of night."

Moreover, the Gospel is not only to be carried to all nations, it is also to be shown that the doctrine of the Church and the practice of Christian virtues are within the reach of all men.

But where are those nations, that we may carry to them the beautiful message of their redemption? Oh, they are hidden in the wild fastnesses of Africa; they revel in blood and slaughter to propitiate their fetiches; they are in far off India and China; they indulge in all the orgies of lust to please their demons; they are hunting one another on the boundless plains of America; they are feasting on human gore on the islands of the ocean. The Church is ready to extend its rule of peace and charity to them, and "all nations shall flow unto it. And many people shall go and say: come and let us go up to the mountain of the Lord and to the house of the God of Jacob and He will teach us His ways, and we will walk in His paths: for the law shall come forth from Sion and the word of the Lord from Jerusalem. And He shall judge the Gentiles and rebuke many people: and they shall turn their swords into ploughshares and their spears into sickles: nation shall not lift up the sword against nation, neither shall they be exercised any more to war." (Isaiah II., 2, 3, 4).

This is the work in which we are engaged to-day and for nearly four hundred years. Therefore we are here, and therefore we penetrate into every country; therefore our missionaries march forth and die to establish the Church among all the nations in every clime and in every zone.

The time did come, my brethren, when it was necessary even to widen the limits of the earth, as the Prophet had foretold. No priest had ever come to America before. New ways had to be opened and they were opened. Columbus discovered America and Vasco de Gama doubled the Cape of Good Hope and found a new route to India and Eastern Asia. In their tracks the Catholic Church had to follow and convert those distant nations. Who could do that best? Who could best be the standard-bearer in the conquering march of the Church around the globe? Who but an order of military discipline and of universal character—a society which is as Catholic as the Church itself? Such an order is the Society of Jesus. Here they are raised by Divine Providence to fight the battles of the Lord of hosts, and they did it, and they do it bravely still.

There was in those days one great empire of which the ruler said that the sun never set within its limits. It was the empire of Charles V. In his dominions the man was raised who founded the Company of Jesus. St. Ignatius Loyola, whose feast we celebrate to-day, was born and bred a soldier. At the siege of Pampeluna, in Spain, against the French, he was wounded. While in the hospital he picks up the "Lives of the Saints" and reads them. He comes to the conclusion, that as those heroes did, he also can do; he can practice the same mortification; he can go to the same labors and humiliation which distinguished their lives. He takes his sword and armor to the Church of the Blessed Virgin and hangs them up there on the altar. Then he retires to Manresa to do penance for his sins and to prepare for a better life. Although a grown-up man, tried on many a battle-field, he goes to school again to learn the elements of Latin. At Paris he meets with St. Francis Xavier and a few other noble hearts. In the Church of the Blessed Virgin, on Mont-Martre, they begin the Society of Jesus. In Rome their undertaking is sanctioned by the Pope.

The constitution of the Order is framed in such a manner that it fits all countries and nations of the world. It does not draw any limit to the activity of the members in the field of Christian life; it includes the whole range of charitable and educational works practiced in the Church. *This character of universality distinguishes this Order above all others, and makes the Jesuits the fit soldiers of the Catholicity of the Church. This is what they are: that is the mission entrusted to them by Providence in the history of the world.* You can view history from many a standpoint; you can see men and things in it in a hundred different lights and shades, but the great outlines of the development of the Church are clearly drawn, and this call of the Society of Jesus is one of the most conspicuous landmarks in the kingdom of Christ.

II.
THEIR MISSIONS.

The first great enterprise of the new Order was to go out as missionaries. St. Ignatius used sometimes to sit in his room with a map of the world spread out before him, and with heaving breast and eyes dimmed with tears, he would sigh because he had not missionaries enough to send to every tribe and people. Only one year after the rules of the Society were approved, St. Francis Xavier was sent to India. You would seek in vain through all history another man to compare with him as an Apostle of heathen nations. Even St. Paul dwindles down in his enterprises when compared with this man. Sometimes St. Francis baptized so many people that in the evening he was so exhausted that he could not raise his arm. He traversed India, he went to Japan, and finally he expired on the coast of China, when God called him to his reward. What glories the Asiatic Church has in those regions, it owes mainly to St. Francis

Xavier. In his steps other members of the Order followed. They preached the gospel with such success that when the persecutions broke out, the number of martyrs was so great, particularly in Japan, that even the persecutions of Nero and Diocletian in Rome in no way gave to the world a grander spectacle of Christian heroism than those half-civilized nations did.

In China the Jesuits were so far advanced in the conversion of the people that the Christian religion was declared by an imperial decree to be a holy law. The Jesuits were admitted as welcome guests among all classes, even the highest, and the imperial palace was not closed against them. A few members of the Society were even numbered among the first and most learned mandarins of the country.

Next they came to America. They did not come here first. The Franciscans and Dominicans preceded them on this continent, for the simple reason that the Order of the Jesuits did not exist when America was discovered. It was about fifty years later that they were formed, but as quickly as they sprang up they were foremost in the missions of America. Who has not admired the life of Blessed Peter Claver, the Apostle of the negro slaves in Carthagena? Nobody can humble himself more than this devoted Saint of the Society of Jesus did among the unfortunate victims of the slave trade.

The missions of Paraguay have ever since their existence deserved the admiration of the whole world. There savages were formed into a nation devoted to the works of peace and piety. No white man, thirsting for gold and bent on the oppression of the poor Indian, was allowed in that theocratic state. Only the beloved Blackrobe ruled those children of nature, and taught them to be self supporting, law-abiding, honest and honorable members of the community. As in the mythology of old, it is reported of Orpheus, that he tamed the fiercest lions with the sweet sounds of his lyre, so the Jesuits subdued the wild cannibals with music and song. They sang their morning and evening prayer; when gliding down the silent rivers in their canoes, they made the lonely banks resound with the harmony of their instruments and voices; at their work in the fields every rock and rill rang with the sweetness of their canticles. And lo! the Indian comes subdued and charmed. He lets spear and tomahawk fall and gives himself up to these masters, who know so well the art of ruling human hearts.

All things were governed according to the Christian religion until the Order was broken up by Pope Clement XIV. Then the missions perished, and the people have lived in misery since that day. It was like a wintry blast over a flowery field in May. To-day, after all their late disastrous wars, the population is decimated to such an extent, that there are twenty women to one man in Paraguay.

In North America, my dear brethren, who were the pioneers that opened the western countries? Who are those who left their names around the lakes? Was it not Marquette and his associates? They were Jesuits. Who discovered the Mississippi and followed its downward course? Were they not also Jesuits? Who penetrated into the Rocky Mountains and are there still to-day, the pioneers of Christian life? The Jesuits. They are found in every region. They were here before your fathers; they have a sacred right to remain and to be honored in a country where their brethren long ago planted the standard of our faith and died martyrs for the sake of Christian civilization. Who dare tell you that they are aliens here? They were received into the Indian tribes hundreds of years ago; they were adopted by the nations of this country before the white settlers had explored its recesses and laid its primeval forests low. The genuine Americans, the Indians, even yet consider you all and every white face in the land as aliens and intruders, except the Catholic priest; he alone of all white men has the freedom of the plains and mountains; he alone can go unhurt over hill and dale, and is welcome in every Indian wigwam. Whereas, if you should dare to show yourselves among the western tribes, you would not be sure of your scalps.

At present the hardest field of missionary life is in Africa. The Jesuits are on the Zambeze River. The mission was tried first by the Trappist Fathers, but they failed. Then the Society of Jesus undertook the task. Its history is a doleful tale of woes. Sixteen, they went a few years ago, but now little mounds, raised over them by friendly hands of negro converts, mark their lonely graves. One of them was lost in the wilderness, and for forty-eight nights slept in trees in order to escape the roving lion. When forty-eight nights were over, he concluded that, lion or not, he would not climb up those trees any more, but would sleep in the jungle below. When he reached at last the mission of the Fathers, he became hopelessly insane and died. Perhaps you fancy that they have given the mission up? Oh, no; they are there again! Taught by the experience of the past, they follow other methods. Whether or not they will succeed, time will tell; but if the Society of Jesus fails there, nobody else need try it again. They will not fail.

I have unrolled before your eyes a truthful picture of the missionary life of the Company of Jesus in many countries, but I have not shown you yet the fiercest battle they have fought and won under the Standard of Christ. The greatest field of missionary life which the Jesuits have ever had, they found in Germany. That was at the time of Luther. We believe that Divine Providence raised St. Ignatius to oppose Luther, as Charles Martel was chosen to crush the Mohammedan hosts on the plains of Poitiers. While in other countries of Europe the Jesuits acted as teachers, confessors and chaplains, in every spiritual and corporal work of mercy, they had to confront the new heresies in Germany. One day St. Ignatius said that he would rather sell himself into slavery than forget and desert the German nation in their gigantic struggle for their Catholic faith. His brave sons saved half that people to the Church. Through this historic fact the Jesuits have exerted the deepest influence upon modern society. They changed the face of the world by making Germany the battle-ground of modern thought. This is a point which I want to explain to you in detail.

There was a time when our fathers stalked around in iron armor, and then their greatest glory was to cleave an infidel in twain from head to foot. When they began to quarrel among themselves about religion, they applied the same sort of argument to one another. Whoever were in the minority had to bleed or to fly. In England, as soon as the Protestants were in the majority, they began to kill the Catholics; they set the same price on the head of a priest as on that of a wolf. In France, the Catholic majority slaughtered the turbulent Huguenots in the night of St.

Bartholomew or banished them by the Edict of Nantes. But in Germany, if that policy had been pursued, the whole nation would have been destroyed, as the people were about equally divided. Therefore, the German nation became the one which had to work out religious tolerance, which is the religious system of modern times. They had to live together; they had to work out rules by which neighbor and neighbor could live in peace and harmony together, whether Protestant or Catholic. They had to find means and ways to abide in the same city, under the same roof, to meet together, to be members of the same city council, to fight in war side by side for the same cause in spite of their religious dissensions. They formed the system of religious toleration, and, my dear brethren, what they fought out, we need not fight over again. It cost the lives of millions of people to come to the conclusions which they arrived at. Before the Thirty Years' War, Germany was the most prosperous and populous country of Europe; the population amounted to 45,000,000. When the war was over, the country was turned into a desert, and only 5,000,000 of its inhabitants survived. Then they became convinced that they had to keep peace together, and that, if they did not, there would not be a single one of them left.

Now, religious toleration is spreading all over the world. It cannot be otherwise. Mankind is fast mixing up in every country; our own land being the type of all for the future. Here we are now living together, Protestants, Catholics, Jews, Indians, Chinese, Negroes; we are from every country of the world. Shall we kill one another? Shall we oppress our neighbors because they do not believe as we do? Shall we destroy them with fire and sword? He would be a traitor who should kindle such feelings among this people. Let your heels stamp on these fanatics and crush them out from all places of influence and authority.

The religious toleration followed by the Catholic Church is as follows : When we go out to Asia, we plant our church by the side of the heathens' temple, whether their god be Brahma or Allah, with Mohammed for his prophet, what is the difference to us? We preach to them the God of Calvary until grass shall grow on the threshold of their mosque and its minarets and dome fall in ; until the screeching owl shall make its habitation there, and "even its crumbling ruins are no more." We have to convince that people, by words of peace and by deeds of charity, that their religion is not good, but that ours is. Therefore we are inclined to peace ; we seek no trouble. Why should they?

Let us all now act here on the principle proclaimed by Gamaliel in the Jewish council: " And now, therefore, I say to you, refrain from these men, and let them alone, for if this design or work be of men, it will fall to nothing ; but if it be of God, you are not able to destroy it." (Act. Ap. V., 38, 39).

III.
THE THEOLOGY OF THE JESUITS.

Now, my brethren, let us view the Jesuits as theologians. When their Order arose, there were many questions, particularly concerning the Holy Scriptures, the Church and Justification, which were not clear then, and indeed they are not all clear yet. Such questions are mainly elucidated and authoritatively defined on account of the opposition of heretics against the truth. In former ages, as a rule, one truth was sifted at one time. Thus, Arius questioned the Divinity of the Son of God, Macedonius, the Divinity of the Holy Ghost, Nestorius, the Incarnation. When Luther arose, a general fire was opened against the Christian religion along the whole line. By his declaration of private judgment as the rule of faith, he opened the flood-gates of all heresies at once. Doctrines which had been overcome and considered as buried forever long before, were revived, and, indeed, there is scarcely a religious system which has not since then been palmed off as the religion of Christ. Even the Salvation Army claims that it forms the kingdom of God.

The modern heresies, therefore, and the fight of the Church against them, imprint on our time the mark of universality, as well as the opening of a new world through Christopher Columbus did in its own way.

There were, first, the Holy Scriptures and Divine Revelation itself. The enemies of the Church charge that we hide the Bible from the people. In reading their statements one would suppose that the popes and bishops and priests had conspired to either monopolize the Scriptures or to treat them as the Jews treated them in the time of Josias, the King: "When they carried out the money that had been brought into the temple of the Lord, Helcias, the priest, found the book of the law of the Lord by the hand of Moses." (II. Par., c. 34, 14).

But you have only to read the works of St. Bernard or the writings of St. Thomas to see what a wonderful knowledge of the Holy Scriptures those Doctors of the Church possessed in the Middle Ages. One feels indeed humbled, overpowered, when comparing one's knowledge with theirs.

Nor is it true to say that the Church as a teaching body has monopolized the Holy Scriptures, keeping them out of the hands of the people. You must not forget that the inventors of the art of printing were laymen and Catholics, and that the first book which they printed was the Bible. There were more than twenty different translations of this book made into the German language alone, before the time of Luther. This ought to be sufficient to show that the accusations of the enemies of the Church against the Catholic clergy are utterly false on this point.

One day, at Nuremberg, a number of Jesuits and their antagonists from the camp of Luther met together to discuss the question of revelation as laid down in Holy Writ. Everything went on quite well until all of a sudden the question was proposed to the Jesuits whether or not it was a revealed truth and therefore an article of faith, that, as is reported in the book of Tobias: "The dog which had been with them in the way, ran before and coming as if he had brought the news, showed his joy by his fawning and wagging his tail." (Tob. XI. 9). Did the dog wag his tail, or did he not?

It was a deep and momentous question. It broke up the conference without result, and opened a controversy which lasted two hundred years. It took the highest authority of the Church to settle the dispute. In itself it seems to be the most trifling sentence of the Scriptures, but Divine Providence allowed it to become a starting point of a beautiful development of doctrine in order to show that nothing is trifling in the Word of God.

The first result was to distinguish between an inspired truth and a revealed truth. It is an inspired truth that the dog wagged his tail. But it is not a revealed truth: it is an historical fact. Are historical facts related in the Holy Scripture articles of faith? Is it an article of faith that Alexander the Great went to Jerusalem? Is it an article of faith that God created Adam and Eve in the manner related in Genesis, or that the deluge took place as described by Moses? Or must we confine Divine inspiration to simply moral and dogmatic sentences?

Two parties were formed at the beginning of the controversy; one party never got over the tail of the dog, and their researches ended in infidelity. They reject the Holy Scripture, regarding it as a book of fables. They have invented a new gospel, of which a main article is that they descend from monkeys and that their ancestors wore tails themselves.

The other party kept up the doctrine of ancient times that the Holy Scripture is really and substantially the Word of God; that each and every sentence of it is inspired by the Holy Ghost, whether relating to moral, dogmatic or historical matter. This is the doctrine of the Catholic Church to-day, as it has been from the beginning, with the great difference that we are more conscious of this truth than our fathers were.

For the Church the controversy had other results. The inquiry was not stopped there. It involved the authority of the Church in defining dogmatic facts, so long and so bitterly controverted by the Jansenists. It led finally to the question whether the Church can declare, authoritatively, which is the actual meaning of a sentence, not as it sounds, but the meaning given it by its author, not only in the Scripture but also in books written about religion at present. Thus it helped to define in its last distinctive lines the authority of the Church in explaining revelation and in teaching faith. In the great controversy between the Jesuits and the Jansenists, which concluded this contest, the doctrine of the former remained the standard doctrine of the Church. This doctrine is that the members of the Church have to abide by her decisions, not only with signs of outward obedience and obsequious silence, but with interior and full adhesion of mind and heart, without reserve or subterfuge, to all her teaching.

The settlement of this point is one of the greatest achievements in theology, and if the skill and persistence in treating the question be considered and compared with those of theologians of times gone by, the noble sons of St. Ignatius deserve a crown with St. Athanasius and St. Augustine.

But in whom does this authority of the Church reside? It was for a long time considered an incontestable fact that this authority resided in a general council of the Church.

Can it be found somewhere else? Luther taught that private authority was sufficient to explain the Scripture, that therefore every Christian—himself included—had spirit enough to become a fully authorized teacher of faith for others, or to explain the Scriptures satisfactorily for himself. He consequently had to place the rule of faith outside of the living organization of the Church; he proclaimed the Bible a rule of faith. The Bible and nothing but the Bible—that is, their interpretation of it, had authority with him and his followers. Now, is it true that the Bible, although it has a Divine character, is the rule of faith? The Catholic Church says: No; it is not the rule, but only a source of faith.

A stone quarry is the source of the material out of which you erect your buildings, but the quarry is no rule for the buildings themselves. The same material may be used for a house or a stable. The rule for the building will be the architect's plan.

It may not be amiss to quote a passage from St. Irenaeus. In relation to this matter he says: "For how should it be, if the Apostles themselves had left us no writings? . . . Many nations of those barbarians, who believe in Christ, do assent, having salvation written in their heart by the Spirit without paper or ink. . . . Those who, in the absence of written documents, have believed this faith, are barbarians as far as our language is concerned; but as regards doctrine, manner and tenor of life, they are, because of faith, very wise indeed; and they do please God, ordering their salvation in all righteousness, chastity and wisdom. If any one were to preach to these men the inventions of the heretics, speaking to them in their own language, they would at once stop their ears and flee as far as possible." (St. Irenaeus, c. Haer. lib. III., cap. IV).

How the heretics, following their own private judgment, treat the *"written documents,"* is described by the same Father in the following beautiful manner: "They disregard the order and connection of the Scriptures and so far as in them lies, dismember and destroy the truth. By transferring passages and dressing them up anew and making one thing out of another, they succeed in deluding many through their wicked art in adapting the Oracles of the Lord to their opinions. Their manner of acting is just as if one, when a beautiful image of a king has been constructed by a skilled artist out of precious jewels, should then take this likeness of the man all to pieces, should rearrange the gems and so fit them together as to make them into the form of a dog or a fox, and even that but poorly executed, and should then maintain and declare that *this* was that beautiful image of the king." (St. Iren. contra Haer. libr. I. cap. VIII).

This shows evidently that we Catholics have not changed our doctrine concerning the nature and authority of the Scriptures since the days of the Apostles, for St. Irenaeus was in almost immediate contact with them, as he states himself throughout his writings.

If you go among the Catholic people, you find the Bible in nearly every house. But they know they have no authority to explain the book. This authority must remain in the hands of the Church, considered as a teaching body. This doctrine of Church authority is the main difference between the Catholic Church and dissenting organizations to-day. If we could make them yield on this point there would quickly follow a conversion to the Church of all but the infidel members of civilized society. But, alas, they are far from seeing the truth.

Nobody has worked more assiduously and faithfully in developing the doctrine of Church authority than the Jesuits. It is their special task in theology to do so. It is particularly to them that the Church owes the definition of the infallibility of the Pope in matters of faith and morals. This definition is the full and final development of the teaching power of the Church. It is not asking much of anybody to believe this doctrine. It first makes every priest and bishop fallible in his own utterances; none of them will ever dare press his special views on anybody else. In the second place, it reserves all final decisions to the best-informed man in the world, for whom special Divine protection and light are claimed, when he is speaking to all Christendom at once, as its head, on the most important matters concerning human existence. How often will he exercise this office? Perhaps not once in a lifetime.

There are ten thousand little popes outside of the Catholic Church who claim the same privilege every Sunday in the year, and you dare not contradict them either, else they will ask you "to what depth you shall descend next?"

These two questions: the inspiration of the Scriptures and the authority to explain them, are settled.

There is another question which is not yet defined. That is, the accord of Revelation and Nature. For us Catholics it is implicitly settled, as all truth is: The accord exists, whatever the discoveries in nature may be; if they seemingly contradict the Bible, it is simply because we either do not yet fully understand the book, or science has to reform its teachings. There must be harmony between the two;

it is not the Holy Scripture, it is not revelation that has to be reformed, but our knowledge of either nature or revelation.

There is a deep discrepancy between the two, as taught by many teachers. Scientists, so-called, have cast their eyes into the depth of heaven and even down into the bowels of the earth, and have discovered things which have baffled their efforts at explanation. Some of them have cast aside all revelation and have gone their own way. They are coming back now and approach us again. Here is the question of the day, who will solve it?

That there is still work left in this field, is an incontestable truth, for nobody has yet given a satisfactory explanation of the deluge. What has been said about it, has been either abortive attempts to justify the Scriptures or impious infidelity.

The Jesuits, of all Catholic priests, have the best opportunity of doing it. They are engaged in the work already. They are among the learned of the priests; they have so many schools and colleges, and teach all sciences themselves. By their colleges the Jesuits are better able to confront all difficulties than other priests are. They have done a good deal already; no difficulty escapes their scrutinizing eye, and there is no science which will succeed in shaking the authority of the Holy Book.

It is a special merit of the Jesuits to have harmonized religion in itself. This harmony of religion is like that of music; it is not the single tone any longer, it is not the practice of the scale, but the sounds are swelling in heavenly chords of harmony, and no discordant note is found.

Now it remains to bring about the same full harmony

between Nature and Revelation. This harmony exists: only strike the key-note and you have it; whoever will solve the question—not to our satisfaction only but also to the satisfaction of the world at large—will immortalize himself for all ages to come.

IV.
THE MORALS OF THE JESUITS.

But nowhere, my dear brethren, have the Jesuits been attacked more than in their moral theology. They are represented as teaching the lawfulness of lying and the horrible doctrine that the end justifies the means. They did not authorize me to make a proposal, but I do it in their name, however. I offer one thousand dollars to any man who is able to find any book written by the Jesuits, or approved by them, or used by them, which contains those doctrines. If there is one among you, or if there is any one outside, who wants to gain that money, I promise it to him in the name of the Jesuits if he can show that they are guilty of this charge. I know that they will not refuse the reward, for it cannot be earned. The accusation is a falsehood.

There is nobody in this whole wide world able to find a book written by a Jesuit or used by the Jesuits in which those doctrines are found. But let me tell you what they do teach: They teach human liberty. That is the point which they have developed most of all. If there is any credit to be given to the Jesuits, as far as moral theology is concerned, that is the one.

Luther taught that original sin is concupiscence itself. If that is the case, he knew well, and you know, that concupiscence is in you after you are baptized. Then we are not justified internally. If original sin is concupiscence, which surely remains after baptism, then justification does not consist in the forgiveness of sins and the restoration through divine grace, but simply in the justice of Christ, thrown about us like a cloak.

Such is the doctrine of Luther. From that conclusion he had to go further. If we are not justified after baptism, except by the justice of Christ thrown about us, we have to come to the conclusion that man is totally depraved. That doctrine of total depravity is the distinctive doctrine of Luther, and it became the starting point of his moral teachings. If man is totally depraved, he has no free will to do right. Luther wrote a book on the slavish will of man (*De Servo Arbitrio*), in which he denied human liberty. Denying human liberty, he had to go further, for, if we are not free to do what we choose, if we are compelled either to do what is wrong or what is right, whether our act is good or bad in itself, it is of no moral value in the sight of God. Luther had to come to the conclusion that good works are not necessary for salvation, and he did. But, my brethren, is not that a horrible doctrine? If it were true, heaven would be peopled with the depraved. It would be a den of thieves and liars and adulterers and murderers, in whom the Most-High would delight, because, regardless of their crimes, he would see them wrapped up in the garb of his beloved son! Think of all the hypocrites on earth! Such a loathsome creation as Luther describes, reminds one of the god of Marcion, who, as Tertullian says, could not even make a cabbage.

If good works are not necessary for salvation, why do you

do them? If you can go to heaven as well by stealing and ruining your neighbor, as by doing acts of kindness and deeds of charity, why should you do those works of charity? If you can go to heaven as well by robbing your brother as by helping the widows and orphans, why should you not do it? These are the consequences of the doctrines which Luther taught, and you cannot get away from them. You have to admit, if you only know the first doctrines of the Christian religion, that good works are necessary for salvation, that there is not a single one of you who will enter heaven if you do not go there with your hands full of works of charity. You must never forget those words of Christ, when he divides men into two great families; where he calls one the "blessed of his father," and why? Because "I was naked and ye covered me; I was hungry and you gave me to eat. I was thirsty and you gave me to drink." But to the others he says: "Depart from me, ye cursed, into everlasting fire." Why? Because they did not do those works of charity. There is no question of murder, or theft, or adultery, but the whole judgment turns upon good works. Did you do them or did you not? If you did not, you are lost forever. That is the Catholic doctrine, and that is the doctrine of every human heart.

The Jesuits examined the question of the fall of man thoroughly, and they came to the conclusion that, although man is fallen, obscured in his intellect and weakened in his will, still he is not that depraved being in whom there is no good, except the cloak of righteousness thrown about him by the Lord. His faculties are impaired, but not to such an extent that he cannot, on natural ground, and by natural means, produce natural virtues of any kind, even the most beautiful. In this point the Jesuits have placed moral teaching in accord with nature ; for your heart tells you that there are many noble thoughts in you and in others which spring from nature and not from faith.

My dear brethren, if you want to learn whether that doctrine of total depravity is right or wrong, read Homer ; he surely stood on natural ground; he surely was not enlightened by the Gospel. How beautiful is the human heart in his description! How noble the virtues of the good! What tender feelings do you find there! How the mother loves her children, and how the children love their parents ; how the stranger is protected, and "sacred misery" is the care of God and men!

Listen to the words of Anticlea, speaking to Ulysses, her son, and admire the love of a mother's heart:

> "For thee, my son, I wept my life away;
> For thee through hell's eternal dungeons stray:
> Nor came my fate through lingering pains and slow;
> Nor bent the silver-shafted queen her bow;
> No dire disease bereaved me of my breath;
> Thou, thou, my son, wert my disease and death;
> Unkindly with my love my son conspired
> For thee I lived, for absent thee expired."
> —*Hom. Od. Book XI.*

Hear now the tender words of the noble wife to her husband :

> "Yet while my Hector still survives, I see
> My father, mother, brethren, kindred, all in thee:
> Alas! My parents, brothers, kindred, all
> Once more will perish if my Hector fall,
> Thy wife, thy infant in thy danger share;
> Oh, prove a husband's and a father's care."
> —*Hom. Il. Book VI.*

Are these the feelings inspired by total depravity?

If you want to find out whether or not it is in accord with nature to teach that man is totally depraved, read that book, and I assure you that you will not be half through it before you will come to the conclusion that man is not fallen so low. His heart is noble still, not only through the grace of God but also by reason of his nature. That is the conclusion the Jesuits have drawn, and nobody has taught that doctrine more beautifully than they have.

In order to do this they had to establish human liberty beyond a doubt. They had to defend it against the Jansenists; against those who teach the doctrine of physical premotion, and against a host of other enemies of every description. If one reads their books on morals he is struck by one thing, their keenness of reasoning in weighing and defining moral acts. One would almost believe they were describing a bargain between the creature and his Maker, and a close bargain, too. Why will you blame them for it? Is it not right to teach where the line between good and evil is, to the breadth of a hair? And also where the limit between strict obligation and a higher life of perfection is? Why should they not point out as sharply as the edge of a sword what in justice you can claim but what in charity you may overlook? In investigating human liberty under every conceivable point of view the Jesuits are better fitted to enter into contact with the modern world than those sour-faced moralists who, like the Pharisees of old, make a beam of a mote and an elephant of a fly. This world of ours is dozing away in a dream of liberty; why do you not fall around the necks of the Jesuits and weep there for joy? They are the friends of liberty, but of a liberty which truly makes you free.

Oh yes, you say, but this calculation of human liberty kills those emotions in which you hear the spirit whisper.

Emotions which make your heart enlarge and your eyeballs grow until you see the glimmering lights of heavenly vision! Well, if it kills them, what of it? There will be that much less fanaticism in the world.

But it would be a mistake to believe that these close calculators are not capable of higher acts of devotion. They teach the highest morality of Christian perfection. There is no order in the Church which has been more devoted to Almighty God than they. As a proof of this I will call your attention only to the devotion of the Sacred Heart of Jesus. They are the ones who have established it in the world.

Do you know what the devotion of the Sacred Heart of Jesus means? As through their doctrine concerning human liberty, the Jesuits make religion a universal interest of all mankind—not of the favored few whom God may have picked out from among the mass, and for whom alone Christ died, as the Jansenists taught—so by the devotion to the Sacred Heart they tone down the dreadful gloom of Calvary, give it a rosy hue, and thereby invite not only heroes but also the lowly to practice the lessons which the Savior has given there. The feast of the Sacred Heart is Good Friday in joyful colors. It is a call addressed to all to come and practice Christian humility and Christian charity; it is a translation into practical life of the doctrine of Christ, published in his sermon on the mount, where he says: "If any man strike thee on the right cheek, turn to him the other also; if any man will go to law with thee and take away thy coat, let him take thy cloak also. . . . Love your enemies: do good to them that hate you and pray for them that persecute and calumniate you." (St. Matt. c. V., 39, 40 and 44).

Such is the devotion of the Sacred Heart. It is the highest type of the Christian law, the practice of the deepest humility and the purest charity.

The Jesuits do not limit their influence upon the morality of the people to their teachings, they also promote piety by showing how to practice these doctrines. They are indefatigable in giving spiritual retreats and missions, during which time old sinners are converted and devout persons confirmed in their righteousness. Nor are they satisfied to appear in the midst of the population, to go again and leave the good seed of their preaching develop itself as best it can; but they organize pious sodalities of the Blessed Virgin wherever it is possible. These sodalities, in which we gather the best elements of our people to make them a shining light to the rest of the congregation, are under the general direction of the Society of Jesus now, as they have been a creation of that Order from the beginning. They are a special feature of the Church to-day, as the guilds were in former times. It is incalculable what a tremendous influence the Jesuits wield in the Christian world through these organizations. But it is an influence exclusively of peace and brotherly love.

The Jesuits practice themselves what they teach others. By their fruits they asked to be judged. On the battlefield, in the hospital, at the bedside of the plague-stricken, in the virgin forests of the new world, in the jungles of Africa, in every country, at every work of charity, at every spiritual and corporal work of mercy, the Jesuits are found.

Look at their galaxy of saints! They have distinguished

themselves by every Christian virtue. Who was purer among common mortals than St. Aloysius, who never looked at the face of a woman? Who was more obedient than St. Francis Xavier, who wrote in a kneeling posture all his letters to St. Ignatius, while he was thousands of miles away from him? Who was more charitable than Blessed Peter Claver, who made himself a slave with slaves, in order to save their souls? Who was more courageous than the martyrs of the Jesuits? And what an army of them! Martyrs of charity and martyrs of the faith of Christ. In the sixteenth century, while the plague was ravaging the country of the Rhine, no less than one hundred and thirty-five Jesuits died of the pestilence inside of a few years, the victims of their devotion. Think of the tortures endured at the stake by the first Jesuits in this country, while the Indians subjected them to all the horrors which their savage cruelty could devise. Remember such heroes as Jogues and Brebeuf and Lallemant. The latter looked calmly on while the Indians ate him up piece by piece. Indeed, St. Lawrence, the Roman deacon, did no better on his gridiron.

Now you, who slander them, come forth and do the like! But, oh, you do not dare! Do you remember plague-stricken Memphis a few years ago! How your coward hosts fled from danger, while twelve Catholic priests died there on that field of honor? Do you remember our own plague-stricken home fourteen years ago, when small-pox decimated the people of Columbus? Which of you dared to approach the pest-house then and visit the sick and comfort the dying? Not one. Why? "Because you were not of the seed of those men by whom salvation was brought to Israel." (1 Mach., c. V., 62).

V.
THE SCHOOLS OF THE JESUITS.

But, my dear brethren, all these glories of the Order dwindle down in comparison with one, which is greater than all: that is their work of education. The Jesuits are the authors of the modern system of education; their bitterest enemies must concede them this honor.

There were schools before them, it is true. The ancient Greeks had their schools. Diogenes was satisfied to teach his wisdom from a tub. The philosophers used academies and porticoes, walking up and down and teaching their disciples in this primitive fashion. There were schools at the time of Christ. His own way of teaching was about the fairest type of the method used by the ancient masters. He spoke to the people from a hill-top, from a ship, in the porticoes of the temple, in the synagogue, at a dinner party, indeed, wherever he could reach them best.

The Romans had their children taught by slaves, unless they sent them to some celebrated masters at Athens, Corinth or other places of like renown. But an organized system of schools did not exist among them.

This system is of Christian creation. What poor beginnings were made by the early Christians! Even the school of Alexandria, in Egypt, was more renowned through the fame of its teachers, than through any notable organization. In the Middle Ages the schools were far advanced over the attempts of ancient times. At the University of Paris, as many as 20,000 students flocked together in a single year. The University of Prag numbered usually 12,000 students yearly. There was also at that time something like organization. The universities were already divided into several faculties. Still they worked under very great difficulties. There was no such organized system of primary and intermediate schools, as we have them, and through which the student has to pass before he can be admitted into a university. This system of intermediate schools is the special creation of the Society of Jesus. By its establishment they also transformed the universities of the Middle Ages into the institutions of learning of modern times. Nor was it only indirectly that the Jesuits thus influenced higher education; they built on their own foundations, and Europe has seen no abler professors in chairs of philosophy and theology than the Bellarmins, the De Lugos, the Suarez and a number of other names, which time forbids to mention here. While the elector of Brandenburg, who had subjected his electorate to the sway of Luther, admitted, with a sigh, that in his dominions a learned man was as rare as a white crow, well-educated youths were issuing by the thousands from the schools of the Jesuits in other countries. And well might they be proud of their pupils! These are drilled under methods which now are the product of the experience gathered for over three hundred years; they are formed under a discipline, better than which no army has seen. The Jesuits shape the mind of their scholars like a diamond drill. In their theological seminaries they practice the art of dialectics and controversy unceasingly; they bring up all the objections since the days of Porphyry and Celsus to those of Voltaire and Bob Ingersoll against Divine revelation, and the student has to answer them.

There is no movement in modern times surpassing in importance and extent the one by which education is rendered accessible to everybody. This movement affects not only civilized nations, but it is felt everywhere. As soon as a nation awakes from the drowsiness of past ages, the school is the first institution to which it resorts as a powerful motor of modern civilization. Even the sleepy Turk is beginning to see that without schools he will be left entirely in the rear

The reasons for this great movement are very clear. Social distinction no longer depends on the sword and physical strength. The time of the battle-ax is over. The time of the predominance of intellectual power is upon us and will never depart. The best educated men will rule this world henceforth. When the art of printing was invented, nothing could stem the tide of education any longer. Education must become the common property of the people. Soon after this great event, the Society of Jesus was formed ; its members became the leaders of the movement immediately. In their steps other religious communities followed, devoting themselves to the education of the young ; they established parochial schools, academies and educational institutions of every description.

Then the nations imitated them. Our public school system is copied from that of the Jesuits. When they were driven away from Spain, France and Portugal, a Protestant monarch, Frederick II., of Prussia, invited them to stay in his kingdom to help in the organization of the national school system, so much admired in our days. The Order did the same service in Russia, even after Pope Clement XIV. had abolished it. By a special request of the Empress they were allowed to remain in Russia as a religious community until Pope Pius VII. re-established the Company.

As they led the van in education in times past, so they are the leaders still in this greatest of all movements of modern times. Do you think that this is saying too much? Well, here is a proposition. The Jesuits have about twenty-five flourishing colleges in this country. Let them select from the number of their students the best trained pupils and confront them with the best students of other institutions of the highest standing; if the pupils of the Jesuits do not win a brilliant victory in the contest, then this eulogy of mine is undeserved. But perhaps you may say: "This contest cannot be brought about." Well, here is one at your command. Take any priest, trained by the Jesuits in the art of dialectics and controversy, oppose to him a whole regiment of yon foul-mouthed slanderers, who claim to know the Alpha and Omega of the Christian religion; bring them up in battle array and the priest will, single handed, put the whole common train to a shameful flight, as St. Michael, the Archangel, sent Lucifer and his swarm of devils reeling down from the starry height of heaven.

Why, then, should we persecute the Jesuits? Why should we talk ill of them? Let this unmanly task be done by those only to whose black hearts every act of virtue is an offense.

At present there is an apprehension among the people outside of the Church that we are trying to destroy the public school system; and, on our part, there is a dread that those outside of the Church want to suppress our parochial schools. Nobody can deny that this mutual distrust exists. But, my brethren, let us all live in peace together. The best we can do is to do our work quietly, each in his own sphere. We Catholics want no strife. This is entirely certain. It takes very little of an argument to convince any fair-minded person of the truth that we do not want to destroy the public school system. Suppose it were destroyed, what then? Who would educate those children who now attend the public schools? What good would it do us to have them brought up in ignorance? At present in the public schools they receive a satisfactory secular instruction, and there is certainly no indication that the people in general are disgusted with the system; on the contrary, it is growing in strength every day. The person who would try to abolish it might just as well try to stop the Niagara Falls from pouring down their mighty floods into the whirlpool below. We shall not undertake the task. Whoever thinks that we are unwise enough to attempt it, is certainly more foolish himself than he supposes us to be.

Let us take realities as they are. The public schools exist; so do our parochial schools; or where they are not now they soon will be. The only sensible policy on both sides is to keep the peace and to push into the background all those who want to disturb this peace. May heaven grant to both Church and State such leaders as will understand one another and will meet in a friendly spirit on this common ground of popular education! It is the most vital question of the day, not only in the United States but all over the civilized world.

Now, you will ask here: "Why should your Catholic children not attend the public schools? Does it not impose on you a crushing burden to build schools of your own and to supply them with competent teachers? If you have not some hidden and unpatriotic purpose in view, why do you not send them also to the public schools? What interest is at stake, that you impose on yourselves such a sacrifice? What do you answer?"

We reply that we have not the slightest objection to the public schools in as far as they are run by the State ; our objections come from another source. There is and there ought to be the greatest *entente cordiale* between the Church and the State. Indeed we can congratulate ourselves on the mutual fair treatment of the two great institutions, at least in Ohio. The State has no better friend than the Church; and should the State ever stand in need of help, it can freely count on every arm of ours.

Let me give you an example of such *entente cordiale*. Here is, within the limits of Sacred Heart congregation, the Ohio State University, one of the best institutions of learning in this country. It is under the control of the State. You never hear a word of hostility against the Catholic Church from the professors in it ; there is not the least objection to their character and spirit as gentlemen. They do not frame their teachings to accommodate any religion whatever, but they frame it to suit facts only ; and in their honest endeavor to be true, they are so near our convictions—particularly in Geology—that there is no reason for dissension. If you furnish them proofs from the ancient Fathers, as for instance, from St. Irenaeus, that the primacy of the Roman Pontiffs is certainly older than the false Isidorian Decretals, they most willingly discard the errors of their text-book and teach the truth.

If such a testimony can be given to the Ohio State University, it cannot be granted to every institution kept up by public taxation in this neighborhood. Here is the Park street public school. From our experience it is a hot-bed of fanaticism. When the Sacred Heart school was built, fourteen years ago, we emptied Park street school of all the Catholic children. Here they were prepared to go to confession, but when their turn came to go to church for that purpose, they began to sob and to cry. When they were asked about the reason of their tears, they informed the Sister that they had been taught in the Park street public school that it was a horrid thing to go to confession.

If the teachers of any public school have an objection to Catholic practices, they should at least have sense enough to remember that the bread on their table is partly paid for by Catholic taxes; they should eat that bread with thankful hearts and let the Catholic Church teach her children her own doctrines. But do not ask us to leave our children in the hands of persons who turn the little ones against the Church! They perhaps will be taught that their parents are idolators, or that we drink blood out of human skulls, or that we are those Romans who crucified the Lord!

Nor does it seem that this spirit has died out in that place, for last year, when our school children marched by it, to take part in the centennial celebration, it was a circus for the Park street school to see them pass. Among all the insulting epithets shouted at them, the following one, uttered by an impudent boy, has fixed itself in my memory and will never leave it: "The penitentiary has broken loose," he cried. And his shout was responded to with a peal of laughter by the assenting audience.

You want to know the truth, well, here it is, as plain as the tongue can speak it : You cannot give us a guarantee, that, as the public schools are now, such things as these will not happen there. Far be it from us to throw a slur upon the high calling of teaching and forming a nation, which is the calling of the teachers of the young; but they must first learn themselves to respect the rights of others and think—not as little of themselves as some of them think of others—but think as much of other as they think of themselves.

Although this is somewhat of a Homeric digression from our subject of "The Jesuits," still it answers in its proper place objections raised against them and us. "We are forming a nation in a nation"—this is the cry of fanatics all around. We do not; we are of the same flesh and blood as our neighbors are; we take an interest in all those things which interest them; we are forming American citizens, with all the literary and scientific information to be had in the public schools, but with the additional advantage of a training in good morals. In this one thing leave us alone. Let us teach our children without restraint what is right and noble according to the ideas of the Catholic Church, whose maxims are the eternal principles of right and justice. Leave our schools alone. They are the nurseries of the Catholic Church, and if you attack them, you will grapple with a question which you never will solve. Stop, for the sake of peace, those sinister attempts made to crush our school system out of existence. Do not consolidate the Catholic vote. Leave it as it is, divided between the two great parties. At all hazards let us have peace. Consider as an enemy of the country any one who dares to disturb this peace which blesses now our great and beautiful land.

VI.
THE JESUITS AS PATRIOTS.

This last remark leads us to a new field. It is that of patriotism and politics. It is claimed against the Jesuits that not only they are not patriotic, but also that they cannot be good citizens of any country. On the other hand, they are accused of continually meddling in politics and disturbing the tranquility of every nation where they are allowed to establish themselves. These are grave charges, perhaps the gravest of all in the eyes of the people. If they be true, it would be dangerous to extend to the Jesuits the hospitality of any community. Are they true?

The same doubts have been raised by the same class of persons against the whole Catholic Church. These fanatics see even in their frenzied dreams the Catholic Church as a bloody phantom rising before them in the stillness of the night!

What is patriotism? For those who talk so loudly about it, it seems to imply that a patriot must be born in this country in order to love it; that he must swear at everything and everybody of foreign origin and get plenty of elbow room to run for an office.

In our opinion, patriotism consists in something else. This virtue has no meaning whatever, if, first of all, you do not respect the rights of your fellow-citizens in every point. You are no patriot if you talk ill of them. You are no patriot if you run an unprincipled business.

But it is not enough to respect the rights of others; if

you want to be patriotic, you must also acquire rights which will make you cherish the place of your citizenship. You are patriotic if you build a home of your own ; if by paying your taxes faithfully, you help to improve your town, your county, your state ; you are a patriot if you help the poor and distressed. What better patriotism do you know? You cannot imagine any better in peaceful times as those are in which we live.

Now, do you not believe that the Jesuits are such patriots, better patriots, indeed, than those lying prophets who, when they have slandered every decent man within their reach, move to other quarters to renew their evil work?

From what you have already heard in the course of this lecture, you can justly infer that the Jesuits are the best patriots which a country can have. If their sentiments were consulted to-day and a vote were taken on the question among them, it is certain that they would unanimously declare the Stars and Stripes the best and most beloved banner in the world. They certainly are in sympathy with the laws, institutions and spirit of the United States. They surely feel at home here, even if the cradle of some of them stood near the lake of Killarney or on the beautiful banks of the Rhine. The constitution of the United States is satisfied with such patriotism ; why would you be more American than the constitution is? Or do you think that those who framed that constitution were imprudent, and that you are so wise that you can make a better one? To hear these patriots talk about the things that they think need reform, the Almighty God Himself is not above their criticism.

The first Bishop of Baltimore, John Carroll, bears a name

as a patriot which any man living might envy. He was a Jesuit.

The only defeat which the Society of Jesus ever suffered, was inflicted upon them in China in the last century. The reason of this defeat was that they had overdone themselves in Chinese patriotism. They wanted to introduce the Chinese language and ceremonies into the Catholic rites of that country in order to make the Catholic worship more sympathetic with the people. It was a mistake, but surely such a one as should honor them in the eyes of every patriot. If their character is above suspicion, it ought to be in this particular point.

Only the most bigoted ignoramus can accuse the Society of Jesus, together with the Catholic Church, of being found wanting in patriotism, as their very character of catholicity makes them feel at home in every clime and among every nation.

The accusations concerning their meddling in politics are just as groundless. The priest is no politician. He may be a Republican or a Democrat, but he will not take part in any partisan political contention. He does not tell his people from the pulpit what ticket they should vote. As long as there are no public questions involving faith or morals, the Catholic clergy stand aloof from the struggles of parties. If the politicians, however, were to drag religion into their contests, they would of course have to deal with us. The sooner they understand this point, the better it will be for them.

The Jesuits are no more politicians than the secular priests are. Why should they be? They do not aspire to any political position; none of them wishes to become President of the United States or member of Congress, or even constable in his own town. You are fully convinced of this. It is a rule of their Order and it has been from the very beginning, that no Jesuit shall ever meddle in politics. This rule was laid down by their founder, and it was sanctioned by a great many of their general chapters.

What the Jesuits have not wished to do, kings and princes have done in spite of them; from time to time they have consulted some Jesuit or other in state affairs. William V., of Bavaria, had such a high opinion of the Order, that he wanted Jesuits to assist at his state councils. Many other sovereigns did the same. Then new and more stringent rules were enacted by the superiors of the Jesuits. It was made a law for the members of the Society, that, if they occupied any position at court, in the capacity of spiritual directors, they should not reside outside of the community house, but should return home daily, if possible, from the palace, as soon as their work was done.

Jealousy prompted their enemies to charge them with all kinds of political crimes: they were accused of killing monarchs and of plotting against the state. The Gunpowder Plot in England was said to be their work, and Father Garnet was put to death on that account. Titus Oates charged them with having conspired against Charles II., in consequence of which accusation six Jesuits were executed. In France they were accused of having organized the massacre of the Night of St. Bartholomew. Among the enemies of the Church it became a fashion to charge the Jesuits with all those things which the people generally disliked, so that in certain parts of the world, even up to our own days, people believe that the Jesuits have horns and cloven feet. You need not be informed that they have no horns; they live in the fierce light of publicity and it is very easy to disprove the charge. The indictment of them for political crimes is equally false, and, for the historian, it is extremely easy to discredit it and to show where wars and massacres had their origin.

An unfortunate book, written by a Spanish Jesuit, gave the enemies of the Order a badly applied argument against the whole society. The argument was badly applied, because it transferred the responsibility of one man to the whole organization.

In the sixteenth century it was a great question among theologians, whether or not it was lawful for any man, by private authority, to kill a tyrant, if there was no other means to get rid of him. Luther taught that it was lawful to do so. So did Calvin, Knox and Theodore Beza, and a great many other Protestant theologians of those days.

In the book of Joshua we read that this great leader of Israel conquered the kings of Canaan and hung five of them after making the people put their heels on their royal necks; and in the life of Samuel we find that this prophet killed a tyrant with his own hand. But their acts were done by God's command and nobody can question His right over life and death. He may, if he wants to do so, command Abraham to kill his own son. But the question is here, whether we may, by private authority, rid a country of a tyrant who ruins the nation. Must the people bleed, or is it right for any one of them to do away with the tyrant?

The doctrine taught by the Protestant theologians above mentioned, was held also by Mariana, a Spanish Jesuit. What in others had passed almost unnoticed, was made in his case a cause for alarm all over Europe. The reason for this disparity of treatment may be found in the circumstance that from Luther down to the last of his disciples in theology, you may expect an extravagance at any time. It is their own private opinion which they teach, nothing more. But from a Catholic priest, and particularly from a member of a religious Order, you expect no vagaries, no wild theories, no eccentric doctrine ; you look upon his sayings as the common teachings of the Church. The opinions of Mariana, as laid down in his book, "On the King and the education of the King," were neither the teachings of the Church nor those of the Order to which he belonged. They were his own private opinions, which he had no right to teach anybody else.

The doctrine that any man may by private authority kill a tyrant, if there is no other means of ridding the country of the monster, is eminently un-Catholic ; for no institution of the world allows less to private authority than the Catholic Church does.

The doctrine is evidently false and pernicious, because it would sanction deeds which all mankind condemn. As for instance, the crime of Guiteau, who, when shooting President Garfield, thought that he was doing a great service to the cause of liberty.

The book of Mariana was condemned by Father Aquaviva, the General of the Society of Jesus, as soon as it reached Rome. The authorities of the Society did more : they passed a law forbidding any member of the Order to teach either publicly or privately, by writing or word of mouth, the condemned doctrine. What more could they do ? This law stands yet to-day since nearly three hundred years.

Still this law did not settle the question itself; tyrants do arise from time to time and nations are distressed to know what to do with them. Shall they condemn them by act of Parliament or verdict of a revolutionary committee and deliver them up to the headsman's ax, or to the guillotine, as has been done in England and in France? These methods of slaying kings do not look any better than the assassination of Lincoln and Garfield, and the Catholic Church does not approve of them. What then shall be done with tyrants? Shall the people groan under their yoke and let Divine Providence remedy the evil? Divine Providence remedies a great many evils, it is true, but God certainly has endowed us with intellect and free-will, in order that we may wipe out all the evils within our reach. Are tyrants one of them?

For the people of the United States it is no question. The constitution of the United States empowers Congress to impeach a President who transgresses the limits of his authority. If you have a tyrant in any office tormenting the life out of you, go to the polls and vote him down. But not every country is blessed with such freedom as ours; in a great many of them the people have no vote.

Soon after Mariana, another Jesuit, one of the ablest theologians of all times, treated this question in a masterly manner. It is Bellarmin. Bellarmin, who was a Cardinal of the Holy Roman Church, has framed the doctrine of the indirect power of the Church over kings and worldly matters, in clear and decisive language. He did not invent the doctrine, as it had been taught before him by St. Thomas and the theologians of the old school, but these theologians did not treat the question explicitly, they only touched it in passing remarks. This doctrine is as follows: The Church, and therefore the Pope as its Chief Pastor, has no direct right over the affairs of this world : it is a matter of indifference to the Church who is President of the United States, who form the Congress, and how many laws are passed there. The Pope has no right to interfere in any election in which purely civil matters are to be decided ; whether the Republicans or the Democrats are at the helm of the State, does not affect him in the least. The Church, being Catholic, and therefore made for all nations, has such a constitution that it will live contented and prosperous under any lawful form of government, whether monarchical or republican.

But there is a common ground on which both Church and State meet each other, as, for instance, in matrimonial matters. To the Church belongs the sacramental part, to the State the regulation of property, inheritances and the like.

Beyond these two fields, namely, the first exclusively occupied by the State, the second, the common ground of Church and State, there is a third one in the exclusive possession of the Church upon which no earthly power has a right to encroach : for instance—Divine worship, the administration of the Sacraments and the preaching of the Gospel.

Now, suppose that earthly powers, whichever they are, do encroach upon the inalienable rights of the Church, what then ? Shall the Church look quietly at the doings of tyrants and call wrong right and right wrong ? "Oh, the Pope may protest," you say. Well, but if the protestation is of no avail ? You may answer : " Have patience and wait till better days dawn again upon this world of ours and let the tyrants have their sway until their rage is worn out." Oh, yes, the Church waited once in patience for three hundred years; she saw her children bleed and die, torn limb from limb, devoured by lions; she looked quietly on, to give an everlasting proof of her pacific intentions. But do not believe that such is her normal condition. Oh, no! If you do, your ideas of the Church of God are unspeakably poor. Christ did not found such a phantom of a kingdom. Before His empire tyrants must tremble and their thrones must shake like the tottering towers of an earthquake-beaten city, if there is no other means any more of preserving the rights of the Church, this bride of Christ and the majestic queen of mankind.

These are the teachings of Bellarmin about the indirect power of the Church over tyrants. It is not my intention to prove the doctrine here. I mention it only to show that the great Jesuit was a friend of liberty and taught a lesson which should swell the breast of every freedom-loving man.

There are people, it seems, born to be slaves and to grovel in the dust. This doctrine of Bellarmin provoked in certain quarters no less opposition than did Mariana's before. Seven years before the theologian died, a book published the story of his death. A fiery goat, so says the book, took him down to hell. From there, according to the book, he issues forth every night on a spirit steed, breathing fire and brimstone and screeching at the top of his voice to frighten the Pope and the Cardinals in their palaces at Rome. This book was printed in 1614 and Cardinal Bellarmin died in 1621. All other stories told against the Jesuits are like this one and bear no more criticism than it does.

VII.
THE LITERATURE OF THE JESUITS.

Not all the books written by Jesuits attracted so much attention as those of Mariana and Bellarmin. Usually their books cause no violent commotion, as a thunder storm does, but they work like a gentle rain on a thirsty field. The reason of this action is very clear. The Jesuits are the most conservative of all men; their literary work is not of an aggressive nature; they do not open fire in an *offensive* warfare, but they keep the ramparts of the Church in a *defensive* attitude. In the point of discussing *Christian* doctrines the Catholic Church cannot be aggressive. She possesses the whole treasure of heavenly truth as a Divine deposit, and all she has to do, is to guard it against attacks, to develop its knowledge among her children, and to preach it to those who live outside of her fold.

Such, also, is the aim of the books written by the Jesuits. They have produced the greatest works of modern times. When you see the volumes of St. Augustine or St. Chrysostom or St. Thomas, you wonder how those intellectual giants of old found time enough to write them. We pigmies cannot summon the patience to read them. A book of more than a hundred pages is beyond our endurance, and what we like best is the truth condensed into a newspaper article.

It is perfectly amazing to behold some of the literary productions of the Society of Jesus. There are the ''Lives of the Saints," the "*Acta Sanctorum*" of the Bollandists. Pope Alexander VII. declared that nobody ever undertook a work which adds more lustre to the Church of God and is of greater profit to the faithful than these "Lives of the Saints." It is the most monumental work of learning of all times.

Father Heribert Rosweid devised its plan and estimated that it would comprise eighteen volumes. He died in 1629. His manuscripts and collections were placed in the hands of three priests, among whom was Father Bolland. From him the work received its name. It is not finished yet.

In 1794 the number of large folio volumes was fifty-two, without counting the "Propylaeum" of May. It was written so far mainly by thirty-two authors. From the year 1794 until 1886 the work rested. Since then six new volumes have appeared, so that now it amounts to fifty-eight folios. It reaches to the twenty-ninth of October. It is an immense library in itself. The maxim of the founder, who said in the preface that "whatever he considered untrue, he freely rejected," has been followed throughout the composition of the work. Thus it has become the most reliable book of reference in existence.

Similar gigantic works were produced by the Jesuits in other branches of learning. Cornelius a Lapide was of marvellous fertility in explaining the Holy Scriptures. Maldonado wrote the best commentary on the Gospels. Suarez produced the most complete theology. His writings were published in twenty-three volumes in folio. The chronological works of Petau, as also his historical theology, are productions of an immortal genius. Father Hardouin continued the chronological labors of Petau; his eccentricities in disputing the genuineness of the works of ancient authors proved finally to be of very great value to him in the collection of the councils of the Church. This collection comprises twelve large volumes and is the most complete of all collections, as it contains the councils from the year 34 to 1714. It was of late continued and brought down to our own times by another Jesuit, Father Schneemann. This splendid edition has in six fine volumes the councils of the last two centuries.

The literature of the Jesuits is not confined to Sacred Science; they have distinguished themselves also in secular branches. Father Kircher was a voluminous writer on mathematics and physical science, while Father Secchi has written some of the best works extant on astronomy. Indeed one would scarcely finish enumerating all the bright literary stars of the Order.

But it is not immense books of reference that exert the deepest influence upon the intellectual life of the world. Little books of pithy substance are far more powerful. St. Thomas used to say: "I fear a man of one book," because such a man has more leisure to study and digest his matter well and bring it forth in a readable form, than if he were writing on a hundred different subjects. Did the Jesuits ever write such little books, which became standard works for the common use of the people or the priests? They did. St. Ignatius himself wrote one of them. It bears the title of *"Spiritual Exercises."* It is a book of thoughts, to be studied over in solitude and peace of mind. It has become the foundation of all retreats and missions preached by the Jesuits. It is a perfect school of spiritual life and has wrought more wonders than any other book of its size ever written.

Blessed Peter Canisius wrote a catechism for the people, which is so plain, so easily taught and learned, that it has stood the test of over three hundred years as a text-book in schools. There is no other work, besides the classics, of which this can be said. On the plan of Blessed Peter Canisius, another Jesuit, Father Deharbe, has in our own days worked out a catechism of the Christian religion, which is a marvel of correctness, completeness and clearness. It has never been equalled as a book of popular instruction. The more a priest uses it in his classes, the more he admires it.

St. Alphonsus Liguori, the founder of the Congregation of the Most Holy Redeemer, has been declared a doctor of the Church on account of his great work on moral theology. But his work is the commentary of another one, written by a Jesuit. His name was Busenbaum, a name familiar to everyone who studies the history of the warfare against the Society of Jesus. He wrote a small book on moral theology, which he entitled: "*Medulla.*" This famous book, burnt often by fanatics, has had more than seventy-five editions. There is no other proof required to show its great value and the immense influence which it has had in shaping moral teachings from its first appearance until our own days.

There have been whole volumes written about the literature of the Jesuits. They are the authors of so many books, and, indeed, such good ones, that if one had a library composed exclusively of them, he would get the best and soundest information which can be found anywhere.

One thing may be said in praise of the writings of the Jesuits in general. which cannot be said about the works of any other body of men: If a certain number of books which are condemned by the Jesuits themselves, as Mariana's, some of Hardouin's fighting works and Berruyer's treatment of the Holy Scriptures in his *Histoire du peuple de Dieu* be excepted, you are perfectly safe in studying all the books written by the Jesuits. You need not question their orthodoxy or their devotion to the Church.

Even our enemies give them the credit of being the best representatives of Catholic doctrines and practices, for wherever they find a priest or layman who is strictly observant of the rules of the Church, they will certainly call him a "Jesuit." Now what greater praise can there be than such an acknowledgment from the lips of those who hate them?

RECAPITULATION.

You have assisted this evening at a lesson on general Church History. You have seen the growth and development of the kingdom of Christ. In thinking of the Jesuits after this, do not believe you heard me say that they have made the Church Catholic; they did not, it was Catholic from the day of its foundation, but they, more than any one else, have shown it to be Catholic. You have followed these devoted sons of the Church to the utmost parts of the earth, where they have carried the light of the Gospel with undaunted courage. They have risen up before you as the staunch defenders of Church authority, particularly in its teaching power; to them the credit was given for the blessing that now the Pope is among us indisputably acknowledged to be the universal teacher—the *doctor universalis*. You have understood how, by their mild and reasonable doctrines in moral theology, they have placed Christian virtue within the reach of every one, and shown it to be the common property of all men of good will, not of only a few chosen heroes. You have seen them as leaders in the greatest of all modern movements—in education ; a movement which has brought down the arrogant Knighthood of the Middle-Ages and displaced the center of gravity in human affairs from the power of the sword to the power of learning and wisdom, and levels mankind with irresistible might. You have learned to appreciate their spirit as citizens and patriots, because their whole life is devoted not to private, but to public, interests. Their great learning was pointed out to you in showing the immortal writings left by them to posterity.

If you sum up all these glories of the Order, the inevitable conclusion presses itself upon your mind, that, what Luther falsely claimed to be, the Jesuits have been in reality, namely, the reformers of the Church. Reformers who boisterously introduce themselves as such, are, as a rule, those who stand most in need of reform themselves ; but quiet and conservative reformers as the Jesuits have always been, are a blessing to the world. We have found no cause against them, but all things in their favor. How, then, can any man talk ill of them? How can any one, claiming to be enlightened, forget himself so far and *descend so low* as to deliver a lecture against these men? Such an ungrateful task reminds one of the words of the poet, who says:

"For so much trash as may be grasped thus;
I had rather be a dog and bay the moon."

CONCLUSION.

I am done, my dear brethren, eulogizing the Society of Jesus. I hope that you have taken these words as an appeal to everybody concerned, for peace and concord.

The insidious attacks against this vanguard of the Catholic Church are certainly unmistakable signs that in certain quarters there is a disposition to pick a quarrel and to provoke a fight. A crusade directed against the school system of the Church, at the head of which the Jesuits are supposed to be, would doubtless find a great number of adherents among the people. But if we arrive at a fair understanding with one another, there is not the slightest reason for distrust or contention.

We have this confidence in the good sense of the people, that they do not intend to do us an intentional wrong. Still there are enemies whom we shall have to watch closely, for fear that they may create a hostile feeling against us.

To judge from observation of public opinion, it is evident that a large majority of the people are absolutely opposed to all strife and religious animosity. Why not let time and peaceful work decide which religion is the best? As soon as we do not do such peaceful work any more, but disturb public tranquillity by wanton attacks upon our neighbors, it will be time enough to preach a crusade against us and fight us down. But that time will never come.

We desire no unjust superiority over our fellow-men; we want to conquer them, it is true, not to oppress them, but to win their intellect by the sunny light of truth, and their heart by Divine charity. Through truth and charity we want to subject them to the yoke of Christ, which we glory ourselves to bear ; for, as the Savior says Himself: "My yoke is sweet and my burden light."

MIXED MARRIAGES.

Their Origin and Results.

BY REV. A. A. LAMBING,

thor of the "Orphan's Friend," "The Sunday School Teacher's Manual," etc., etc.

THIRD EDITION.—REVISED AND ENLARGED.

"Did not Solomon, king of Israel, sin in this kind of thing? and surely among many nations re was not a king like him; and he was beloved of his God, . . . and yet women of other ntries brought even him to ruin."
—2 ESDRAS, xiii, 26

NOTRE DAME, INDIANA:
AVE MARIA PRESS.
1878.

PREFACE.

The Prophet Jeremias, lamenting the calamities that had befallen the chosen people, exclaimed; "*With desolation is the land made desolate, because there is no one that considereth in the heart.*" The same remark may with equal truth be applied to all the evils which afflict the family, society, and the Church. The want of serious reflection is the fruitful source of innumerable disorders. Lead men but to reflect, and the foundation is laid for reformation. In proportion as the world becomes more material in its views and pursuits, will the feelings and passions encroach on the domain of reason and usurp the province of prudent consideration. The more important the matter engaging attention, the more deplorable are the consequences likely to be. No one, it is presumed, can be insensible to the force of this truth when applied to the affair of selecting a partner to share the joys and sorrows, the prosperity and adversity incident to a wedded life, and bear the trials inseparable from the education and training of a family. To a forgetfulness of this, more than to any other cause, are to be attributed the many disorders that have connected themselves with the Sacrament of Marriage,—disorders which destroy the peace of families and grieve the Church in the present, while they threaten even more in the future. Could parents be induced to impress upon the minds of their children the holiness of the married life, and could the young be led to ponder more carefully the same momentous question, it would contribute in no small degree to their own mutual happiness, and would, at the same time, advance the interests of the Church in this country.

It is with a view of aiding in so laudable a work that the following pages—which are a reproduction, with some alterations and additions, of articles published by the writer some years ago in the AVE MARIA

MIXED MARRIAGES.

I.

MATRIMONY VIEWED IN THE LIGHT OF THE CHURCH AND THE REFORMATION.

"When we consider that Matrimony is the axis on which the whole social economy revolves, can we suppose it to be sufficiently sacred, or too highly admire the wisdom of Him who stamped it with the seal of religion?"—*Genius of Christianity*, Part 1, Book 1, Chap. x.

He who attentively studies the manner in which the Church is accustomed to deal with the important subjects which pertain to faith, morals and discipline, cannot but conceive a deeper reverence for her, and discover more clearly the presence of an intelligence more than human directing and controlling her movements. So deeply were many of the early Christian kings inspired with an idea of her wisdom that they gloried in reproducing in their civil codes certain important decisions emanating from her. The names of Charlemagne and Alfred the Great may be given as illustrious examples, who, though model statesmen, were yet willing to receive light from her. Where there exists the greatest apprehension of the rebellion of man's fallen nature, her hand directs him with special care, neither driving him to desperation by unbecoming severity, nor encouraging him by a reprehensible indulgence. This remark applies with peculiar force to the Sacrament of Matrimony, in which the vicious inclinations are least disposed to brook restraint. "In nothing, perhaps, is the influence of the Spirit of Truth more evident in the teaching of the Church than in the care with which she has protected this great Sacrament."* So beautiful is the Sacrament of Matrimony in the Church, and so deformed beyond her sacred pale, that it may with propriety be made the subject of a few remarks. And the more appropriately, as the ideas which now prevail among us are so greatly at variance with her doctrine and dis-

---

* Pastoral Letter of the Second Plenary Council of Baltimore.

cipline. If, however, the subject is one of interesting, it is, at the same time, one of no less useful investigation. For nothing has tended so powerfully to increase the evil consequences arising from a perversion of this holy rite as the forgetfulness of parents and the young to ponder them maturely. "The holiness of Christian Matrimony is connected with our most sacred associations and duties; and it cannot be lost sight of, in however small a degree, without entailing the most serious consequences."*

Yet more solemn are the words of the Sovereign Pontiff who is now happily ruling the Church. In the first Encyclical Letter that he addressed to the Hierarchy of the Christian world he makes use of these words in relation to the Sacrament of Matrimony,—words remarkable as well for the profound wisdom they contain, as for the august source from which they emanate: "The family," says the Holy Father, "so deplorably disturbed in our time, can be re-established in its dignity by no other means than by the laws according to which the Divine Maker established it in the Church. Jesus Christ in elevating into the dignity of a Sacrament the ceremony of marriage, which He wished to use as a symbol of His union with the Church, has not only rendered more holy the conjugal union, but has prepared for the parents as well as for the children the most efficacious aids by which they may arrive, by accomplishing their mutual duties, at the possession of temporal and eternal felicity. But when impious laws, having no regard to the respect due to this great Sacrament, have placed it in the same category as purely civil contracts, the result is the deplorable consequences that the dignity of Christian marriage being violated, some citizens have substituted legal concubinage for the legitimate union; the married couple have neglected their mutual duties of fidelity, the children have not observed the respect and obedience which they owe to their parents, the ties of domestic affection have been relaxed, and, what is a most detestable example, the gravest prejudice to public morals, pernicious and regrettable separations have very often succeeded to an insensate love."

There is something so pleasing in the contemplation of a well-selected and happy union that few can regard it without feelings of delight. "Who," asks Tertullian, "can express the happiness of that marriage which the Church approves, which Sacrifice [the Mass] confirms, and which blessing seals—angels announce it, and the Father ratifies?"

That which is so pleasing for man to contemplate attracted the heart

---

* Ibid.

of our Divine Saviour, and induced him to honor the privileged couple of Cana in Galilee with His presence, and even to work a miracle lest a cloud of disappointment and humiliation should darken the sunshine of that happy day. Congratulations, not such as are usually offered, but heartfelt and sincere, flow upon those whom God has already blessed, and a long life overflowing with every innocent joy is the only wish and prayer of relatives and friends. To these the happy parents unite in adding their blessing, and over all the good priest raises those hands consecrated to impart heavenly benedictions. Nor is it only for a time that sunshine lights their path. Poverty with its attending privations, sickness with its variety of suffering, and adversity with its train of misfortunes, may in turn or together cross the path of the husband and wife; it is vain,—nothing can rob them of Christian cheerfulness. For it is not the fruit of health, wealth or prosperity; it is the flower that springs from the soil of a pure heart cultivated by prudent discipline, and moistened with the dews of prayer and the Sacraments. If the imagination, passing over a few years, pictures the fireside surrounded by a group of smiling little faces, cheering the heart of the parent by their innocent prattle, or lisping a prayer at the mother's knee and receiving from her lips lessons of saving truth, it is only anticipating the prayer of the Church begging Almighty God to bestow upon the newly married couple the blessing of seeing their children's children even to the third and fourth generations before He calls them to an eternal inheritance. When life has at length fled, and the parent is stretched on the bed of death, what can be so consoling, after the last rites of the Church, as to see the dying couch surrounded with dutiful children, imbued with sentiments of deep filial affection? The prayers put up for the departing soul are dictated as well by a sense of gratitude as by a desire of aiding the soul in its last terrible struggle.

We need not be surprised at the celestial beauty of this Sacrament, seeing the noble union by which it is typified,—a union pointed out to us by the Apostle Saint Paul. When, " in the fulness of time," Christ descended to earth to ameliorate the condition of His fallen creatures, it was by a fruitful union that He accomplished the regeneration of those whom Adam had begotten by a carnal generation. In the chaste womb of Immaculate Mary He wedded His Divinity to our frail nature, that from these fruitful nuptials might spring the children of God. Having by His death finished the work given by His eternal Father, He again espouses another chaste bride, the Church, who will ever remain submissive, obedient, and fruitful. The fostering care of

Christ for the Church, and her love and regard for Him, are the models for the Christian husband and wife. "Husbands, love your wives," says the Apostle, "as Christ also loved the Church, and delivered Himself up for it." "Let women be subject to their husbands as to the Lord." And as the Church was formed from the side of Christ sleeping in death upon the Cross when His Sacred Body was pierced with the lance, so the mother of the human race was not formed by separate creation, but but was derived from the side of the sleeping Adam. Hence she was claimed by him, as "bone of his bone and flesh of his flesh"; and hence also does the Apostle say that "he who loveth his wife loveth himself." "For this cause," declares the Holy Spirit, "shall a man leave father and mother, and shall cleave unto his wife: and they two shall be in one flesh."* In confirming this law in the New Dispensation, our Divine Redeemer declared in these explicit words the indissolubility of the marriage tie: "What therefore *God* hath joined together, let not *man* put asunder."† He at the same time abrogated forever the privilege of divorce permitted the Jews by Moses on account of the hardness of their hearts, because "from the beginning it was not so."

With an archetype so pure and holy, it is not difficult to know the essential qualities of a union that would begin and continue happily. It must commence in the heart and affections before it is consummated by the joining of hands and the blessing of the Church. It were vain to expect a life of happiness if nature has endowed the two persons with dispositions of such a character as will not coalesce into one, unless the dews of Divine grace have softened and smoothed down the asperities of natural temperament. Any opinion or belief of either party antagonistic to the other on an essential or even an important point, must, while it continues, entail consequences fatal to happiness. In two cases in particular must this be the inevitable result: when their views of the nature of this Sacrament differ, and when their religious convictions are not the same—questions which generally, though not necessarily, merge into one. A moment's reflection will clearly show that marriage is not a matter in which only the affections or caprice are concerned, but rather a subject to be viewed in the light of both reason and religion; it is, in a word, one of the most important events in the life of a man or woman. A forgetfulness of this great truth will expose the contracting parties to the danger of a lifelong misery, and will even place their eternal happiness in jeopardy;

---

* St. Matthew, xix, 5. † Ibid., verse 6.

strange ideas for one to entertain in the nineteenth century, but nevertheless true. So long as the Church was permitted to exercise perfect control in matters relating to marriage, all moved smoothly on; for although abuses appeared at times, they were known to be such, and opposed. "The Church has shown in reference to this subject a spirit of watchfulness and solicitude which alone would entitle her to the gratitude of man, and cause her to be regarded as the most faithful guardian of public and private morality."* Rather than relax in an essential point her sacred discipline, she has witnessed the defection of entire peoples; but the wisdom of her course always appeared in the sequel.

A lamentable change was ushered in by the dawn of the Reformation. The eagerness and haste with which the first heroes of Protestantism desecrated this Sacrament borders on the incredible, and offers to historians a problem of very difficult solution. Their first act was a species of divorce, that of repudiating their first spouse, the Church, to whom was vowed the chastity of their bodies; and of infidelity, in uniting themselves to another bride. They next permitted the unnatural and unchristian state of bigamy, allowing Philip, Landgrave of Hesse, to take a second wife during the life of the first. The latter was a species of crime which the public conscience, still Catholic, or deeply imbued with Catholic ideas, was not prepared to tolerate beyond the shadow of the royal sceptre. The former was encouraged, because it struck a death-blow at the sacredness of vows, and degraded the royalty of that servitude which consecrates the body yet pure to the divine service. Then they "made the members of Christ the members of a harlot," and so far from evincing a sense of shame, they gloried in the crime, and encouraged others to throw off the yoke and follow their example. Writing, as I do, for those who believe, I shall not delay to prove the harmony that exists between the Catholic doctrines, on the one hand, and reason and revelation, on the other. I cannot, however, forego the pleasure of presenting a few extracts from the writings of the Father of the Reformation, which, being enhanced by his example, cannot fail to convey a sad picture of the moral degradation of those who pretended to be instruments in the hands of Providence for restoring religion to its primitive purity.

The *Table-Talk* of Luther—that sink of immorality—affords us this pithy extract in regard to his *reformed view* (as a poor Augustinian monk he thought differently):

---

* Pastoral Letter of the Second Plenary Council of Baltimore.

"Though I should make a thousand vows, though a hundred thousand angels,—to say nothing of that miserable being they call the Pope, should tell me that I ought to remain without a helpmate, that I ought to remain alone, what weight would these vows and these angelic commands have with those words of God: '*It is not good for man to be alone.*'"

It was not, however, from a desire of elevating the married state above life in a cloister, but rather of opening an avenue for the indulgence of the most degraded sensual appetites, that caused them to treat vows with so much contempt; else why did they so soon trample on the sacredness of Matrimony, as we shall presently find they did; else why did Luther preach his infamous sermon on Matrimony,—a discourse which the most ardent of his admirers have never dared to present in an English dress, and one which places his views on the sanctity of marriage in such a light as to demonstrate, beyond the shadow of a doubt, that whatever object he proposed to himself in attempting a reformation, it was not that of giving his followers a more exalted idea of it than that which they had previously entertained.[*] If anything could possibly be more unblushing and better calculated to show the mind of the reformer, it is the nuptial mass composed by Andrew Carlestadt for his own marriage.[†]

Next hear the Father of the Reformation on polygamy: "The Scripture prevents me," he wrote to the Chancellor of the Duke of Saxe-Weimar, "from forbidding anyone to take several wives at the same time; *it is a commendable practice; but I would not be the first to introduce it among Christians.*" Neither the fear of God nor respect for His holy law, neither self-respect nor religious conviction prevented the apostle of the Reformation from anticipating Joe Smith in his shocking immorality; but only the fact that as yet *the people were too Christian in their ideas.* With the precedent which their master had transmitted to them, and their knowledge of the principle on which he had acted, his disciples found little difficulty in proceeding ere long to the extremes which propriety had forbidden to him. So far vows and polygamy. We shall now turn to divorce, the remaining wound inflicted on public morality and domestic happiness.

If there be any force that can effect the ruin of our republic, it is the laxity of morals in this particular. The association of one man with one woman is the foundation of all society, and the groundwork of the nation. Remove the foundation-stone, and it must result in the

---

[*] Audin's Life of Luther, vol. ii, p. 19, etc.   [†] Ibid., vol. i, p. 387.

ruin of the superstructure. To do this was among the first acts of the Reformers. The Fathers of the Second Plenary Council of Baltimore were fully alive to the importance of preserving the purity and indissolubility of marriage, when they addressed these words to their respective flocks : " We refer with pain to the scandalous multiplications of these unlawful separations, which, more than any other cause, are sapping the foundations of morality and preparing society for an entire dissolution of the basis on which it rests." It is painful to bear witness against brethren, but the true nature of the malady and its origin must be ascertained before the antidote can be applied with a well-grounded hope of success. The prevalence of divorce, and the facility with which it is obtained in this and most European countries, is truly deplorable, and makes the ceremony of marriage beyond the pale of the Church a very mockery. In every State of the Union, divorce, not from cohabitation, but from the bond itself of marriage, is recognized and permitted by law; and not only is the power of severing the bond exercised by the Legislature, it is also placed within the jurisdiction of the Courts, with the sole exception of the State of Maryland, a vestige of the ruined edifice of ancient Catholic legislation. The necessary amount of crime varies from adultery, extreme cruelty, and habitual drunkenness, to the kind complacency of the State of Iowa, where "divorce may be granted when it is evident that the parties cannot live in peace and happiness together, and their welfare requires a separation." When the exercise of clemency involves the surrender of no principle, it is a commendable virtue; but in a matter of this kind it is an incentive to the commission of the most revolting crimes. However unchristian the conduct and legislation of those may appear who have embraced the principles of the Reformation, they contain nothing that should raise a blush on the cheek of their ancestors. For if the German Reformers taught mankind to trample on vows and to disregard the bonds that bound them during life to one only partner, Henry VIII in England demonstrated beyond all doubt the advantage of divorce to a man of a tender conscience. It is unnecessary to place before the reader an account of the manner in which this unprincipled monarch disposed of his different wives,—a man who, as he acknowledged on his death-bed to Feller, "had never refused any man's life to his hatred, nor any woman's honor to his lust." The intrigue to which he was forced to have recourse, and the difficulty and final refusal he met with in his attempt to have the Church pronounce his divorce from the virtuous Catharine of Aragon, shows the strength of unbridled passion and the necessity of wholesome restraint. But they show, upon the testimony of one of her fiercest enemies, the firmness of the Church where principles are involved. I had thought to make some further remarks in this place on the facility with which divorces may be obtained in every civilized nation, and to lay before the reader statistics to show that this unholy liberty is eagerly sought after. But figures such as I am prepared to give would appear incredible. Suffice it to say that any one who wants a divorce can obtain it without difficulty, and even without a reason, as may be seen by Chicago advertisements in many newspapers. For divorce statistics let the reader consult Chapter V of *Divorce and Divorce Legislation*, by *Theodore D. Woolsey, D. D., LL. D., President of Yale College*. I would not wound the reader's sensibility by asking him to contemplate the sensual depravity by which the principles of the Perfectionists and Fourierists would undermine the foundations of society. But I would insist that all these repulsive disorders are the legitimate and necessary fruits of the principles promulgated by the Reformers. By destroying the principle of submission to authority, and establishing that of private judgment, they not only prepared the way, but, much more, they encouraged corrupt nature to rush into every extreme, and prepared in advance a justification for the most repulsive sensuality. "*By their fruits you shall know them.*"

Having stripped Matrimony of sacred dignity as a Sacrament, it was only a matter of form to take from it the name. Calvin accomplishes this feat with one stroke of the pen. Hear him: "The state of marriage is no otherwise good and holy than that of the farmer, the mason, the shoemaker, and the barber, which states are not Sacraments." * It has now degenerated to such an extent among the Sects as to be regarded as a civil contract only, and, being such, serious doubts are entertained, by some, of its validity when entered into on a Sunday. This degradation of Matrimony was expressed with admirable candor by the New England Puritans in the following enactment found among the Connecticut Blue Laws (Barber's Collection): "37. No Gospel minister shall join people in marriage. The magistrates only shall join people in marriage, as they may do it with less scandal to Christ's church." The civil magistrate in our day performs almost as many marriage ceremonies as the ministers. Encouraged as human weakness and depravity were by the Reformers, no other result could have been expected; and it may truly be said that all the disorders—and their name is legion—that have marred the beauty of this sacred rite

---

* Institutions, Book IV.

both in the Church and beyond her pale, are due to this criminal laxity. Human nature, doubtless, was the same in the Church before the sixteenth century as it has been since that period: but, on the one hand, Matrimony is a Sacrament in the Church, and, like all the obligations which Almighty God imposes upon us, carries with it the supernatural assistance necessary to render it sweet and agreeable; and, on the other hand, the laws of the Church are supported by a sanction which prevents them from being transgressed with impunity. But the Church is a mother, not a tyrant. Hence she has always been accustomed but *for the gravest reasons only* to permit the husband and wife to separate *a toro*, that is, from cohabitation; yet she says distinctly, "the bond of marriage is never broken but by death; and should either contract a new alliance, the offender is guilty of the crime of adultery,* and incurs the sentence of excommunication." So stringent is the law of the Church on this point, and so rigidly enforced, that some, despairing of ever being separated from an uncongenial partner, have not hesitated to take such a one's life to open an avenue to a new marriage. Here, too, the vigilant eye of the Church followed them, and an effectual barrier was interposed by raising this unlawful act to the dignity of a diriment impediment—*impedimentum criminis*—which makes a marriage contracted under such circumstances null and void.

A precaution such as this is wholly uncalled for among our reformed brethren. Divorce, a coin of par value among them, answers the purpose much better. The prevalence of this evil shows an alarming degree of corruption, and makes us refuse to class that body among the followers of Him who so severely censured the divorce permitted by Moses to the Jews.† Yet it was free from many of the evil consequences attending the divorce now in vogue among Protestants. True, a trivial offence on the part of the wife was all that was needed to put it in the husband's power to apply for a bill of separation; but so numerous were the conditions required for the validity of the document, that even the size and form of the parchment, the style and character of the letters, were prescribed, under the penalty of nullity.‡

---

* St. Mark x. 11, 12. † Deut. xxiv. 1.

‡ The following Note from P. De Ligny's *Life of Christ*, (Eng. trans. p. 125,) is given for the information of the curious and those desirous of instituting a comparison between *condemned* Jewish and *reformed* Protestant divorce:

"For granting a bill of divorce the Jews required the following conditions: 1. It could not be granted, except with the permission of the husband. 2. The husband should transfer the deed to

Under the lax system introduced by the Reformation, some of the most important impediments to marriage had been abolished, the Sacrament had been stripped of every vestige of its sacred character, contracting parties so far from meriting the benediction of Heaven incurred its severest maledictions, and even when the union was consummated it was in the power of either one to dissolve it. Marriage, in a word, was an action of no greater importance than the buying or selling of a horse. What wonder if some evil-disposed Catholics envied Protestants their privileges, and sighed for the flesh-pots of Egypt! At first the impediments and restrictions would begin to be looked upon with diminished reverence and respect; then complaints of undue severity would be made against the chaste Spouse of Christ; next, the evil would assume a defiant aspect, and transgress the sacred canons; and finally, the rebellion of individuals would settle into a habit. The development and grounding of such a habit would depend in a great measure upon the associations and training of those whose minds were in the course of formation.

Taking the world as it is at present, there are, from whatever sources they spring, three irregularities in marriages among the laxer sort of Christians: Marriage before a minister of the sects, or a civil magistrate; marriage within the forbidden degrees of kindred; and mixed marriage, by which I mean marriage of a Catholic with anyone who is not a Catholic.

The first is sometimes resorted to as a means of contracting a marriage that would not be permitted by the Church, or the permission for which would be obtained with difficulty. For although she grants dispensations in the case of certain impediments, it is always with reluctance, and within a limit beyond which she will not extend her clemency. Bad as it certainly is, and forbidden and severely punished by the Church, it is of comparatively rare occurrence, and is not without a remedy. This fact, together with the utter abhorrence in which it

---

the woman with his own hand. 3. There should not be less than three witnesses, and all the witnesses should affix their seal to the instrument. 4. The recital should set forth three degrees of generation of the man, and three of the woman. 5. The paper on which it was engrossed should be of greater length than breadth; the letters should be written in a round hand, and separated from one another; there should be no erasures; and if a drop of ink fell on the paper, it would make the act a nullity. The husband, on giving the deed, should say: 'Receive the act of divorce; be separated from me, and let any one be allowed to marry thee!'"

"The formula read thus: I, Rabbi N., son of Rabbi N., son of Rabbi N., such a day of such a month of such a year from the creation of the world, being in such a place, of my own full and free determination and without being constrained to it, have repudiated N., daughter of Rabbi N., son of Rabbi N., son of Rabbi N., and I have placed in her hands the deed of divorce, the schedule of separation, and the testimony of division. She may go wheresoever it pleaseth her, without any one offering her any opposition, conformably to the constitution of Moses and the people of Israel."

is held by all who lay claim to the observance of ecclesiastical precepts, will prevent the instances from ever becoming numerous.

The second abuse is of rarer occurrence, but has the misfortune of being irreparable. I do not refer to those cases only which take place in defiance of the Church. All cause her grief, although she permits them in certain cases. But if clandestine and mixed marriages are a violation of ecclesiastical law, these are contrary to the law of nature, and nature is loth to grant dispensations. The Church has manifested the greatest wisdom in prohibiting them, as the following statistics and observations will abundantly show:

"These marriages are the most prolific source of simpletons. Howe observed seventeen marriages among blood relations, from which there came forth ninety-five children. Of these children *thirty-five* were simpletons, twelve were affected with the scrofula, one child was deaf, and one dwarf. According to Remiss about 15 per cent. of all the simpletons in the insane and benevolent asylums of the United States are the offspring of marriages between blood relations. Rameau found that the French families that inhabit New Brunswick mostly intermarry. In one of these families—the father and mother of which were first-cousins—of seven children, six were simpletons."

These statements are confirmed by the following letter:

"To THE EDITOR OF THE LONDON TIMES:

"SIR: I beg permission to give the testimony of my experience as regards the sad results attending the marriage of first-cousins, which consequences ought to be well known, so that they may be avoided; and you will confer a favor upon humanity by giving a warning.

"The marriage of first-cousins is undoubtedly the most prolific cause of congenital deaf-mutism known, and it frequently affects the sight, the general constitution and the mental capacity as well. I am personally acquainted with numerous instances of this affliction in families. In one, that of a working-man, out of nine children eight were deaf and dumb, and were, moreover, of such weak constitutions that at one time the three youngest (all born singly) could not walk. In another, a clergyman's, out of eight children four were afflicted, one being deaf and dumb, with imperfect sight; another deaf, dumb and idiotic. In a third there are four deaf mutes. In a fourth, two out of four cannot hear; and in a fifth, three children who are deaf mutes, with imperfect sight.

"It is needless for us to multiply instances; there is no doubt whatever on the subject. The only requirement is that these consequences may be universally known, that such calamities may not be entailed upon offspring.

"I am, sir, your obedient servant,
"SAMUEL SMITH, Chaplain, &c.,
"The Royal Association in aid of the Deaf and Dumb."

Having traced mixed marriages to their source, we are prepared to examine them in the results which they produce in the Church, in society, and in the family.

II.

THE ACTION OF THE CHURCH IN RELATION TO MIXED MARRIAGES.

In her solicitude for the purity of "the Faith once delivered to the saints," the Church experienced great difficulty in treating the matter of mixed marriages; a subject which Luther, with his characteristic freedom of expression, disposed of in the following summary manner, marking at the same time a line of conduct for those who in later times should adopt his religious principles: "If it is allowable for me to trade with a heathen, a Turk, or a heretic, why may I not marry one? A heathen, male or female, is still a man or woman, beautiful and created by God, just as much as St. Peter, St. Paul, or St. Lucy."* Not so the Church. Her light is from above, and her course of action must be directed according to it.

Those who first clear away the forest and break the soil of an unreclaimed territory, have many inconveniences to endure and many privations to suffer. Special provision must be made for them by the State, and time is required by the new colony before it is sufficiently advanced to take its place among its sister States. As time rolls on, it will lay aside the habiliments of childhood, forget the toys that amused it, and adopt the regime of maturer years. So it has ever been with nations newly converted or in process of conversion to Catholicity. The clemency of Mother Church for her children placed in such circumstances is in harmony with her other wise regulations; but, like them, it is liable to be abused by the indifferent or malicious. It is in favor of some of her children residing in places where the Catholic population is limited, and where it would consequently be difficult, if not impossible, for those contemplating marriage to meet with suitable companions of their own religion—and this is the principal motive that induces her to grant dispensations—that the Church in particular instances, and with certain restrictions, permits her children to contract marriages with persons of an heretical communion. So reluctant is she to use this power, that the exercise of it is reserved to the Supreme Pontiff alone, and only delegated by him to a limited extent to the other Prelates. It must not, however, be imagined that all who marry beyond the pale of the Church do so with her consent. The readiness with which persons influenced by an unbridled passion defy and trample upon her laws is well known.

---

* De Vita Matrimoniali.

Mixed marriages are contrary to the natural, the divine, and the ecclesiastical law.* They are contrary to the natural law, because of the imminent danger of perversion on the part of the Catholic; the fear that the children will be either without religion or be instructed in the tenets of a sect condemned by the Church as heretical; and also on account of the peril in which the peace of the family is placed by the union of elements so discordant. Experience demonstrates beyond the possibility of doubt that these dangers are not imaginary, but real. A more ample treatment of this part of the subject will, however, be found further on. That they are at variance with the Divine law is yet more apparent; for, if Christ, at the price of His Incarnation, labors, sufferings, death and resurrection, established "one fold," out of which there is no salvation, He has, by the very fact, imposed upon the members of that fold the obligation of preserving by every means the treasure which He has confided to them, and of transmitting it to their children. Nor are the Scriptures silent. The Apostle of the Gentiles, in numerous passages of his Epistles, warns the Christians against the pernicious consequences of too intimate an association with those who are "enemies of the cross of Christ; whose end is destruction." "Bear not the yoke," he tells them, "with unbelievers." "A man that is a heretic . . . avoid." Speaking of the privilege enjoyed by a woman, whose husband is dead, of marrying another, he says: 'Let her marry whom she will; only in the Lord." The fathers and commentators generally explain these texts as forbidding mixed marriages; and they require but little explanation to convey that meaning.† The Old Testament expressly forbids mixed marriages, on account of the peril to which the faith of the Jews would be thereby exposed. When the chosen people were about to enter the land of promise, the following was among the solemn admonitions given them by God in reference to their intercourse with the surrounding nations. 'Neither shalt thou make marriages with them. Thou shalt not give thy daughter to his son, nor take his daughter for thy son. *For she will turn away thy son from following Me.*"‡ With good reason, humanly speaking, was this command imposed on the Jews; for it is extremely difficult for two persons to pass a lifetime in each other's company, more especially in the intimate companionship which marriage presupposes, without sooner or later bringing their opinions and

---

* Vide Scavini, Theol. Moralis, De Matrimonio.
† Vide Estii Commentarius. ‡ 4 Deut., vii, 3, 4.

views to coincide. Domestic happiness demands it as a necessary condition. The strongest attachment may at first exist in the hearts of each for personal creed and tenets; but the corroding power of time alone, all other agents prescinded, is incalculable. Time mocks at the poignant grief of the true heart at the grave of a loved one; for he well knows that his might is able to obliterate every trace of sorrow and dry the cheek bedewed with tears. The mass of mineral cast into the furnace will ere long lose its color and will be clothed in the red glare of the flames; and the frozen stream will unbind its fetters in the genial rays of the sun in spring. The same must naturally be expected in regard to the religious convictions of persons united in a mixed marriage. Should the husband ask the wife, or she the husband, to leap over the chasm that lies between them, the demand would be met by a simple refusal. But "continual dropping will wear a stone"; and that which is more than the work of a single day may be less than the work of twenty or thirty years.

The numerous decrees of the Church, illustrated and explained by her constant practice, leaves no one in ignorance of her antipathy to mixed marriages. "The danger of perversion," says F. Nampon, "is the ground of interdiction; now this danger is almost inseparable from marriages which are not blessed by a common religion."* In the first ages of the Church we find the subject engaging her attention. The fifteenth, sixteenth, and seventeenth canons of the Synod of Elvira, held in the fourth century, forbade Christians to marry with pagans, Jews, and heretics.† The Synod of Arles, in Gaul, which met a few years later, confirmed these prohibitions in its eleventh canon.‡ Similar to these are the fourteenth canon of the Council of Chalcedon and the thirty-first of that of Laodicea. It is not, however, with the ancient Church, but rather with the modern, that we are concerned in the present inquiry. The religious revolution which resulted in the birth of Protestantism not only shook the Church to her foundation, but also obliterated every trace of former heresies, or gave them an entirely different coloring. When the Church at length commenced to gather into her fold some of those, particularly in the North of Europe, who had strayed from it in the beginning, the affair of mixed marriages demanded great attention. It was a critical juncture. The

---

* Catholic Doctrine, p. 588.
† See Hefele, History of the Councils, vol. 1, p. 144.
‡ Ibid., p. 190, the author says: "We may look upon the assembly at Arles as a General Council of the West, or of the Roman Patriarchate."

reins of discipline should be relaxed, but not too much; they should be held, but not with too firm a grasp. The wisdom of the Spouse of Christ was equal to the task. But can man control the waywardness of his free will? It is hardly possible. Liberty, though an inestimable boon, is yet a dangerous one. The Church acted with reluctance; and, had the necessity been removed which compelled her to act, would gladly have relapsed into her time-worn groove. But it was not permitted. The disorder, so far from diminishing, was on the increase. Instead of resting satisfied with the concessions made by the Church, society continued to encroach on forbidden ground and demand more ample indulgence. Frequently did the Vicar of Christ raise his voice in solemn protest against the wanderings of his flock; but they were not restrained. Out of the fourteen Sovereign Pontiffs who, beginning with St. Leo the Great and extending to the present august Head of the Church, labored by briefs, decrees, and other official declarations to arrest the ever-increasing disorder, the names of Benedict XIV, Pius VIII, and Pius IX stand conspicuous. The first of these, one whose name is synonymous with whatever is learned or illustrious in the Sovereign Pontificate, was the champion who began the struggle after the Reformation. His Instruction of November 4, 1741, before declaring that these marriages are to be regarded as valid, notwithstanding the unlawful manner in which they had been contracted, continues: "His Holiness, deeply lamenting that there are among Catholics persons who, shamefully demented by an insane love, do not from their hearts abhor, and are not led entirely to abstain from these detestable nuptials, *which holy mother Church has unceasingly condemned and interdicted;* and praising very much the zeal of those Prelates who strive by the severest punishments enacted by the Church to prevent Catholics from uniting themselves in a sacrilegious bond with heretics, seriously and earnestly exhorts and admonishes all Bishops, Vicars-Apostolic, curés, missionaries, and all other faithful ministers of God and the Church, to prevent, as far as they are able, Catholics of both sexes from contracting such nuptials to the *ruin of their own souls*, and by every suitable means to break off and hinder the same."* The same learned Pontiff, in his Encyclical of June 29, 1748, which is perhaps the most comprehensive document on the subject that has yet emanated from the Holy See, after citing numerous decrees, etc., bearing on the question, says, speaking of dispensations which were sometimes given

---

* Declaratio super Matrimoniis Hollandiæ. Denziger, Enchiridion, p. 667–8. The italics are ours.

without requiring the abjuration of heresy as a previous condition: "These concessions were, in the first place, very rare, and the majority of them for contracting marriages between princes, and were not granted except for the most urgent reasons, and these pertaining to the public good." He concludes in words that will strike the modern ear as novel and peculiar: "Finally, from what has been said it is evident that in all cases in which permission or dispensation is asked from the Apostolic See for contracting marriage by a Catholic with a heretic, the same Apostolic See, as we have said above, *always disapproved and condemned, and now also abominates and detests such nuptials, unless abjuration of heresy precedes.*"* Passing over numerous Briefs of the Holy See, involving and explaining the doctrine contained in those already given, we reach, in the early part of the present century, the Pontificate of Pius VIII, when the subject assumed a form hitherto unknown, resulting in a conflict in the Prussian dominions between the secular and the ecclesiastical powers. As usual, the representatives of the latter suffered both in their own persons and in their flocks, on whom they saw injuries wantonly inflicted. Recourse was had to Rome, the centre of unity and the source of consolation and wisdom. The Head of the Church replied in an able Brief, in which, as his successor, Gregory XVI, remarks, "the Holy See had pushed indulgence so far that it may truly be said that it reached the limits which cannot be passed without prevarication." In the course of his epistle the following passage occurs, which shows the mind of the Church to be still unchanged: "We need not tell you, versed as you are in the sacred sciences, that *the Church has a horror of these unions which present so many deformities and spiritual dangers.*" A little further on he points out the three conditions which are always required, and from which, as Pius IX remarked in a late instruction, the Church can never dispense, since they are founded in the natural and divine law. His words are these: "It has been the constant habit to add to the dispensations granted, the express condition of requiring, previous to the marriage, necessary guarantees, (1) not only to preserve the Catholic party from being perverted by the non-Catholic, (2) the former being, on the other hand, required to use every effort to withdraw the other from error; (3) but also that the children of both sexes, to issue from the union, *should be brought up exclusively in the sanctity of the Catholic religion.*"†

* Denzinger, Enchiridion, pp. 672-3.
† See "Lives of the Popes," vol. ii, pp. 761-4, for a translation of this important document, and an account of the circumstances which called it forth.

It may not be out of place to state here a fact of which some young Christians are ignorant, who inconsiderately make a promise of marriage with a Protestant or an infidel; but who regretting it and repenting afterwards, and finding it difficult to extricate themselves from the embarrassing position in which it places them, marry reluctantly, because they deem it wrong to break off the engagement. What I would wish to tell such persons is this: It is a sin as well as an imprudence to make an unconditional promise of doing anything forbidden by the Church; and such a promise, when made, is not binding. Of this nature are unconditional promises to marry a person not a Catholic. Hence the breaking of such an engagement is not only not a sin, but is a positive duty, just as much as it would be a duty, for example, to break a promise of attending a Protestant meeting on Sunday instead of going to Mass.

It were superfluous to add more. The spirit of the Church is clearly seen from the words of her supreme Pastors. Every tribunal which the Christian is bound to respect and obey, has pronounced in the most explicit manner against them. How the children of the Church can still marry beyond her pale, it is difficult to imagine. True, many of them ask for and receive a dispensation; but, on the other hand, there are others whose criminality proceeds to such an extent that a union is necessary to redeem their character and conceal the effects of unbecoming intimacy. But even when a dispensation is granted, the Church does not conceal her displeasure and regret. At each mixed marriage she affords a further confirmation of her former decrees and prohibitions in the extreme measures to which she resorts to show the utter abhorrence in which she holds these unholy alliances. It is admirably symbolized in the gloom—for I can give it no name more appropriate—with which she surrounds such an union. A Christian burial service is more consoling. The persons are not permitted to enter the contract in the church, before the holy altar,—no, not even in the sacristy; the Holy Sacrifice is not offered up, nor does the blessing of the Church descend upon them as a fructifying dew; no candle burns as an emblem of faith—their faith, alas! burns too faintly. If the minister of God is permitted to be present, it is only as a witness, divested of every insignia of his sacred office; the sombre color of the tomb is all that is wanting to complete the picture. What if the Catholic so far forget his sacred dignity as a Catholic as to go before a civil magistrate or an heretical minister? If now the lamp of faith burns so faintly, will not the rude blasts of temptation and adversity be more than sufficient to extinguish it entirely? No trace of religion may remain in after years, but the melancholy reflection which will at times force itself upon the mind, that a priceless treasure has been lost. The children may learn to use the phrase so suggestive to the Catholic hearer, yet so common in many parts of the country: "I am a friend of the Catholics, for my father was once a member of that Church," or, "my mother ought to be a Catholic." Expressions of this kind bear a sad testimony against the person leaving the true fold, and tell of an immortal soul bartered to satisfy the cravings of an unholy love.

III.

SOME OF THE CAUSES OF MIXED MARRIAGES AT THE PRESENT TIME.

The better to arrest the growing evil of mixed marriages, it will be necessary to point out some of the principal causes from which they spring. It were impossible to enumerate all of them. Some, though local, or depending upon the condition or circumstances in which individual Catholics are placed, may yet have greater weight with them than causes which in general exercise a more wide-spread influence. Nor do I profess to point out all of even the greater causes; I shall content myself with indicating and commenting upon a few only,—but these, it is believed, will, if removed, destroy the influence of nearly if not quite all the others.

1. Foremost among these must be reckoned the absence of a true Catholic spirit, or lively faith among many Catholics. Of the terrible consequences which the principle of private interpretation gradually but necessarily introduced into the world, none is more fatal than that which, undermining the faith of man in the supernatural, weakens the influence of supernatural motives of action. And so powerful and insidious are the workings of this false principle, that Catholics, though professing to hold it in abhorrence, are yet influenced by it to a far greater extent than they are willing to acknowledge. Does the reading of the lives of the early martyrs, who so heroically laid down their lives for the Faith, create in our minds the same feelings as it did in the minds of Christians five hundred years ago? Or does it not rather read like a myth, and do not some persons claiming to be Catholics regard the joyful rushing of the martyrs to death as the result of an imprudent enthusiasm that should have been repressed? Some among us are almost cold enough in faith to excuse apostasy under circum-

stances so trying. We wish, indeed, for a place in heaven beside them, but we shrink from the thought of purchasing it at what we consider so dear a price. We too readily forget the words of Christ: "You are not of the world, as I am not of the world." I do not of course deny that there are many now living in every part of the Christian world who are animated by the true Catholic spirit; what I maintain is, that "the faith of many has grown cold," as St. Paul predicted it would, and that hence follow in society the consequences pointed out by the same inspired writer.

There must ever be in the nature of things an essential antagonism between truth and error; and much more between the purest truth and the basest error. Now, the only teacher of revealed truth upon earth is the Catholic Church, for to it alone was sent the Spirit of Truth to teach it all truth to the end of time. That all men are bound under the pain of eternal damnation to hear, believe and obey that divinely appointed teacher, is manifest from the words of Christ: "He that hears you, hears Me; and he that despises you, despises Me"; and "He that will not hear the Church, let him be to thee as the heathen and the publican." Nor is man at liberty to accept certain doctrines and reject others; for all depend alike on the same divine authority. Hence our Divine Redeemer in giving His Apostles—and through them the teaching Church to the end of time—their commission to instruct, commanded them to preach to all nations, "teaching them to observe *all things* whatsoever I have commanded you," and He further declared that "he that believeth not, shall be condemned." It is a lively sense of the authority upon which the teaching of the Church and the promises she makes to her children rest, that has inspired true Catholics in all ages with an affection for her bordering on enthusiasm. As Christ, who is the way, the truth and the life, abiding in His Church, makes it "the pillar and ground of truth," so Satan, "who is a liar, and the father of lies," acting on the depraved heart of the proud—that is, of those who prefer their own private judgment, according to the false principle of the Reformation, to the authority of the Church—makes it the source of every error. This lively faith in the teaching of the Church and correct idea of the nature of error must necessarily prevent mixed marriages. Hence St. Paul in forbidding them in the words "Bear not the yoke with unbelievers," immediately gives the reason: "for what participation hath justice with injustice? Or what fellowship hath light with darkness? And what concord hath Christ with Belial? Or what part hath the *faithful* with the *unbeliever?*"

The influence of a lively faith upon mixed marriages is strikingly illustrated in another way that is deserving the reader's serious attention. No person contemplates a mixed marriage so long as he is advancing in the way of perfection. It is only when his piety begins to grow cold that it begins to be thought of as something possible. Again, if a person who has contracted such a marriage begin afterwards to lead a more regular and exemplary life than he did at the time of his marriage, it will invariably be seen that, in proportion as his piety increases, in the same proportion will his regret for having married one not of the true Fold increase, and with it his appreciation of the difficulties in which it has involved him.

2. Allied to this want of a lively faith is the absence of a genuine hatred of heresy. To some persons such a hatred may appear impossible; to others it may seem a relic of the dark ages altogether unsuited to the present enlightened and liberal state of society. We are forced from necessity to live in the midst of heretics of every shade of unbelief, and to associate and traffic with them; and we find them good neighbors, and apparently in every respect the equals of their Catholic fellow-citizens. Even in the practice of their erroneous forms of religion we cannot but admire their seeming sincerity. And how can we be asked to hate that in which we can discover so little that is worthy of condemnation? But the fact that we do not detect any evil is no evidence that it does not exist; but is rather a proof that our consciences are not so sensitive as they should be. Besides, we must not permit ourselves to be caught by a fallacy, and imagine that we are required to hate our heretical neighbors. It is the heretical doctrines to which, consciously or unconsciously, they adhere, that we are required to hold in abhorrence. If we reflect on the true nature of heresy, it will not be difficult to hate it. Let the reader, then, bear well in mind that the antagonism between truth and error is and must be always the same, and cannot be toned down by the lapse of time or the character or manners of those who profess them. Catholicity cannot cease to be right because some of those who profess it do wrong; nor can heresy cease to be bad because some naturally good persons adhere to it. Jesus Christ has said of Christians, "It must needs be that scandals come"; and, "Have not I chosen you twelve [Apostles], and one of you is a devil." Good heretics are not such on account of their heretical doctrines, but in spite of them. Our daily intercourse with Protestants makes it no easy matter to entertain an undying hatred of their errors. And although there are many reasons why we must do so, I shall adduce those only that rest upon the inspired words

of the sacred Scriptures. But first let us ask, What is heresy? It is the choosing of a religious belief for one's self, and consequently the rejecting of that which the authority of the Church would impose; it is the practical application of the Protestant principle of private judgment; it is the rebellion of man against the Church, of pride against authority, of Satan against God. Now, the Catholic, so far as his religion is concerned, is the representative of the authoritative teaching of God; and the heretic, so far as his is concerned, is the representative of the rebellion of the devil. Awful as these expressions are, the words of Christ and His Apostles can be understood in no other way; and they are sufficiently clear to appeal to the understanding of the most illiterate. Says Christ to His Apostles: "He that hears you, hears Me; and he that despises you, despises Me." The Catholic hears; the heretic does not. Again, "He that will not hear the Church, let him be to thee as the heathen and the publican." The same remark once more applies. "He that is not for Me, is against Me." The heretic is not for Christ, hence he must be against Him. Again, says Christ: "Go, teach all nations, ... teaching them to observe all things," etc. The Catholic observes all things; the heretic does not. Again, "He that believeth and is baptized, shall be saved; he that believeth not, shall be condemned." Here, too, the Catholic and heretic are on opposite sides. The words of St. Paul breathe the same spirit as those of his Divine Master. Reproving the Galatians for permitting themselves to be deceived by false teachers, he says: "There are some that trouble you, and would pervert the gospel of Christ. But though we, or an angel from heaven, preach a gospel to you besides that which we have preached to you, let him be anathema." And in the next verse, to add force to his reproof, he repeats the same terrible words. Even the beloved disciple, St. John, is carried away by the heinousness of the crime of heresy of those who denied the divinity of Christ; and he forbids the Christians to associate with them. He says: "If any man come to you and have not this doctrine, receive him not into thy house, nor say to him: Welcome." Finally, that I may not burden the page with quotations that necessarily breathe the same spirit, I shall conclude with the words of Christ in the Apocalypse, to the Bishop of Ephesus, whom He reproves for his lukewarmness: "But thou hast this, that thou hatest the deeds of the Nicholaites, which I also hate." Here a man otherwise rebuked partially redeems his character even before God by his hatred of heresy.

It were superfluous to quote from the Fathers of the Church, the decrees of Councils, or the utterances of Sovereign Pontiffs: they would perfectly accord, as they necessarily must, with the words of Christ and His Apostles. It is, then, the duty of every Catholic to hate the errors of all those who wander from the one true Fold, of which he has the privilege of being a member; and the better Catholic he is, the more must he hate them; for he cannot love and prize the truth without holding in abhorrence that which would assail it. It is self-evident that this hatred must effectually prevent mixed marriages. But should it grow cold, as it has to a lamentable extent among Catholics at the present time, the barrier is removed, and mixed marriages lose that feature which has ever made them "abominable" and "detestable" in the eyes of the Church.

3. Another cause of mixed marriages is the attendance of Catholic children at the public schools. Catholic parents are sometimes so captivated with the outfit of these schools, where elegant buildings with commodious rooms and the latest improvements in school-furniture greet the eye, as vainly to imagine that for this reason the children must advance more rapidly in knowledge. Besides, the Protestant children who attend these schools are sometimes better dressed, and present a more genteel outward appearance than the poor children of the Catholic schools. It is much to be regretted that so many of our parishes are as yet unable on account of their poverty to supply better school-accommodations; but it is much more to be regretted that any Catholic parent should imagine that costly furniture, and not rather personal exertion, is requisite for advancement in learning, or that respectability consists in fine dress and liberal views, and not rather in a good moral character and a thorough knowledge of man's duties to God, to his neighbor, and to himself. The attendance of children at these infidel schools weakens their attachment to the Faith, and prevents them from conceiving a true appreciation of the place which religion holds; and in doing so it imparts erroneous views of the heinousness of the crime of rebellion against the authority of the Church. It lowers the standard of morals, and turns the mind of the child more and more aside from the pursuit of "the one thing necessary," to that of wealth and "respectability"; and—to pass over a host of other evils—it forms a circle of Protestant and infidel friends, and gives rise to companionships that in many cases ripen into mixed marriages.

4. A fourth cause of mixed marriages is the force of bad example. The greater the number of mixed marriages, the more powerful will be the force of the bad example given to the Catholic community; and youth, who find all restraint uncongenial to the ardor of their age, will find a partial justification of their conduct in the thought that so many

others are as guilty as they. If the parents themselves of the youth were parties in a mixed marriage, the example will have additional weight. And here let me state an important fact that may have escaped the attention of persons studying the question of mixed marriages. It is, that the children of a mixed marriage, where the Protestant party to it was afterwards converted, will be far more likely to contract mixed marriages than the children of Catholic parents. This is accounted for in part by the force of example, and in part by association with the friends of the parent who was originally Protestant. From the most careful personal observation, extending over many years, as well as from that of other persons of experience, I make no hesitation in affirming that the marriages of such children who were raised Catholic will be two with Protestants to one with Catholics. However startling this statement may seem, I have no fear that any person of extensive acquaintance with the subject will be able to call it successfully in question.

5. A further cause of mixed marriages is the manner in which persons passing from childhood to maturity become remiss in the reception of the Sacraments of Penance and the Holy Eucharist. For a few years after the child receives its first Communion it is generally a regular monthly or more frequent communicant; but as it grows up, and its passions begin to gain strength, and its need of the grace of the Sacraments increases, it unfortunately becomes, as a rule, less frequent in its reception of them, and falls a more easy prey to temptation. This is especially true of girls living out in cities, whose parents are sometimes too indifferent as regards the selection of places for them, and are not sufficiently vigilant in watching over their conduct. Such girls are frequently out at unseasonable hours, lose correct ideas of duty and self-respect, and become an easy prey to un-Catholic and unprincipled young men, who take them to fairs, balls, picnics, theatres, and other places of amusement. The consciences of such persons gradually become hardened, and their knowledge of duty indefinite; and, worst of all, they will not in many cases mention in confession the dangerous companionships in which they are entangled until the eve of their unhappy marriage, when little hope of arresting their imprudent course remains.

6. A sixth cause of mixed marriages is found in the literature of the day. The greater part of the stories found in the papers and novels commonly devoured by the young, are of such a character as in one way or another to attack the sanctity of Christian marriage. And so low is the standard of morality in the world, that this is done as a

matter of course, and no one is shocked by it. The young reader devours them in the same spirit, and unconsciously undermines the foundation of true morality and the correct idea of the sanctity of marriage in his mind; so that when the time of marriage comes for himself he has no higher idea than was learned from the heroes of the tales he read. These harmonize so well with the cravings of his sensual appetites that he is ready to follow them without hesitation. But it is not this class of reading that must plead guilty of ill-disguised immorality. It is sometimes to be found in literature of the highest order. The poet-laureate of England has built up one of his most celebrated poems, *Enoch Arden*, on an instance of conjugal infidelity of a shockingly immoral character. Yet his sin is readily pardoned by his enraptured admirers.

7. Finally, one of the principal causes of mixed marriages is a want of serious reflection. This will become sufficiently apparent to all who reflect on the evils of these unions, even as they are traced in the narrow compass of these pages, to require no further illustration. Properly considered, no step in life is more momentous than that of marriage. It is a matter in which the light of divine grace should be sought by earnest and persevering prayer; in which the counsel of a prudent director should be obtained; in which the advice of parents and prudent friends should be asked; in which the natural dispositions of the contracting parties should be carefully considered; and upon which, in a word, all the natural and supernatural light possible should be shed to prevent irreparable mistakes where most of all they are likely to be made. Yet, in fact, there are few steps taken with more reckless precipitation than this; and the following words from the Pastoral Letter of the Bishop of Hexham apply more forcibly to this country than they do to England: "We find that marriages of Catholics with Protestants are sadly prevalent among you, and that many seem to look upon such unions as if they were a matter of course, and unobjectionable. The engagement is made, the preparations are completed, the wedding-day is often fixed, and then a dispensation is asked for as a mere formality, without any attempt to plead some cause why the solemn laws of the Church should be thus set aside. Nay, so completely is it taken for granted, that your pastors sometimes fear that the shock of a refusal may be too much for your faith, and plead the danger that exists of driving you into a sacrilegious rebellion and open defiance of the Church."

IV.

UNHAPPINESS AND MISERY THE NECESSARY CONSEQUENCES OF MIXED MARRIAGES.

Much of the unhappiness and misery which haunts the steps of the married couple, and attends the training of their family, proceeds from such a difference of natural disposition in the man and woman, as has been said, as will not coalesce to form an agreeable companionship. It is difficult to imagine how so important a matter could have escaped the attention of persons about to form a most intimate union for life. But the hasty and thoughtless manner in which they proceeded is sufficient to account for it. An unrestrained passion, a foolish fancy, it may be, was the only motive present to their minds, without a moment's reflection on the lifetime to be spent in each other's company. Divine grace, it must be admitted, has much to do with the future of every one of us. But God is accustomed to employ human means and channels, so as not to interfere with the harmony which His wisdom has established in the universe. If human weakness and folly can mar the beauty of a Christian marriage, over which the Church extends the mantle of protection and pours the treasures of divine grace, will it not vitiate much more those in which religion has no part?

The Christian marriage invokes a blessing on the husband, wife and children; unchristian nuptials entail a threefold misfortune. Put the case of perhaps the most frequent occurrence, that in which the husband is the non-Catholic. Suppose him to be either a member of one of the denominations generally regarded as the respectable portion of the Protestant community; or, which is more probably the case, a mere sensationist, ready to attach himself to the preacher who for the time is commanding the largest share of public attention in his neighborhood; or, finally, let him be a declared infidel, an enemy of religion in every form. In any case he cannot hope to enjoy the pleasures of a good husband and father. If he reflect at all before contracting marriage, it is not as a Christian—at least not as a Catholic; and however well his conduct may seem to accord with the maxims of human prudence, there is an essential element of happiness that can never be found in the cup which he would fain put to his lips. He differs essentially from his companion in his manner of thinking. Both the present and the future are viewed from different points : what should be all to her, is of trifling importance to him ; he lives for time and the world—she for eternity and God ; in a word, they remain as before marriage—not one, but two.

Let us turn, however, to the case of the wife—with whose condition our sympathies should more properly be enlisted. The future looms up darkly before all save the unfortunate victim, from whom a merciful Providence, kind even to the erring, conceals much of the sorrows and afflictions in store for her. Her temporal happiness may be looked upon as irrevocably lost, her eternal salvation is placed in the greatest jeopardy, and she is forced to submit to become the mother of children who may never see the face of God and the resplendent mansion of the blessed. At present all is sunshine, and not a cloud appears to intercept the view; promises are readily made, to be as readily broken. Alas, for human weakness! Like the exile in a distant land who dreams that he again witnesses the scenes made dear by the sports of childhood, and enjoys the company of those loved ones whom he never more expected to meet on this side the grave, it only renders the reality of his situation the more grievous when he awakes to find that all has vanished with the return of day.

If the husband be indifferent in matters of religion, or disposed to regard the Catholic Church with a favorable eye because his wife is a member of that body, she will enjoy the greatest liberty her condition can afford. Still, how many difficulties may he not put in her way that will render the practice of her religion difficult, not to say impossible? The Catholic, it is well known, will at a great temporal sacrifice locate himself near a church in order to have his wife and family in a place where they may be able to hear Mass regularly and witness religion surrounded with all the ceremonies and attractions capable of pleasing the senses and elevating the heart; where the children, even, on the lap of their mother may be present; and where the knowledge and practice of the Catholic religion will grow with their growth and strengthen with their strength. Not so the Protestant husband. With the best dispositions, he is a stranger to the importance of religion; for the system to which he belongs, if he belong to any, has so hewn down and lopped off the essential doctrines and practices as to make it a matter of trifling moment whether a man believe or practice any or not; he may, if he feels so disposed, doubt the existence of God and a future state, and be still a passable Protestant. It is not difficult to understand how such a one cannot appreciate the longing of the Catholic heart for the regular attendance at Mass and reception of the Sacraments, and how he will be indisposed to sacrifice worldly interests for the sake of one whom he may sincerely love. She is in this manner placed at a distance from church, and is forced to bear it in silence; to feel her love of the Church grow cold with the lapse of time, till she comes at length to be indifferent in affairs of religion. All arise from the absence of that unanimity of sentiment, that sameness of interest which must ever be wanting, that knitting together of souls, without which the ceremony of marriage is little better than an empty form, and wedded life a species of penal servitude. If she entertain for him the love which is a part of her duty, she will find it difficult to resist the temptation that would whisper in her heart that, after all, his religion cannot be heretical; that the Church is too severe in condemning it; that he is good, practices virtue, and that virtue merits and will receive a reward. This is the first step in the way of perversion; the second differs but little from it. He has frequently gone with her to Mass, and now he requests her to return the compliment and attend his church. Besides, she is curious to know what is said and done there; what is meant by Prayer Meeting, Love Feast, Taking the Sacrament, etc. She has no intention of taking part in the exercises; she is impelled by curiosity. The second and third visit will be followed by less remorse of conscience; in a word, the work has been begun, and the experiences of the past show in a vision what the end will be. But suppose she resists temptation, represses curiosity, and remains faithful. Suppose she continues to view his religion in the same light in which it is regarded by the Church: the thought that he is treading the broad road to ruin must ever be a subject of most poignant grief. When sickness comes upon him, and her days and nights are consumed at his bedside, that work of love will be embittered by the consideration that she cannot afford assistance to the immortal part of his being, that must, ere long, appear before its Judge and receive a final sentence. No sad yet consoling word is heard bidding her call in the minister of God; no anxious friend inquires whether or not he has received the last Sacraments and consolations of religion. No: he is a stranger to these supernatural aids, and never did the afflicted wife realize this truth so vividly as now. The waters of Baptism, the preliminary step towards entering the assembly of the faithful on earth, and the indispensable requisite for gaining admittance to the realms of endless bliss, perhaps never flowed on his brow. The body will soon repose in the tomb,—but the soul, what portion shall it receive? Let the veil be drawn over what God has reserved for His own eye and those of His angels.

But the greatest affliction the poor wife will be forced to endure will be found in the contemplation of her isolated condition. What a sense of loneliness must overpower her when time and familiarity with her new mode of life have removed the fatal delusion! Yet this is only the beginning. She has yet to sound the depths of her soul, and learn the capabilities of enduring that may lie concealed in its numerous folds. The moment when this depth will be laid open to her is when she turns from the cold, inhospitable world to prostrate herself before the throne of Him who alone can pour the balm of consolation into the bruised and bleeding heart. Here, too, the partner of her life is far from her. For if she prays, it is alone; if she assists at Mass and receives the Sacraments, it is alone; if she strive to overcome the temptations incident to her state of life, it is alone; in serving the family, in adoring God, she is alone. "There is none to comfort her among all those that were dear to her." In health, in sickness, in death, in the grave, in eternity, she is alone; separated from him for whom she should be ready to forsake all,—home and country, parents, relations and friends. What can I say more? Even the supernatural joys which the Church affords her children at certain seasons are to her days of mourning. If the Christian heart leaps with gladness on celebrating the birth of our Redeemer, she must sit at home and weep over her inability to share in the universal rejoicing. The same takes place at Easter, Corpus Christi, and during the beautiful season of the devotion to Mary, when the Christian soul is renewed like the blooming year. If she have a family, it only serves to increase her sorrow. How deeply she rues the day on which she followed her own counsel, rather than listen to the admonitions of her parents and the warning of the Church! Yet this is the most favorable light in which a mixed marriage can appear; it is making the Protestant a mere negative in contributing to conjugal felicity.

Proceed a degree further, and imagine the husband to be a member of one of the sects, zealous for the creed in which he was schooled. Instead of regarding her religion with indifference, he seizes every opportunity to ridicule and oppose it. When the time approaches for making the Easter Communion or of performing any other particular duty, his mockeries, scoffs, and threats increase; the wife is forbidden to perform it, and if she still does it, it is by stealth, and will furnish a plentiful source of contention for weeks to come; if she does not, he has gained a victory at the expense of her peace of mind. Perhaps he makes the minister of his sect, or some religious friend, a frequent visitor at his home, where, as a matter of course, innumerable circumstances will tend to make the religion of his wife a subject of common and annoying conversation. If this be so, she will soon be a stranger to happiness, and will learn to sigh for death as the only alleviation of her sufferings, the only rest for her weary soul. On Sunday she follows one street to church, he goes by another; she is taught to regard the salvation of her soul as the "one thing necessary,"—that "he that loves husband or wife more than Me is not worthy of Me." She is told to turn a docile ear to the voice of the Church; for "he that will not hear the Church, let him be to thee as a heathen and a publican." The duties she owes to her family are also commented on, since "if any man have not care of his own, and especially of those of his house, he hath denied the faith, and is worse than an infidel." He, on the contrary, is entertained with a discourse on universal salvation, or regaled with a tirade against the Pope, whom the excited minister modestly terms the Beast of the Apocalypse, or a lesson is read on the selling of Indulgences, worshipping the Virgin Mary, etc. Her children, if she have the misfortune of becoming a mother, must be baptized by stealth, if at all, instructed but imperfectly, and their adherence to the Church here, and their eternal salvation hereafter, must ever be a matter of deepest anxiety.

Going still further, it sometimes happens that the husband scoffs at the very mention of God and religion. If so, do not ask for a picture of the future. The bent-down form and faltering step; the emaciated countenance and hollow eyes; the cheek furrowed with tears, and hair silvered before the prime of life is reached; or, worse, the struggle carried on for a time amid adversities of every kind, till at length the broken heart yielded to despair; the lost faith, and forgetfulness of eternity tell, more plainly than words could do, the melancholy tale. It frequently happens, however, that there is no struggle; and that the person who should be a Catholic calmly gives up all idea of complying with religious duties, and becomes practically an infidel. I once knew a Catholic lady of exemplary regularity become so enamored of a young man as to marry him although he hated the Catholic religion so much that he would not permit a priest, no nor the Bishop, to marry him. Yet she drifted immediately in the current with him. I was again called upon to visit a woman who was married to a Protestant by his preacher, continued to attend his church with him, and had a family. While the children were yet small, she was taken suddenly ill, and died without being able to give the least sign of repentance. Almost every priest is able to furnish similar examples.

If the picture will admit of a still deeper shade, it is found in the dying request of the wife to have a priest summoned to her bedside coldly refused; in the soul going forth from the body, after exhausting itself in fruitless cries for the assistance which can alone avail in that dread moment; in the melancholy reflection that even the lifeless clay will not be permitted by the heartless husband to rest in consecrated ground and share in the suffrages of the Church and the faithful. I have known instances in which the Protestant or infidel husband threatened violence to the priest who had the courage to present himself at the house to administer the last rites of religion to the dying wife, whose cries and groans from an adjoining apartment would have been sufficient to move a heart of adamant. Among other instances let me give that of a husband who presented himself at the door with a revolver in hand to meet the priest, who was forced to retire. A second visit, though hardly less perilous, was yet more successful. Another priest, after travelling eight or ten miles through inclement weather, found the husband ready to meet him with a large carving knife. Hundreds of such instances might be furnished if it were necessary. Yet these husbands no doubt made many fair promises before marriage; and, if they were married by the priest, must have promised to afford every facility to the wife whom they now wished to exclude even from heaven.* But I am forced to say that blame is

---

* An important case has recently been decided by the British Courts, which affords a striking evidence of the little regard to which the wishes of the wife are entitled before the law, and the ease with which the promises made by the husband before marriage may be broken whenever he sees fit to break them. The court has decided, in fact, that it is his duty, in certain circumstances, to break them, although they were the sole conditions on which the wife consented to the marriage, or the Church permitted it. The case is briefly this, as stated and commented upon by the *Dublin Review* (Jan., 1879, pp. 208-223): In 1863, Mr. Agar-Ellis was paying his addresses to the Hon. Miss Stonor, a daughter of Lord Camoys. He was a Protestant; she a Catholic. On making a proposal of marriage, he was informed of the conditions required by the Church: but he refused for two years to consent to comply with them. At length, however, he consented, and the marriage took place. The children, the fruit of the union, received instruction in the Catholic Faith, but were compelled by their father to attend at Protestant places of worship. But upon a certain Sunday morning they rebelled, and refused to go with him. This incident led to the initiation of legal proceedings on the part both of the father and the mother. Mrs. Agar-Ellis presented a petition to the court, alleging that her husband had threatened to send her children away in order to be educated by a Protestant clergyman in the country, and praying that such direction might be given for their custody and education as should prevent them from being deprived of her society and care, and permit them to be brought up in the Roman Catholic religion. This petition was dismissed. Mr. Agar-Ellis constituted his children wards of the court, and took out a summons for directions with reference to their education. Upon this application, Vice-Chancellor Malins made an order declaring that the children should be brought up as Protestants, and granted an injunction restraining the mother "from taking, or procuring, or permitting to be taken the infants, or any of them to confession, or to any church, or place of worship where service was performed otherwise than according to the rites of the Church of England." The order was the subject of an immediate appeal: but the Court of Appeal affirmed the order.

Such was the result for the Catholic mother and her helpless children, because—as was stated in a similar case—" It is on principle settled so as to be beyond question or argument, that *the ante-nuptial promise is, in point of law, absolutely void.*" The italics are mine. Let the Catholic contemplating a mixed marriage reflect on this; for, although it occurred in England, the law of this country, so far as I am acquainted with its tenor, is of the same spirit. The following are the conclusions which the *Review* draws from a consideration of the case:

frequently to be attached to the wife. If she were more firm and resolute in demanding the rights of conscience when she first finds her husband disposed to break his promises, she would in many cases do much to ameliorate her condition in the future. I do not say that she should quarrel; but I do say that when she finds herself ensnared she should energetically and courageously demand those rights of which slaves themselves cannot justly be deprived. But such a person often holds a place beneath that of the slave. Oh, that an angel would come and show to those contemplating a mixed marriage the terrible fate that awaits them, here and in the world to come! But the disregard with which they commence life too often remains with them during it, and rather deepens into utter oblivion of God and heaven than dissolves into tears of compunction. Of what avail is the voice of God's minister when they disregard the lessons of experience?

Over this mockery of a union stands the ghastly form of Divorce, ready with a drawn sword to sever the slender bond, and launch the unfortunate wife a helpless wreck on a new ocean of misery, vast and fathomless. For, what is matrimony from a Protestant point of view? This is a question of paramount importance, and cannot be answered more suitably than by citing the words of M. de Stolberg, and supporting and illustrating them by the statistics of the Divorce Court,— material ready at the wish of any inquirer who will be at the slightest pains to collect it. Writing to a young person whom he was endeavoring to dissuade from a mixed marriage, he says, after enumerating some of the trials to which she will be exposed: "And he who demands such a sacrifice from you does not pledge himself to be your husband forever. His religion authorizes him to forsake you in order to contract ties which Jesus Christ declares to be adulterous. And this husband who *lends* himself to you, while you *give* yourself to him, is either without religion, and then he leaves you without security for his

---

"1. That an agreement entered into before marriage by a husband to relinquish to his wife the religious education of their children is absolutely void." But we have seen from the words of the Holy Father given in the text that this is an agreement without which the Church cannot sanction a mixed marriage. Yet the Protestant who makes it and the Catholic who receives it must regard it as a mere waste of words.

2. "That while the father is alive he is the sole judge whether danger is to be apprehended in disturbing religious impressions already acquired," etc.

3. "That in the case of a conflict the court will actively assist the father," etc. "What comes out more prominently than anything else, in all these cases, is the absolute subordination of the wife to the husband, and her total extinction, social and moral." "In the management or education of her children she has no right beyond what her husband benignantly permits." I need add no comments to this practical illustration of the lamentable condition of the children of a mixed marriage, or the helplessness of a mother, with the best dispositions, to ameliorate it. When she appeals to the law, she is told there is no law for her but the will of her husband.

fidelity, or he is attached to his false worship, and in that case he will soon repent of having married you." Should he repent, he can with little difficulty and with hardly the shadow of a reason obtain a divorce in any part of this country, as I have elsewhere shown. This facility with which divorce may be had adds one of the most appalling features to mixed marriages. Let the young lady who contemplates such a marriage, or to whom the temptation of such a union is presented, reflect seriously upon this.

The whole matter resolves itself into such a result as this: A thoughtless young girl confides herself to a person in the most perfect and unreserved manner possible, and submits to the possibility of every imaginable grievance and injustice, and the great probability of eternal ruin, and yet she may be deserted at any moment. What fate then awaits her? What is to become of her children? This one reflection, were there no other unpleasant consequences to be anticipated, should make the Catholic party, before contracting marriage, pause and consider: " He whom I marry to-day may forsake me to-morrow. And while I dare not enter into another marriage during his lifetime, I may be forced to endure every privation; perhaps I may even find it necessary to beg a morsel of bread. The consolation of having my children —should God in time bless me with any—by my side, may not be granted; I may be forced to confide them to unfriendly hands." But it is enough. Let us turn to consider the condition of the children.

V.

THE CHILDREN OF MIXED MARRIAGES.

Having devoted so much space to considering the case of the parents, let us now briefly glance at that of the children. However grievous may have been the portion of the Catholic parent, it was willingly submitted to, at least by anticipation, in embracing that state of life. But the children had no part in shaping their destiny. Before their birth, they were doomed to a probable life of heresy or infidelity, with its consequent train of evils both in the temporal and eternal order. Of what crime, we may ask, were these helpless innocents guilty, that with the life of the body they should inherit from an unreflecting parent the probable death of the soul, in so far at least as it lay in the power of the very ones to give it, to whom God and nature united in intrusting the proper education and training of the young mind? If there be [any creature worthy of compassion, it is surely this tender, unsuspecting, helpless infant; if there be any calamity that should call forth our tears and the tears of angels, surely it is this act of injustice committed against the helpless and unsuspecting. I would not arouse the feelings of the reader or call forth his tears; I would only move parents and the young to reflect seriously on the terrible evil of mixed marriages and the unchristian and inhuman crime, the crying outrage which they sometimes willingly commit against their own flesh and blood, and the terrible account which they prepare for themselves when the time of repentance and satisfaction shall have passed forever. At present it is only the probability of a great evil;—the remedy is still in their hands; return in a few years, and the actual occurrence of the evil may appear, to rend the heart and bedew the cheek. Perhaps the reader has already learned to lament the frequent recurrence of this appalling crime,—for who that feels an interest in the growth of the Church and the welfare of his fellow-men has not learned so much; if not, he may have witnessed the tears of others flow. Let us, however, repress the rising force of feeling, and proceed with deliberation to the discussion of our subject.

The habits of man, as is well known, are formed by imitation. Before it is conscious of what is transpiring, the child will have formed from imitation habits which the vicissitudes of a long life will labor in vain to eradicate. It is a gross error, and evinces an ignorance of human nature, to imagine that a child is ever too young to receive impressions. Are we not frequently astonished at the inquiries and replies of a child of four or five summers, and struck with the correctness of its conclusions? Nothing escapes its attention. Its observation extends even to matters of religion, which the difference of opinion of father and mother makes a topic of frequent and, perhaps, disedifying conversation. How readily will it not perceive that a want of unison exists between them in this particular! Imagination will readily furnish the reader with a picture, more or less vivid, of the course of reasoning the young mind will naturally pursue. Nature has impressed it so deeply with reverence for the authors of its mortal being, and with deference for their opinions, as to render it impossible for the child to think that either is capable of error. To what conclusion can it arrive? The father attends this Church, the mother that; the children attend one, to the exclusion of all others; or they visit both indiscriminately; or the father takes the boys, and the mother the girls. And here let me protest against the criminal inconsiderateness of the Catholic who before marrying with one not of our holy Faith, deliberately agrees to claim the children only of her sex, leaving the religious training of the others to the care of her uncatholic partner. Is not the soul of a little girl as precious in the sight of God as that of a boy? and is not the soul of a boy as well calculated to enjoy the delights of paradise as that of a girl? The Catholic must believe that in her religion only is salvation attainable; yet she deliberately gives up half the children to what she knows to be error and heresy, and—must it be said—to almost certain eternal perdition. Surely this is a most inhuman atrocity, which only the implied renunciation of the Catholic Faith can justify in the eyes of reasoning men, which nothing can justify in the eyes of God. Whence is the child to seek a solution of the problem? It is unable to weigh the arguments that respectively support the two religious systems, and thus to determine for itself which is true, which false. The voice of natural love forbids it to believe that either parent is in the wrong. This much only it knows with certainty, that of two contradictory propositions one only can be true. Affection at this season of life is more powerful than reason. Religion, it must conclude, is, after all, a matter of trifling importance, else why should father and mother differ so widely in regard to it?

And here let me note another circumstance that like many others connected with mixed marriages escapes the popular eye. If a young lady is so unfortunate as to marry out of the Church, people will still congratulate her if she gets a good husband. Yet so far as the religious training of the children is concerned, this is rather a misfortune than a blessing. If the husband is a bad man, the natural law imprinted on the souls of the children will not be slow in telling them that his conduct cannot be an example for them; and hence they will listen the more readily to the teaching and follow with greater docility the example of the mother. But if the husband is a good, religious man after his own way, it will be impossible for the children to decide between the relative merits of the two religions, and their ideas of the importance of religion at all will be the more thoroughly subverted, leaving them skeptics of the most hopeless sort.

Nor can the Catholic parent avert the deplorable consequences. A partial success may attend her efforts; but she can never inspire her children with the firm faith and profound reverence found in the heart of the Catholic. The child's respect for the parent is also undermined; for if the motive of its submission and obedience is not, after the promptings of nature, the fear and love of God, "from whom all paternity proceeds," they will not long retain their purity, simplicity and force. External agencies, too, will be busily engaged in perverting the young mind and in sullying the young heart. Its relationship with Protestants will frequently bring it into their company; they will besiege it with inquiries and puzzling questions, comment on the difficulty of practising the Catholic religion, while theirs demands so little sacrifice from poor human nature; even the Protestant parent will often take occasion to express his doubt in the mysteries of our holy religion, in the Real Presence, the power of the priest to forgive sins, the necessity of hearing Mass on Sundays, fasting, etc. Notwithstanding the fallacy of his arguments, they will still appear formidable to the child, unable as it is to refute them or discover their weak point. Unable to answer them, it will acknowledge their force, and begin to doubt the teaching of the Church; which, united to the difficulty it meets with in the practice of religion, will ere long make Catholicity seem a burden, which it is to its interest to cast wholly aside. While this is taking place in the heart, the mind is being poisoned by the pernicious ideas of morality which are afloat in the unholy atmosphere of the infidel schools which it is accustomed to frequent. If the child that is well instructed finds it difficult successfully to withstand the fierce attacks on religion and morality now so common, where will the ill-instructed offspring of a mixed marriage be?

If the bigoted husband forbid the baptism of the children, the trouble and anguish of the mother will be increased a hundredfold. And this is very common. There are few neighborhoods in which instances of it are not to be found. So common is it indeed that examples are wholly uncalled for. The mother must steal out with the child, or confide it to a friend to have it baptized, when the husband is absent from home; and this is not done perhaps until the child has passed several months without the Sacrament, and in daily peril of dying deprived of all right to heaven. When the husband at length discovers, by some accident—for the matter is carefully concealed from him—that his child has been baptized, he becomes enraged, blasphemes the Church and all that belongs to it, abuses, perhaps beats his wife, and makes her life miserable for weeks to come. It will also tend to make him the more vigilant to prevent the child, when it begins to grow up, from being instructed in the rudiments of Catholic doctrine, and from practising the duties of a Christian. Hence the young mind will expand and the character will be formed without the first principles of religion,—wholly ignorant of its duties to God, its fellow-men and itself. And when the age comes at which a youth commonly begins to reflect seriously, and the few imperfect lessons received in early life come up dimly from the storehouse of memory, the baser passions will have begun to acquire strength and to urge their claim to indulgence. Having never fully, or even imperfectly, comprehended what it is to be a Christian— having never been taught to restrain the waywardness of fallen nature —having never been convinced of the necessity of chastising the body and bringing it into subjection—having never, in a word, known that the life of man is a constant warfare, he will hardly give promise of an honorable and Christian career.

If, on the other hand, the mother is the Protestant, it will be almost impossible for the father to instil into the minds of his children the dews of Christian doctrine. At a time when the deepest and most abiding impressions are usually made, the child is constantly in the society of its mother, while the father spends but little time in its company. She can readily counteract any instruction he might then impart; for, together with a more favorable opportunity, she possesses a more captivating manner.

But the period when the imbecility of the Catholic parent against an enemy of the Church most clearly appears, is when the youth is to be prepared for receiving the Sacraments. Imagine a father instructing his son on the necessity of confessing his sins, the preparation to be made, and the manner of undertaking the important work. He next essays a lesson on Communion, going as well as he can over the ground usually reviewed on such an occasion. Perhaps he is to a great extent ignorant of what he would teach, and gives the child good reason to conclude that he is not in his proper element; perhaps his practice of religion is not wholly free from censure; or despair of success may cut short all, and the child be left "till it has better judgment." At best, what will it infer from the inestimable importance and advantage of receiving the Sacraments, contrasted with the conduct and belief of the other loved parent, who will not be slow in declaring the strong disapprobation with which the lesson was heard?

But it is the pastor, to whom is confided the care of the soul, that perceives the deep wound inflicted on the young heart. When undertaking the same work of preparing the child for the Sacraments, and particularly for First Communion, he readily notices the difference between those who were blessed with Catholic parents and those who were not so fortunate. The child that received its first lessons of religion on the lap of its mother, and afterward united religious with secular learning, has a firm foundation for its faith, receives the instruction with docility, and learns to regard the Sacraments and sacred rites of the Church with reverential awe. Even the child of Catholic parents left in total ignorance will readily open its heart to the saving knowledge of religion, and receive with an unwavering confidence the explanation of the Divine Mysteries. But the one in whose heart all ideas of religion have been destroyed by the domestic disputes which it has always been accustomed to hear, will regard with a sceptical eye the words of its instructor. In vain is the lesson repeated and reiterated by the patient instructor; it vain is the example of the saints and holy youths laid before him in the most attractive manner: his heart has never been warmed with the breath of true piety; it has never been moistened with the gentle dew of prayer, lisped at the knees of a good mother. Do what the zealous instructor will, the soil remains barren. *The child is a stranger to reverence.* If, by dint of repeated explanations and discourses on the paramount importance of the act which it is about to perform, the attention of the child is finally arrested, and it appears to appreciate, in a certain degree, the work in which it is engaged, its feelings will usually spring from the thought that it is preparing for something unusual, rather than that it is the stupendous privilege which faith teaches us to esteem it. In general, the Sacraments, if at all received, will be approached in a mechanical way, without even an approximate idea of their value. A greater misfortune than this drying up of the fountains of faith, piety, and reverence, can hardly be imagined. Yet the pastor daily meets it among the disorders of mixed marriages, and daily laments his inability to apply an effectual remedy.

In connection with the above features of this important topic is another consideration, which generally escapes attention, though following as a natural consequence: it is that the children of a mixed marriage, though trained up to the knowledge and practice of the Catholic religion, fall away from the Faith more readily than the offspring of a Catholic union. This assertion is sustained both by the evidence of reason and the facts of the case. For the best instruction that can be given is almost nugatory without the force of example. The example of a devout father or a pious mother constantly rises up to upraid the negligent child with dishonoring the memory of one whom it is bound to honor; and even when the child has attained to maturity, the memory of a departed parent survives, and the soiled or worn out prayer-book may tell him of one in whose footsteps he should glory to tread.

But what will the vision of the past call up to the child of a mixed marriage? Religious disputes; known duties neglected, or performed in a perfunctory manner; Sacraments received at the time only when the Church prescribes it under pain of excommunication; and Mass heard when there could be found no excuse for absence. Or, it may be, an heroic though unhappy life, a continual sacrifice offered for the love of God and the Church to one who continued ungrateful to the end. Such noble examples as these are unfortunately not the rule, but the exception.

VI.

THE PRACTICAL RESULT OF MIXED MARRIAGES.

While the most zealous opponent of mixed marriages must acknowledge that they are the means of converting to the true Faith some persons who might not, humanly speaking, have come to a knowledge of the Church, it must, on the other hand, be confessed that not a few are by the same means perverted, with their families, and turned away from the right path. If the example, the love and prayers of the Catholic member are instrumental in so good a work, it is only to a limited extent; the number of such converts bears no proportion to that of those who fall away and are lost. And granting that a vast majority were converted, is not the loss of a single immortal soul, "for whom Christ died," a calamity to be averted by every possible means? The danger of perversion is always present; it is the event which reason would lead us to expect, and if it does not so happen, it is because the grace of God, seconded by personal efforts and sacrifices, succeeds in turning nature from her proper channel. The principle is bad; it is the seed; the tree and its fruits are in the world around us. These, which speak the language of facts, are more convincing than mere speculations. Take the following general and particular statistics, which have been collected and arranged with scrupulous care, and which are free from any exaggeration, however incredible they may appear:

There is a congregation in one of the Middle States (and the Middle States, it is natural to suppose, are no worse in this respect than the other States of the Union) which, containing about one hundred and seventy-five families, has the appalling number of *fifty-seven mixed marriages*. These afford the following statistics, which place the dreadful disorder of which I am treating in its true light, and offer a comment which the most irrefragable arguments would fail to produce. The number of converts resulting from all the means that have been employed is only *six;* while those who have forsaken their religion and gone astray count *twenty-two.* There are still others whose case is at present doubtful, some of whom it is but reasonable to suppose will turn in one direction, some in another. But the ratio already given naturally fills the mind with apprehensions which an acquaintance with the condition of affairs is not calculated to dispel. Add to this the sorrow, anxiety and care yet to be endured by those who, sustained by divine assistance, will persevere till death; and then turn to the children. As regards them, there are at present found *fifty-four* who are being instructed in the rudiments of our holy religion, with the prospect of adhering to the practice of her doctrines; as a counterpoise for which, we have *one hundred and thirty-seven* who are receiving their religious training in one or another of the sects, or are left to grow up in utter ignorance; and *thirty-one* whose ultimate end is yet doubtful. Many of these families, it is proper to observe, are still increasing, some for good, others for evil. Finally, as a further result, there are presented *four* Catholic, *seven* mixed, and *twenty-nine* Protestant marriages emanating from the same baneful source. To sum up in a few words. The number of perverted Catholics is nearly four to one against the converts; the Protestant children, nearly three to one; while those whose case is uncertain is as one to two. The mixed marriages are nearly two to one, and the Protestant more than seven to one against the Catholic marriages.

If the above figures appear to be too general, take the following particular ones, in which an Irish and an American couple figure. They are, I admit, extraordinary instances; but they show to what an extent the evils of mixed marriages may reach in a single family. And perhaps similar instances are not so rare as people imagine. The principal reason they are thought to be rare is because people have not the opportunity or do not take the pains to trace them out in all their ramifications. My limited experience, so far from leading me to think them of unusual occurrence, makes me, on the contrary, feel assured that so far from being rare, they are very common. But to come to the two families in question; and first, of the Irish. The wife was the Catholic, and she has persevered in the midst of difficulties and trials that are and can be known only to God. Nor is she remiss in her religious duties: on the contrary, she is most exemplary. Their union was blessed with ten children. A part, I know not how many, were baptized by stealth; but only one made any attempt at leading the life of a Catholic; which, however, he has long since abandoned. He was twice married to Protestants, the first of whom was converted before her death. Of his large family a part was baptized, but no member is now of the one Fold. The rest of the original family all married Protestants, except one who is as yet unmarried; two of them married twice each, and another one three times. All but one have large families, and some of these grandchildren, perhaps fifteen, are also married. To sum up, then, we have: the husband, who lived and died a Protestant; one convert; three or four apostates; half a dozen or more children baptized, but never raised in the true Faith; two mixed marriages, and perhaps thirty (the number is uncertain) Protestant marriages; between seventy-five and a hundred Protestant children; at least fifteen, perhaps many more, young, increasing families; but *not one Catholic*. "*By their fruits you shall know them.*" Now, take the American couple. Here, too, the wife was the Catholic, and has persevered in the practice of her Faith in the midst of trials and persecutions more than sufficient to win a martyr's crown. This couple were married about forty-five years ago; and had six children, all of whom were baptized, and trained for a time to the practice of their religion; some, if not all, receiving their first Holy Communion. The only one, however, that persevered to adult age, married out of the Church, soon after apostatized, and is raising a Protestant family. Four of the others married Protestants, one of them twice. The remaining one first married a Protestant, and upon his death, soon after, returned to the practice of the Catholic religion, marrying in succession two Catholics, and is now raising her family in the true Faith. The outcome of this union is a fathomless ocean of sorrow for the wife; five apostates; five families of say twenty-five children being raised Protestants; *no convert;* one Catholic family of four or five children; and two Catholic, one mixed, and six Protestant marriages. "*By their fruits you shall know them.*" Yet this havoc in the Church, dreadful as it is, is the work which two mixed marriages are capable of effecting in half a century. What will the next half effect? Further, it is not to be forgotten that in all these cases the wife was the Catholic, which is the most favorable aspect in which a mixed marriage can be presented. Should the wife be the Protestant, the Christian training of the children would be almost a hopeless undertaking.

The following, condensed from the *West-Virginia Catholic Messenger*, is an instance in which the father was the Catholic, and it falls in nothing behind those already given. Richard Reeder, of Wood County, W. Va., died in 1878, at the age of 103 years. He had been brought up in the true Faith, but at the age of 24 married a Protestant, and, falling away from the practice of his religious duties, did not become reconciled to the Church until a year or two before his death. "A trustworthy account," says the *Messenger*, "gives their issue as follows: thirteen children, eighty-five grandchildren, one hundred and seventy-five great-grandchildren, thirty great-great-grandchildren—in all, to the date of Mr. Reeder's death, 303 souls. . . . . They are all Protestants of various hues. But one-seventh of them, at most, belong formally to any sect; the rest are scattered around." No account, it must be remembered, is here made of the number of Protestant marriages—for there was no Catholic nor mixed marriage—nor of the number of families still increasing. Here too the mixed marriage was unattended by intemperance or other external agent to aid it in working out its lawful destiny. "*By their fruits you shall know them.*"

Can anyone after this accuse the Church of severity in the enforcement of her discipline? can anyone censure the Bishops and Clergy for warning their flocks, and disclaiming even with unwonted severity against this blighting disorder? But it may be argued, and with some apparent plausibility, that in communities where the Catholic population is proportionately larger, the influence on the mind of a Protestant united with a Catholic to bring him to embrace the Catholic religion would be comparatively greater than where Protestant ascendancy prevailed; and where mixed marriages, by reaching the numbers found in the first instance given above, had lost nearly all appearance of deformity and established a prescriptive right for those to use their liberty who contemplate a change of life. To balance this argument, it may with equal truth be asserted that a Catholic so uniting himself to one not of his own religious convictions is more inexcusable; in other words, is less strongly attached to his creed and consequently not so apt to exercise an influence for good on the mind of his partner, but, on the contrary, more likely to follow her. What will she discover in the conduct of one whose normal state in the present is that of rebellion against the Church, that is calculated to impress her with the truth, beauty, and sublimity of the Catholic religion? Besides, the Protestant who marries a Catholic conceives a lower opinion of him from that very act, because she knows that in doing it he is guilty of infidelity to what he knows to be his duty to his Church and his God. But the opinion entertained by many persons, that mixed marriages in a community where the Catholic religion predominates, are attended with less pernicious consequences than where Catholics are greatly in the minority, is a dangerous delusion. They are everywhere the same, and like their author carry their deformity as an inheritance with them. Let those who doubt it give the matter their attention, and be at the trouble of collecting statistics, and their eyes will be opened.

But the length to which this essay has extended warns me that it is time to conclude. Still, I cannot regret having said so much. I have endeavored to give a simple, unimpassioned treatment of a few of the evils from this prolific source. If the feelings sometimes gained a momentary ascendancy, it was when the picture darkened beyond the reach of silent endurance. But it is not a picture drawn from the imagination. "Not the half has been told," as those whose lives and energies are devoted to stemming the tide or repairing its ravages will unhesitatingly acknowledge. Happy would it be for many a Catholic had he gone to his grave instead of to his nuptials. Then he would have to render an account for but one soul; now, a thousand may rise up in judgment against him.

It is only when we view the matter in detail, and illustrate it by the fruits of its production, which are seen in the world around us, that its magnitude can at all be properly estimated. A good family, founded with the blessing of the Church, and growing up under her shadow, multiplies souls for heaven. But a family such as we are now considering multiplies, indeed, but only as enemies of God and the Church. Here again is presented a new phase of the disorder. When the unfortunate Catholic is sleeping in the dust,—his soul saved or lost, as the case may be,—the effects of his misguided choice are, and to the end of time will be, a standing record against him. It is incredible that a Catholic should so far disregard the solemn command of the Church, so far defy the known will of God, and despise the warning of conscience, as to involve himself and his posterity in such a labyrinth of temporal and eternal misery.

A. M. D. G.

BY

RIGHT REV. BISHOP IRELAND

DELIVERED IN

CENTRAL MUSIC HALL,

CHICAGO,

Wednesday Evening, January 17th, 1883,

UNDER THE AUSPICES OF THE

ST. PATRICK'S SOCIETY.

CHICAGO:
PRINTED FOR THE ST. PATRICK'S SOCIETY.

1883.

Right Rev. Bishop Ireland

— ON —

"INTEMPERANCE."

The immense audience gathered in Central Music Hall, Wednesday Evening, January 17th was a gratifying earnest of the active interest felt by the citizens of Chicago in the work which engaged the zeal and enlisted the labors and eloquence of the Right Reverend Bishop Ireland.

The significant presence of upwards of fifty Catholic clergymen of the city and vicinity, headed by the Most Reverend Archbishop Feehan, besides being a graceful compliment to the distinguished lecturer, demonstrated at the same time the sympathy of the Catholic ecclesiastical authorities in the cause of temperance and total abstinence.

On the platform were seated the leading priests of Chicago, and others from neighboring cities and states; several clergymen of the Protestant denominations; Rev. S. Humphrey Gurteen, of the Charity Organization Society; Rev. Dr. Thomas; Rev. Dr. Burroughs, of the Chicago University; Hon. Judges Moran and Barnum; Ex-Judge S. M. Moore; Hon. Francis Adams, Counsel to the Corporation; Hon. DeWitt C. Cregier, Commissioner of Public Works; Hon. Thomas Hoyne, Hon. John N. Jewett, Hon. John Mattocks, Col. Wm. P. Rend, Hon. M. J. Dunne, Hon. Wm. H. Condon, Jno. J. McGrath, Jno. Gaynor, M. W. Kelly, P. H. Rice, W. F. McLaughlin, H. T. Maguire, Wm. A. Amberg, William J. Onahan, and other well-known citizens.

Numerous letters expressing the warmest sympathy in the purpose of the lecture were addressed to President Onahan, of the St. Patrick's Society, by gentlemen who had been invited to attend—in several instances inclosing bank checks for sums in aid of the charities named as the beneficiaries of the lecture—the Little Sisters of the Poor, and the St. Vincent's Infant Asylum.

Messrs. John R. Walsh, President Chicago National Bank; John B. Drake, Grand Pacific Hotel; A. A. Carpenter, President Commercial Club; O. H. Tobey, Tobey & Booth; James H. McVicker, and Judge Lambert Tree, were among the foremost in generosity.

At the request of the St. Patrick's Society, his Grace, Archbishop Feehan, presided on the occasion, and having announced the subject of the lecture, introduced Right Reverend Bishop Ireland to the audience. The Bishop was welcomed by demonstrations of applause, which were repeated again and again during the progress of his eloquent and forcible address.

The following report presents the lecture in full:—

INTEMPERANCE.

"OUR DUTY IN REGARD TO THE EVIL."

Your Grace, Ladies and Gentlemen:
Permit me to give expression to the feelings of deep gratification which this evening fills my heart. I love the cause of temperance; I have pledged to it the services of my life. Temperance I consider one of the great vital questions of the times, believing that under whatever aspect we view the interests of the people, whether social economy or public morals, the State or the Church be the immediate subject of our thoughts, temperance must receive a very large part of our attention, if we seriously seek to protect and advance those interests. I am gladdened, and Heaven is thanked by me, when I witness hopeful tokens of triumph for the cause, significant manifestations of popular favor in its behalf.

This magnificent gathering in the city of Chicago, to do honor to temperance, is a most auspicious event, truly a red-lettered occasion in the history of the movement. Chicago is the metropolis of the great West. States and territories, within the area of which at no distant day all problems regarding the potency of the human race will receive solutions which the world heretofore has never afforded them, obey the impulse your city imparts. They cast their eyes toward her for guidance and inspiration. She reigns in the region of thought, as well as in commerce. When, therefore, the news shall have sped far and wide that a meeting such as I now witness has been held in this metropolis, imposing by its numbers not more than by its high representative character, comprising within its circle leading and influential men, the lawyer and the financier as well as the mechanic and the laborer, the public official together with the freeman citizen, the clergyman and the layman, under the honored leadership of the zealous and revered Archbishop, for the purpose of paying noble and willing tribute to the cause of temperance, and promising powerful aid amid its battlings,—the movement throughout the entire country will pulsate with new life; an era of vigorous strength and buoyant hope, the preludes to glorious victory, will have dawned for it in America. It is an honor which I highly prize that I am allowed to address you during this most important demonstration in favor of temperance.

THE TEMPERANCE CAUSE.

The temperance cause, Ladies and Gentlemen, deserves your homage. It is a cause most pure, most holy. Its appeal reaches the noblest, the most generous, the most heavenly instincts of the soul—charity for suffering fellow-man, devotion to country, sacred love of religion. So strong and so direct is its appeal to those profound and ever responsive instincts: the sole reason why the millions of true men in the country have not long ago arisen in their might to do valiant service under the standards of temperance, must be that they have not heard its piercing accents, and that their eyes have not rested upon the scenes of woe which compel them. The baneful feature in the dreaded evil which the temperance movement seeks to combat is that it succeeds in covering up its fierceness from casual observation. We walk over and amid smouldering fires of hell, unconscious of harm done or of danger to come. Meanwhile, advantage taken of our unfortunate security, the forces increase for a final effort to break up the whole social fabric, with all the hopes of the human race for earth or Heaven. No; men are not aware of the extent, and the power of the evil. They who are the most fitted to war against it, often know the least about it. The most effective work in the temperance movement is to lay bare before the public gaze the facts of the case; public indignation and public resolve to remedy the evil will follow.

The evil is the drink plague. Plague I will call it, not finding a better name to express its inhuman hideousness, and its demon-like power to harm men. It is ubiquitous. It has shot through the whole land its poison-bearing arrows. It holds in cities pompous court, riots amid wild revelry in burg and village, breaks in with savage howl upon the quietness of rural homes. It obtains dominion among all classes in the social scale. The poor man's garret, the marble palace of the wealthy open equally their doors. Peasant and prince, merchant and laborer, man and woman, child and adult are in turn stricken down. Not the ignorant alone feel its deathly touch; over brightest minds it casts its stygian shades. Wherever it enters, the plague debases and degrades. It scatters broadcast disease and death. Poverty and vice form its retinue. It demolishes homes, blasts the happiness of wife and child, laughs at the purest affections, delights in the ruin of virtue and innocence. It fills jails and asylums, carts victims to morgues and gibbets. It eats into the very foundations of civil society, and defies strong governments, whose arms it paralyzes. It annuls the potent ministrations of religion by locking against them the minds and hearts of men. All forms of evil and misery are its allies and march in its track. Worse, ten thousand times worse, than all other plagues that ever stalked over the earth, it transmits beyond the grave its fatal curse. Having racked and mocked its victim in this life, it casts him, while he is without reason and incapable of receiving God's pardon, sin-laden and unshriven before the dread tribunal of eternal justice. The plague is a vast deep sea of suffering, of woe, of sin. It has deluged the country and its billows are ever rising bolder and higher, battering down the stoutest obstructions, reaching out for fresh hetacombs of victims, rendered by each new conquest more daring and more cruel. It is the demon let loose among men, the demon rioting on earth, warring everywhere against light and virtue, exhaling everywhere darkness, sin and misery, and its name should be Demon. "O, spirit of wine, if thou hast no name, I will name thee Demon."

ALCOHOL: THE USE AND THE DANGER.

The material producing and feeding the drink plague is alcohol. Under this word I comprise brandy, whiskey, beer, wine—all liquors of an intoxicating nature. Alcohol in the liquor is the intoxicating element. It is this, and not other ingredients, that men seek in their draughts of brandy, wine or beer; indeed, fermentation and distillation conserve few other ingredients, and those only in minute quantities, beyond alcohol and water.

It is unnecessary, I assume, to tell you that I do not consider as wrong in itself the use of alcoholic drinks. It is evident for the christian moralist that there are limits within which such use does not conflict with the moral law. Physicians, too, no doubt, will assign limits, however restricted, within which alcoholic drinks do no harm worthy of notice to man's physical frame. The abuse, not the use, is wrong and forbidden. Upon those points there is no room for dispute.

But while I make this statement in favor of alcohol, I am compelled to add that in the whole domain of truth there are few principles demanding from us, in their safe application to practical morals, more cautious attention than the one which allows within due limits of moderation the use of alcoholic liquor.

The line separating in practice the use of alcohol from the abuse is shadowy; the many are unable to perceive it. The territory, too, within the limits of illicit use or moderation is narrow. Experience proves that but little drink has been taken, when physical injury occurs for the body, and the workings of the mind become confused. With these results the abuse begins, and the brood of alcoholic evils at once obtain life, acquiring strength as the abuse increases, until the climax is reached, at first in acute, then in chronic drunkenness. It is a perilous error to fancy that the alcoholic plague does not rage throughout all intermediate stages from the first act of immoderation to the moment of absolute drunkenness, though, of course, only in corresponding degrees of virulence. Millions have been murdered soul and body by alcohol, who were never drunk, as the word is commonly understood. Then, too, the nature of alcohol is most peculiar. Once admitted into the mouth, even in most moderate doles, it labors as it were with conscious purpose to create an appetite for itself, to enslave its host and fasten around him its serpentine coils. Watchful eye and powerful will may, I grant, defeat it. But eye and will frequently forget their cunning; vigilance and strength fail them. Whatever fancied pleasant effects alcohol produces result from the quickening of the nervous system, and the rapid circulation of the blood through the veins. A reaction follows from this irregular condition of the body, leaving behind a morbid languor and a deep feeling of uneasiness. A fresh draught will relieve the pain and repeat the pleasure. Why not take it? the appetite suggests. It is still the use, whispers the tempter alcohol, not the abuse. The fresh draught is taken; in it lurked the abuse. The reaction the second time is more painful, the demand for a third draught more imperious, conscience and mind meanwhile made weaker. The stumbling-block was the abstract principle that there is a licit use of alcohol.

Gradually, link by link, the drinker forges the adamantine chains which, countless as the lines of nerves in his body, at last inwrap him round and round from head to foot, and lash him in abject helplessness to the chariot of the most cruel and the most insatiable of conquerors, alcohol. Using alcohol is sailing down the Niagara. At first there is no danger; but, insensibly, even while the placid surface of the waters still lulls you into the belief that all is right, the current beneath has gained giant strength, and when, the deepening waves causing alarm, you twist the rudder, the maddened river laughs at your vain effort, and your bark in violent leaps reaches the precipice. "Look not at the wine which is yellow," counsels the Inspired Page, "when the color thereof shineth in the glass. It goeth in pleasantly ; but in the end it will bite like a snake, and will spread abroad poison like a basilisk."

THE IMMODERATE USE.

Taken beyond the strict limits of moderation, alcohol is a poison. The epithet usually applied to beverages which contain it is "intoxicant"—poisonous. It poisons body and soul, mind and heart. Amid all the torments to which man has subjected earth's creatures, he has extracted from them no element so fatal to his happiness, to all that he values or esteems in himself. The poison of poisons is alcohol.

It wrecks the body. The tottering step, the palsied hand, the bleared eye, the hectic flush or the death-like pallor on the cheek, indicate its secret workings. Nerve and muscle shorn of their power, the blood clogged with impurities, the tippler's body becomes an inviting field for all diseases that inscribe the page of a medical vocabulary, and if, as time went by, some one fell disease or another has not overtaken him, alcoholism ends his life, exacting from him, as if to punish his long resistance, the most unnatural torments. The delirium tremens is the final development of the terrible poison which cancer-like has been all the while consuming the habitual drinker of alcohol.

Into man's mind, the God-like faculty which raises him so far skyward that no measurement is possible between him and mere animal or material creation, alcohol injects its venom, disturbing and suspending its power of action. It rushes the blood to the brain, the material seat of the mind. There is first a whirl of rapid thought. The drinker mistakes the effect for mental vigor. Fatal delusion ! He quaffs another glass: the wheel of thought now spins too rapidly ; there is confusion, and soon complete suspension of reason. The image of God is for the time being effaced from the soul ; dooms-day's darkening of the sun is as noontide to the heavy shades of night that settle upon it. The drunkard is no longer a rational being.

The mind is the power in man to control his lower appetites. Man in his higher being is made to God's image and likeness; in his animal nature he owns the vilest and most untamed passions, which are ever seeking to break loose and satiate themselves in sin. Reason aided by God's grace can alone repress them. Suspend reason—the barriers are broken down, the pent-up torrent of iniquity is free. Worse yet—and this is the special demoniac feature of alcohol—it pours copious oil upon the burning fires of passion, and turns man into the furious beast. The good within him is silenced, the evil intensified and emboldened. Alcohol is that demon of the Gospel who having taken possession of man's heart, sends message to hell for seven other demons, that they, too, may abide with him, and render his conquest the more secure and the more lasting. Pure lips will, amid the fumes of alcohol, pour forth blasphemy and obscenity ; loving hearts put on tiger-like ferocity ; mildness lifts the hand in murderous assault ; innocence, reverence, honesty, give place to vice, to fraud, to lawlessness. The demon is the spirit of evil, and the demon is never so fully humanized as when he enteres with alcohol into the body of man.

EXTENT OF THE LIQUOR TRAFFIC.

This alcoholic poison floods the land. Distilleries and breweries to produce it, saloons to distribute it for immediate use, surpass in number the centres of any other branch of traffic. The whiskey and beer business is the coveted investment for capital and labor. Laws are controlled in the interest of the production and the supply. Alcohol is king. The report of the Commissioner of Internal Revenue for 1881 shows as distilled in the United States during one year, 117,728,150 gallons—over two and one-third gallons of brandy, gin or whiskey for every man, woman and child in the country. The twenty-first annual session of the United States Beer Brewers' Congress, held in Chicago last year, reported 13,347,110 barrels of beer manufactured the previous fiscal year, or 413,760,410 gallons—over eight gallons of beer to every person in the population. In addition to the home supply of distilled and fermented liquors, large quantities of spirits and wines were imported from foreign countries. The custom duties upon imported spirits and wines for the year ending June 30, 1881, amounted to $6,469,643. Nor are we at the end of our count. We have yet the native wines produced in the country, and especially the unlimited quantities of whiskey and beer upon which the government does not collect revenue. The whiskey frauds, we know, are extensive.

The Commissioner of Internal Revenue, in his report for 1880, tells us that during the previous period of four years and four months, 4,061 illicit distilleries had been seized, 7,399 persons had been arrested for illicit distilling, and that in suppressing demonstrations of violence against the government officers on the part of illegal distillers, 26 officers had been killed and 57 wounded.

SALOONS AND SALOON-KEEPERS.

Saloon-keepers, the professional distributers of the alcoholic fluid, are posted at all street-corners of cities and villages, hard by all places of public gathering, with glass in hand, and honeyed words on lips, coaxing men to buy and drink. I need not describe a saloon. Do not, however, picture to yourselves, in the high regions of the abstract, an ideal saloon. The ideal saloon-keeper, an upright, honorable, conscientious man, will never sell liquor to an habitual drunkard, or to a person who has already been drinking and whom another draught will intoxicate; he will never permit minors, boys or girls, to cross his threshold; he will not suffer around his counter indecent or profane language; he will not violate law and the precious traditions of his country by selling on Sunday; he will never drug his liquor, and will never take from his patrons more than the legitimate market value of the fluid. Upon these conditions being observed, I will not say that liquor-selling is a moral wrong. The ideal saloon-keeper is possible; perhaps you have met him during your lifetime; may be Diogenes, lamp in hand, searching through our American cities would discover him, before wearying marches should have compelled him to abandon the search. I have, at present, before my mind, the saloon as it usually now-a-days exhibits itself, down in an underground cellar, away from the light of the sun, or, if it does open its doors to the sidewalk, seeking with painted windows and rows of lattice work to hide its traffic from public gaze, as if ashamed itself of the nefariousness of its practices. The keeper has one set purpose—to roll in dimes and dollars, heedless whether lives are wrecked and souls damned. The hopeless inebriate and the yet innocent boy receive the glass from his hand. He resorts to tricks and devices to draw customers, to stimulate their appetite for drink. Sunday as on Monday, during night as during day, he is at work to fill his victims with alcohol, and his till with silver and gold. This is his ambition; and I am willing to pay him the compliment that he executes well his double task.

According to the report of the Commissioner of Internal Revenue for July, 1881, there were at that date in the United States 4,112 wholesale dealers in distilled liquors, and 170,640 retail dealers. A report for the year 1880 stated the wholesale dealers in fermented liquors as 2,065, and the retail dealers exclusively engaged in the sale of fermented liquors, 8,952. Those figures, you understand, should be made much higher to represent correctly the facts of the present time. But accepting them as they read, we have in the country wholesale and retail dealers in liquors, distilled or fermented, 185,769—one dealer to 270 souls of the entire population, women and children included. The retail dealers in distilled drinks, brandy and whiskey, average one to 293 persons. In the First Revenue District of Illinois, which embraces Cook (including Chicago), Du Page and Lake counties, there had been issued for the year ending July 1, 1881, 4,990 licenses to sell distilled liquors. The population of the three counties was in 1880, 647,954, giving 130 as the average of population to a whiskey saloon. "These figures" remarked lately the *Chicago Tribune*, "were for one year ago, and the subsequent increase in the number of saloons has kept pace with that in the population. The First District includes two rural counties without cities; it also includes several towns in Cook county where saloons are prohibited. Nevertheless there is a saloon for every 130 of the population."

The number affrights you. Yet the official figures of the government do not tell the full truth, either for the country at large, or for your own immediate territory. You must add to the number of saloons paying tribute to the government the unlicensed rum holes, which are everywhere most numerous. Nor can you leave out of the computation the home-saloons. There are thousands of men and women in your city, whose ideas of social respectability would not permit them to enter into a common, public saloon. They have their saloons in their own houses: their sideboards are laden with bottle and decanter. Their liquors come directly from the wholesale dealer; purchasing wholesale by keg or case, in the code of fashionable etiquette, is not rated as demeaning or vulgar. For my part, I perceive no difference between the corner and the home saloon, as regards the consumption of alcohol and the dangers of the alcoholic plague, except, perhaps, that in the home saloon, because of its continuous presence, the temptation is more powerful. The sideboard is honored when we rise in the morning, when we retire at night, before and after meals, when friends call, when we feel fatigue or exhaustion, amid sadness and rejoicing, when projects succeed or fail, whenever, in one word, we feel the craving of the alcoholic appetite.

THE VICTIMS OF THE DRINK PLAGUE.

The direct and immediate effect from this deluge of alcohol is that millions fall victims to the drink plague. Could I but gather into one vast multitude a single year's holocaust, show their numbers, exhibit them writhing in all the miseries of the various stages of intemperance from their first immoderate cup until the grave has closed upon them, you would turn aside from the most horrid accidents, from fire and tempest, war and pestilence, and declare that there is no evil for the human family to be likened to the evil of the drink plague.

Dr. William Hargreaves has published a book, "Our Wasted Resources," in which very carefully weighed figures are given in connection with intemperance. He estimates to each retail liquor dealer through the country "four customers who are drunkards," *i. e.* helpless habitual inebriates. The figure, I assert, is by no means too high. This rate, taking as the basis of our calculation only the retail whiskey saloons, gives us in the United States 722,560 drunkards. Every year, it is computed, 100,000 of those unfortunates roll into dishonored graves, and from other ranks of the intemperate 100,000 come up to take their places. In Chicago and her suburban territory we would have 19,960 of those drunkards.

We have in the country one whiskey saloon to 293 persons; in this First District of Illinois, one to 130. Taking from these figures of the population the children who cannot drink, the large number of minors and women who do not drink, the adult males who are abstainers or who patronize only home saloons, we find remaining to each saloon an average of about twenty-five customers. Saloons will subsist only on large sales,—the business would not pay. We must, consequently, calculate that the twenty-five customers of each saloon drink beyond all moderation, and, if they are not "drunkards," we have to rank them as advanced alcoholics. Men who belong to this last class are often those who do the most harm in society, sufficient alcohol being consumed to stir up their savage passions, while reason has not so far departed as to render them incapable of further wrong-doing, as they would be if they were more fully overpowered by drink. If to the hopeless drunkards we add advanced alcoholics, our figures should be for the country at large over 4,000,000, and for your own city and suburban territory over 124,000. In this calculation, you will remark, we are leaving out the drunkards and the advanced alcoholics both of the beer shops and of the home saloons, which, no less than the public whiskey saloons, furnish their strong proportion in the general quota of immoderate drinkers.

But higher yet, beyond all possibility of exact computation, you must build your figures in estimating the extent of the plague, when you take into account, as you should, the millions of men and women who have not reached either one of the stages we have described, but who are nevertheless the victims of alcoholism. I refer to the men and women, who as yet fancy themselves masters of their will, believing that they have the power to control at any moment the alcoholic appetite, but who in reality are its slaves, and are rapidly progressing towards the more dreaded stages of the disease. This class of victims, says Dr. Richardson, "constitutes among us a widespread, obvious community." That it is "widespread and obvious," you will certainly confess, if you adopt the writer's diagnosis of the case. "By persons in this stage," he tells us, "alcohol is felt to be a frequent daily necessity, an urgent necessity. They depend on alcohol. They are tremulous under effort until they get it; they are easily affected by sense of cold until they get it; they have a knowledge that they cannot digest a meal until they get it, and so they preface each meal by a drink of it; they have a keen sense of oppression after a meal, until they take a drink." No one of us need travel far to meet numerous people to whom those words apply.

REPORTS OF POLICE COURTS.

The reports of police courts help to form an estimate as to the extent of the plague in America. Much drunkenness, we must allow, never becomes public among us, and is never dealt with by the authorities, which, however, is probably even a more fertile source of misery, poverty and degradation than that which comes before the courts. Drunkards, too, in many cities, even when the offense is public, are not arrested by the police, if they are not boisterous in their conduct, or if they are socially respectable. Some cities are particularly lenient in this regard. Still, the arrests reported for drunkenness are alarmingly large. How far more numerous must be the actual cases of drunkenness? A few instances will suffice. In San Francisco in one year the total arrests were 25,669, of which 19,500 were for drunkenness, or for disorderly conduct in connection with drunkenness. In Suffolk County, Massachusetts, which includes the city of Boston, the total number of sentences passed by the courts from September, 1879, to September, 1880, were 16,897; of these 12,221 were for various grades of drunkenness. The arrests in New York for a year were 71,699, of which 48,191 were for intoxication and disorderly conduct. In Philadelphia, for 1881, 44,097 arrests were made—for drunkenness 23,094, for drunkenness and disorderly conduct 4,205—altogether for drunkenness 27,299. In Brooklyn the arrests for 1881 were 28,882, of which 12,971 were for drunkenness, and 1,118 for drunkenness and disorderly conduct. Chicago had in 1881, 31,713 arrests. Of this number only 2,014 are scored as "drunk," and 1,424 as "drunk and disorderly." The number is small apparently. But I am told by one of your officials, the more polite term "disorderly," has in Chicago the meaning elsewhere given to "drunk," and, as a consequence, your arrests, classed as "disorderly," rate sufficiently high—12,533.

FACTS FROM THE DAILY NEWSPAPER.

The newspaper, "the abstract and brief chronicle of the times," by its daily report, now from one point of the country, now from another, reveals also, in a way, the extent and the virulence of this malady of the age. It re-echoes but the more startling eruptions of the evil—enough to tell how deep it lies and how fatally it works. I read your city papers for the first ten days in January in search of reports of drunkenness. I noticed for Chicago two suicides: one purchases a bottle of whiskey in a State street saloon, goes out and shoots himself; another leaves behind him a paper upon which is written "Whiskey, whiskey." One man, aged sixty, dies under a stairway from cold and whiskey; the corpse of a poor fellow is discovered in the basement of a saloon, death coming, the coroner said, from alcoholism. One drunkard falls and breaks his leg; another is pitched down a stairway and receives serious injury; yet another is precipitated into a basement. Some ten were arrested for drunkenness, or for assaults while drunk; of these, two were man and wife, whose home whiskey had changed into a bedlam; one was a gentlemanly, well-dressed man who had arrived in the city from Europe a few days previously; and another was an unfortunate soldier from the plains returning to his home in the East. There were four cases of stabbing in saloons. A miserable fellow goes home drunk, quarrels with his wife, and stabs the kind-hearted neighbor who sought to protect the poor woman from the brutal husband. Three cases were of the most aggravating nature: men fired with alcohol sought the lives of your police officers—one received a pistol shot, one was stabbed, and saloon thugs cruelly beat another with bottles and beer glasses. And while all these horrors are taking place we stand by with silent tongues and idle arms; whiskey men hang over their rum-holes the flags of "personal rights" and "civil liberty," and the country rushes in a wild race toward a hopeless abyss of lawlessness and crime! Your papers, for the same period of ten days re echoed the doings of alcohol in other parts of the country. At Streator, Illinois, an officer of the law is killed and the murderer blames whiskey. At St. Louis a policeman is stabbed in a saloon; a wife sues for a divorce because the husband is a drunkard. The nephew of a millionaire, the proprietor of the Inman steamships, was found dead in a cell of the police station of Toronto, where he was confined on a charge of habitual drunkenness. In Philadelphia a famed navigator who had escaped from the icebergs of the Arctic, returns home to find, he says, his wife an inebriate. At Louisville a man commits suicide from drink. In a village of Canada a drunken spree occurs in the presence of death; whiskey bottles are flourished around the corpse, whose "wake" the brutes were keeping; the house takes fire and two women are burnt to death. In Milwaukee a drunken policeman must be discharged from the force; in a frontier village of Minnesota there is a whiskey brawl, and murder is committed. At Baltimore a drunkard is found dead in his prison cell. And thus, from East to West, from North to South, the demon alcohol riots over the land, all the other demons of hell forming his retinue, defying law, order, religion; polluting, destroying whatever he touches; reaching out his accursed hand to desecrate all that we hold dear and sacred for this life, or the life to come.

A PAINFUL REVELATION.

One painful revelation, which accounts of intemperance in the country put before us, deserves special attention. Intemperance, we have to learn, has invaded the ranks of youth, and has not paused even in presence of womanhood. What will the future be, if minors, boys and girls, are taught to be drunkards, and women in whose keeping the purity and the happiness of our homes must ever remain, begin to love the poisoned draught? Seven thousand youths under the age of twenty, some even under ten, are annually arrested in Chicago, the very great majority of cases being for drunkenness, or for offenses in which they indulge after getting drunk. A number of those seven thousand are young girls. Among the arrests for drunkenness in cities when the sex of prisoners is stated, the arrests of women are sometimes as high as one-fifth of the total number. The home saloons, too, furnish their female drunkards, and these are seldom arrested.

INDIRECT EVILS OF THE PLAGUE: THE DRUNKARD'S FAMILY.

The victim of alcohol does not live alone in the world : he is a son or a father, a brother or a husband ; there is around him, encircling him in his misery and receiving from him the fruits of the poison, a family. My God! Can we view the seething sea of woe and suffering, without being moved to pity, and aroused to action? God's blessing, we know, follows the wiping away of sorrow's tear, the healing up of broken hearts : " Religion, pure and undefiled, before God is this, to visit the fatherless and widows in their tribulation." Convert but one drunkard, save but one family from the effects of the plague, and grateful prayer will ascend for you to the throne of grace. A young man staggers by you, unheeded and, you may think, deserving to be unheeded. Aye, but he was once a mother's joy and pride ; she cared not for wealth or empire, when she pressed her boy to her bosom. Now, he is a drunkard, and her old age is steeped in sorrow. This next one was the hope of a father's declining years: he spent upon him riches of hand, and affections of heart ; to-day the father is friendless and famishing, and the son's heart has but one love—whiskey. How often the happy bride of yesterday finds herself, ere the voice of holy promises spoken before God's altar has ceased to reverberate in her ear, the wife of a drunkard ! For years she leads a life of sorrow and misery, the horrors of which no one realizes who has not witnessed them. He had pledged undying affection, knightly protection : when he comes home from the saloon, his mouth opens to curse, and his hand rises to strike. Only alcohol could produce the hellish scene of a weak, timid, loving wife, weltering in her blood, and a brutal man, her husband, gloating over the scene ! And the little ones ! Is there no spark of human feeling left in the drunkard? No. The tiger of the forest, the lion of the desert, feed and protect their young : a drunkard leaves his children to starve, if he does not in his cruelty hasten their death. A drunkard's home—outside of hell in all created space, there is no other such place of despair and agony. The father's steps approach: it is a signal for the child to crouch away timidly into a corner. Fear and misery never permit a smile to wreath its lips, its heart to beat with one joyful sensation. We have known the child to scream from hunger, and the father would take the last cent from the house to purchase drink. We have seen the child laid out in cold death, and the father still demanded alcohol. We have met children, in rags, roaming the streets, a prey to vice and crime, and in reply to our questionings, they would say : Father drank and home was not endurable. We have seen maidens as pure as the snow falling from the clouds; whose hearts had known but the most innocent affections—we have seen them driven, O, Heaven to hideous vice, and, again the reply was : I could not stay at home, because father drank. The home is the fount of happiness, the guardian of virtue, the sanctuary of religion. Alcohol desecrates and wrecks it. The burning lava of Vesuvius does not leave behind it ground more barren, more shorn of beauty, life and promise.

INTEMPERANCE AND CRIME.

Intemperance brings dire disaster to the whole social fabric. It loads down our criminal calendar. We are living in a fortunate period of time ; the country is at peace with foreign nations ; there is no civil strife within its own borders ; no agrarian war, no conflict of classes has occurred. Yet, our jails and workhouses are crowded ; our criminal courts are never void of culprits ; our police forces though large are too small for the work allotted to them. What is the cause ? I answer : Alcohol. Intemperance is not the sole crime of the day, nor is it the sole cause of other crimes which men commit. But as Chief Justice Noah Davis of New York says, "among all the causes of crime intemperance stands out the unapproachable chief." In addition to specific rum crimes, alcohol begets numberless others, inasmuch as it awakens the lower appetites, and breaks down all moral barriers. It is the fruitful feeder of immorality, theft, rapine, murder. It suggests to the mind the thought of crime ; it gives the animal excitement needed for deeds of violence ; it silences conscience when the deed has been done. How often after horrid crimes, which affright in his sober moments the wrong-doer himself, we hear from him the excuse,—Whiskey did it !

In an article prepared by A. S. Fiske for the Report of the U. S. Commissioner of Education, A. D. 1871, on crime in New England, we find stated as an undeniable fact that "from 80 to 90 per cent. of our criminals connect their course of crime with intemperance." A committee report in the Dominion House of Commons, in 1875, says : "We find on examining the reports of the Prison

leads to intemperance, of all that is allied with intemperance. Oh! the thousands of souls that daily damned through drink! And for those souls Christ died, and we are not alarmed at th[e] loss! If men are carried away by the rushing waters of a flood, we endeavor to save them: wh[en] ruin is the deluge, and hell the death, we are motionless. Alcohol has wrested millions of so[uls] from God's Church; and devotion to Church should be, with her children, the most powerful of motives to wage war against it.

THE NEED OF THE HOUR.

We are men, citizens, christians; as such, debtors to humanity, to country, to religion. I[s] not our solemn duty "to sound an alarm?" Is it not the need of the hour, to rouse men to a se[nse] of the danger which is overwhelming us on all-sides? What most frightens and discourages me presence of modern intemperance is the singular apathy—inexplicable, I confess, to me—of good and moral portions of the population towards the evil. They do but little, if anything, a[nd] but little, if anything, were to be done. There are even those among them who seem to regret t[he] efforts are made against the reign of alcohol. Temperance workers are called by them enthusia[sts,] fanatics, and, microscope in hand, they scrutinize our plans and minute workings, to seek matter censure. If a mistake is made along our lines, they rejoice. Are temperance workers, we mi[ght] almost ask, or saloon keepers the enemy? No careful scrutiny is made of the plans and worki[ng] of alcohol, which, while we are disputing on details, is sending destruction through the land, a[nd] filling hell with souls. We have scruples lest we hurt its minions overmuch, or some abstract rig[ht] of theirs be forgotten. I sometimes think that our apathy is but another sad proof of alcoh[ol's] conquests. We are afraid to enter the lists against it, so potent has it become in the halls of leg[is]lation, in the marts of commerce, around the very doors of our churches. Perhaps, too, I sometim[es] imagine, we deprecate the logical consequences which the war would force upon ourselves in o[ur] daily life. We pat with tender touch our own social glass, which our feelings persuade us we u[se] but never abuse; and we tremble lest, in a general war upon alcohol, some stray pebble mig[ht] strike and shatter that cherished glass. But surely I am mistaken: the reason of our apathy is th[at] we have not reflected sufficiently upon the evils of alcohol.

THE PRESENT CIRCUMSTANCES EXCEPTIONAL AND EXTRAORDINARY.

It is well to bear in mind that the modern alcoholic eruption is an extraordinary crisis in t[he] history of social morals. Intemperance there has been always in the world since the days of No[ah] and at all times, as we learn from the warnings of Holy Scripture, alcohol, even, in its mildest di[ctates,] demanded most cautious handling. But never was intemperance so widespread and so viol[ent] as it is to day. The evil has been steadily increasing since the discovery of the art of distillatio[n] and the consequent introduction into popular use of ardent spirits. The last century seems b[ad] enough, as we view it through the chronicles of the time, which tell us of stout drinking parti[es] even to most shameful excess, among the upper classes of society. Drunkenness, we would fanc[y,] was then a sort of social virtue. We are far worse off to-day. Cultured social opinion may fro[wn] more severely upon excess; but drunkenness is to-day far more universal, and its effects far m[ore] brutal. Intemperance has taken hold of all classes; it weighs as a fatal millstone upon the nec[k] of the masses; it has entered into all the arteries of the social body. And annually is the gia[nt] evil gaining in destructive power. "In 1859," said lately Cardinal Manning, "the number of liqu[or] shops in England was 50,000. To-day it is 200,000. It has increased four-fold, while the popu[lation] has not more than doubled itself." The American saloon, we can have no doubt, has been multipli[ed] in similar ratio. Until very recently, the drink-plague had chosen as its peculiar ground the nor[th]ern latitudes of Europe and America: more southern countries were comparatively free from [its] ravages. Even over these is it now spreading with alarming rapidity. Drunkenness is becomi[ng] quite common in Belgium, France, Germany and Switzerland. The populations of those countri[es] are using ardent spirits in large quantities. As a consequence the taste for alcoholic drinks of [all] sorts is disordered and abnormal. Beers and wines are consumed in most unnatural draughts. T[he] beer product last year in the German empire was 830,000,000 gallons, the consumption in Bava[ria] averaging 200 quarts to every person in the population, women and children included. An imper[ial] commission is at present working in Russia to seek out and propose measures for the diminution [of] intemperance in the empire. The closing years of the nineteenth century has its plague, wor[se,] far worse, than the Black Plague of some centuries ago. All those facts before us, is it not absur[d,] when the temperance question comes up for discussion, to argue in the abstract, or to consider on[ly]

...t would be useful or sufficient, right or wrong, in ages and in countries separated altogether in the ...re and the extent of the disease from the case with which we must deal to-day? This abstract ...oning is, I put it, one of our worst curses, as it excuses our apathy and self-indulgence, and ...s us to misrepresent the activity and the motives of zealous, earnest men. We need, if we ...ld do good, to be practical and to deal with problems as we find them at hand.

IS PROHIBITION THE REMEDY?

Certainly temperance workers, also, must be practical in the means which they propose. We ...not lose time in dreaming about measures which present public opinion will not allow us to en-...e. Neither must we, by remedying one evil, introduce another. Our principles of action should ...lways philosophically and socially correct. In dealing with the alcohol question it is of no pur-...e to say that the use of alcohol is always wrong, or that the selling of alcohol for drink is, also, ...insically wrong. The propositions are not true. What is true is that the use of alcohol, the ... of alcohol, are things most perilous, and strong precautionary measures should be taken in both ...s to prevent evil results. When civil communities, like families, agree, by free option, to ex-...e from their territory, completely and forever, all alcoholic drinks, my blessing attends them. ...o such general agreement exists, how far one portion of the population has the moral right to ...rain by law the sale and use of liquor, is the great question in temperance politics. The sole ...cal plea upon which prohibition can ever seek to obtain a hearing is this,—that liquor selling has ...ome among us such a nuisance that the most sacred interests of the people, the salvation of the ...mmonwealth itself, are imperilled, and that all other means, less radical, have been tried in vain ...vert the calamity. It must be borne in mind that under our free government it is a very dan-...us proceeding to infringe to any considerable distance upon private rights and liberties under ...plea of the public welfare. The very essence of our republican government is, that it will res-...t as far as it may be at all possible, private rights. Individual taste as to what we are to eat or ...k is one of the most personal of our natural rights, one of the very last subjects, indeed, even in ...eme cases, for public legislation. The case is, certainly, supposable, when matters should have ...e to such a pass, as I believe they have in China as regards the use of opium, that nothing but ...ibition would suffice: then, *Salus populi suprema lex*, would be my principle. Even then, how-...r, we should have to consider whether public opinion had been so formed, as to warrant the prac-...l enforcement of prohibition. The first work must at all times be to appeal to the intelligence ... moral nature of men. Legislation by itself will be idle speech. It has its purpose: it removes ... lessens temptations; it assists and strengthens moral sentiment; but alone it neither creates, nor ...s the place of virtue. So far, in America, I imagine, public opinion is not prepared for prohibition; ...have we with sufficient loyalty tried other less radical measures, to be justified in invoking the for-... hope—absolute prohibition. If in the future, however, the country shall be precipitated to-...ds extremes on the liquor question, the liquor dealers will themselves have brought about the ...s: they will reap the whirlwind where they have sown the wind. By resisting, as they do ...resent, all rational and moderate measures for the suppression, or diminution of the evils of alco-... they will have forced us to cut them off as men madly and incurably opposed to the interests ...e commonwealth.

HIGH LICENSE.

What is at once practicable, and would be most serviceable in diminishing the evils of intemper-...e, is to demand of liquor sellers high license-fees. There are two grounds upon which we base ... plea for high license. One is the economic ground: if a traffic of any kind puts unusual imped-...nts in the wheels of government, state or municipal, and increases to an inordinate degree its ... enses, the traffic should be made to bear its due proportion of those expenses. Before saloon-...pers have reason to complain of injustice, or harsh treatment, they should be made to pay over ...ee-fourths of all sums spent annually in maintaining police forces, criminal courts, jails, public ...rities. In allowing them to pay but trifles of those sums, the state or city is guilty of deep in-...ice towards the sober citizen, who is taxed to repair the harm inflicted by liquor upon society. ... second ground for high license is the moral consideration that it is the duty of government to ...vent as well as to punish wrong-doing, when no principle is violated by such prevention, and to ... restrictions upon a traffic which is dangerous to public morals. Saloons are numerous beyond ...ustification, and in most cases are in the hands of reckless individuals. High license will reduce ... number. Not many, who would be candidates for a bar, could pay $1000, or $500; nor would the wholesale dealer be anxious, as he is now, to advance the license fee. High license w[ill] drive saloons from the outlying districts into the more central portions of the city, where police [con]trol is more effective. It would end the unholy alliance between groceries and liquor, and the laborer or his wife could buy a pound of tea or sugar without being invited to buy also a gla[ss of] whiskey or beer. The impecunious fellows, ashamed to beg and too idle to work, willing, howe[ver] to sell whiskey, are often the men most careless of consequences: their idea is to make mo[ney.] They would be kept out of the business. A salutary fear would rest upon all liquor dealers of [vio]lating city ordinances, lest they lose their license, which has some value when it costs $50[0 or] $1,000. Nor would so many drink, if we had high license. There are men who will seek out w[his]key or beer wherever it is and pay any money for it. There are many others, however, who [will] not drink when temptation is not thrust upon them. The poor working-man after his day's [work] will not walk several blocks to find a saloon. If it is next door, and the selfish keeper, envying [the] dollar he has earned so hard, invites him with a sickly smile and a shake of his clammy han[d to] cross its threshold, the poor man will yield, and get drunk. Diminish the saloons, and you dimi[nish] the number of drinkers. A low license fee is an open encouragement to the indefinite and [irres]ponsible multiplication of rum-holes in every street and in every block of our cities.

ENFORCE EXISTING LAWS.

Then we should see that the laws already enacted for the repression of intemperance be ri[gidly] enforced. There are laws forbidding the sale of liquor to minors, to habitual drunkards, obli[ging] saloons as well as other places of traffic to close their doors on Sundays. These laws if allow[ed to] remain a dead letter on the statute book paralyze the whole social machinery, the consequence b[eing] that law in general is not respected or feared. Why, in a special manner, are laws rega[rding] the sale of liquor, permitted to be violated? Does it not appear that saloon keepers place thems[elves] above the law, and are practically a law to the whole community? The blame rests with the pe[ople] at large; it rests with you, my hearers; it rests with the conservative, law-abiding citizens. The[y do] not speak, and the officers of the law either believe that public opinion warrants the violatio[n of] liquor laws, or, receiving no support from the moral elements of the community, they have no[t the] courage to face the evil. A city government does the expressed bidding of the citizens. If bu[t one] class speak—the saloon keepers, their bidding is done.

PERSONAL TOTAL ABSTINENCE.

Something more, however, than the exercise of your political power in favor of tempera[nce] will I ask of you—a personal tribute to the cause, by abstaining totally yourselves from the u[se of] intoxicating beverages. Personal temperance in the present extraordinary crisis of the plagu[e, to] be sure and effective, must take the form of total abstinence. I am talking, I know, to men [and] women who are safe in their own persons from the alcoholic plague: but, I assume too, I am tal[king] to men and women who are conscious of a duty to their fellow-men, to their near neighbors, to [their] relatives, perhaps to their own children. We desire to do our share in saving and protecting t[hem.] For them total abstinence is a necessity. Those who have at any time fallen victims to the pla[gue] cannot taste alcohol without almost a certain relapse. Thousands of others have never yet bee[n in] a state of intoxication: but they show a fondness for the glass; their system is already worke[d up] from continuous potations to such a pitch of nervous excitement, that the frequent draught is a n[ecessity.] May be they are simply, as yet, untried in life's battles: from very inexperience they must fea[r the] contagion, total abstinence should be their rule. Drinking alcohol for them is clinging to a preci[pice;] it is treading downward the steep ascent of an Alpine range, over which trained mountaineers [fear] to travel. Honey-combed as society is with drinking customs, pressed at every step to d[rink,] encouraged by high example of parents and esteemed neighbors, laughed at by companions if [they] refuse the glass, the weak, the young, are so completely exposed to danger, that their escape is [next] to the miraculous, unless they are teetotalers. Shall we preach total abstinence to them without b[eing] ourselves total abstainers? We are speaking in the air. Practice alone renders our words effec[tive.] They, to whom we are speaking, will draw no line between our strength and their own weakn[ess,] and they will pass us by as idle talkers.

THE SOCIAL CUSTOMS OF THE DAY.

Our personal total abstinence will remove the great stumbling-block in the pathway of tem[per]ance—the social customs of the day. Alcohol has succeeded, divesting itself purposely of the g[ross]ness which it usually wears, in obtaining social favor, the approval of fashion. The power of

with the multitude is fashion; good and evil gain favor according as they are more or less
 ionable. Drink has been and is fashionable. It occupies the honored place on the tables of the
 ders of society; at public banquets the toast of the occasion demands a copious libation; visit a friend,
 l simultaneously with the chair as a signal of hospitable welcome, the decanter appears; when
 uaintances meet, a treat is offered; at wedding and at christening, liquor flows. Alcohol has con-
uted itself the test of friendship, the token of joy, the comfort in sadness: it has gained the seal of
ial dignity. It demands as a right these social honors; he who refuses them is deemed cold, heart-
 , singular, eccentric. He feels out of place in the world, and unless his moral courage permits him to
 wn upon all foes, he discards total abstinence. Why, men and women, young and old, are, as it
 e, compelled to drink. In this way drunkards are made; in this way the reformation of drunkards
omes impossible. The so-called decent customs of society create and foster the appetite, and
the never interrupted streams that fill up the sea of misery and sin, the drink-plague.
There is no hope of arresting this evil until the whole order of social ideas upon the use of
 ohol has been reversed. Drinking must be declared unfashionable; alcohol must be made to
 ir its true colors in the gilded parlor as well as in the poor man's cabin, amid the banquetting
 ongs as well as in cellar saloons. Men must come to feel that they do no favor to those whom
y press to drink; friends must resent as an injury such invitations. When this shall have been
omplished, the era of intemperance will be nearing the evening of its course. The fashion will
 k downwards through all classes. The saloon-keepers themselves, in numbers, finding that no
 ger can they be pillars in Church and State, will heed their remaining instincts of self-respect
l will abandon a business that disgraces themselves and their children.
This change is to be wrought through the influence of men and women such as I am honored
 eing permitted to address this evening. Each one has his influence, and with each one influence
 talent, for which an account shall be demanded by the Supreme Judge.

OUR CATHOLICS OF INFLUENCE TOO SELDOM HELP US.

To silent example add, as time and opportunity will permit, active work. Speak, exhort,
 lain, as the case may be. Reach out the hand to some struggling neighbor to sustain and direct
 . Take part in associations formed for the spread of temperance, for the proper enforcement
the laws, for the distribution of healthy literature on the subject of temperance and other kindred
 ues. There is power in associations which the members working separately do not own. In
 i instance let me express my high appreciation of well-known societies, the representatives of
 ich throng the hall this evening, and whose zeal and persevering energy I know from intercourse
 h them—I speak of the societies connected with the Catholic Total Abstinence Union of America.
ey have done a noble work among the Catholics of the country, ; . id many difficulties, often
 h slight encouragement from the communities whose battles they were fighting. I pray that
 i blessings may attend them, and that with new energy they may reach out to wider fields of
or, with promise of most abundant harvests. The obstacle to the success of these societies here-
 ore has been that the more influential Catholics, those of more affluence, of higher social positions,
 e kept aloof from them. The laborer, the mechanic, the poor man, in one word, has been
 rged with the duty of fighting the whole battle. This is not as it should be. I do not discard
poor man, God forbid! but I would enlist in our ranks the rich as well as the poor. If God has
ced us in more elevated stations, we owe Him more loyal service. There is a tendency, which is
 according to God's ways, that as men ascend in society they sever themselves from their fellow
 n, do not feel the same sympathy with their wants, and are afraid to come in contact with the
 sses even for the furtherance of noble causes. In the temperance warfare I make a special appeal
 men of affluence and of influence; they can do much for us, and we need their aid.

A SPECIAL WORD TO IRISHMEN.

A few more words and I will have done. I wish to address them to those of my hearers for
 ose ears, as for my own, the name of the Isle of Saints is music most sweet. All that I have said
the evils of intemperance assumes in my mind a peculiar depth of meaning, when I view intemper-
 e as among the Irish people. Then more than ever do I feel my heart swelling under feelings of
ense hatred, and my whole soul bending all its energies in war against alcohol. The true Irish
 riot must ever signalize alcohol as the chief enemy of his race; when he is alcohol's subject,
 ether by yielding to it his own appetite, or by obeying in aught its influence, he is a traitor to his
 intry's best interests.

Our misfortune in this country—to speak now but of Irishmen in America—is that so often o
the doorways of saloons Irish names are inscribed, and too often do Irishmen visit saloons. The
derive all the ills from which we suffer, and which at times cause us to lower our heads in sha
If there are Irish inmates in jails and alms houses, if Irishmen throng the tenement-house and
cellar in the impoverished districts of our cities, if more Irishmen do not attain, in America, the h
places in commerce, in statesmanship, in wealth, and in fame, to which their strong arm and brilli
mind entitle them—the cause is that they drink. If among other races three-fourths of the cri
and the pauperism with which they are debited result from the use of alcohol, I do not fear to
that among Irishmen ninety-five per cent. or more would be the correct figure. So good are the Ir
people without liquor; so bad are they with it. Their warm blood cannot endure the stimula
and with but limited draughts they are more subdued by the demon of intemperance than oth
who would imbibe larger quantities.

No people bury beneath the wreck which alcohol produces brighter and more valued virtu
Were we all sober we could challenge, for our noble gifts of mind and heart, the admiration of
world; our temporal and social prosperity would be at once assured. The pity! O, the pi
that the great Irish race, amid the wondrous opportunites which America unfolds, should not rise
its full stature in the glory of earth and heaven! What are its hopes? The best—if we remem
the lessons of Ireland's great benefactor, Rev. Theobald Mathew. What are its hopes? I h
none—if we continue to pay tribute to alcohol. Did I not read aright the signs of the times, whe
believe that the Irish people are determined to give battle to this inveterate foe, and to honor the
selves by their strict adhesion to temperance, I would, for my own part, abandon all efforts
raise them upwards, and fold my hands in despair.

As we love our race, as we would gain for Irishmen honor from our fellow-citizens of ot
nationalities, as we would brighten the sky over the old island home itself, I beg of my Ir
hearers to labor with me to hasten the day when no Irishman will keep, and no Irishman
patronize, a saloon.

[NOTE.—It is worthy of remark that the lecture netted over one thousand dollars;
Right Reverend Bishop Ireland having characteristically declined to receive any compensat
whatever, the St. Patrick's Society divided the amount realized equally between the Little Sist
of the Poor and the St. Vincent's Infant Asylum, which was a welcome aid to those deserv
institutions.]

TWO LECTURES

ON

NEWFOUNDLAND,

DELIVERED AT

ST. BONAVENTURE'S COLLEGE,

JANUARY 25, AND FEBRUARY 1, 1860,

BY

THE RIGHT REV. DR. MULLOCK.

New York:
JOHN MULLALY, OFFICE OF THE METROPOLITAN RECORD,
No. 419 BROADWAY.
1860.

FIRST LECTURE.

LADIES AND GENTLEMEN,—The subject on which I have the honor of addressing you this evening is one of particular interest to us—it is the land we live in, Newfoundland, the native or adopted country of all here present. Of all the feelings implanted in the heart of man, next to religion, there is none so strong as patriotism : the *dulce et decorum est pro patria mori* (it is sweet and honorable to die for one's country), is not alone the expression of the pagan moralist, it is the universal feeling of all people in ancient and modern times : nay, more ; we know that our Divine Redeemer himself, when foretelling the destruction of the capital of his people, Jerusalem, pointing out from the summit of Mount Olivet the glories of the Temple, the golden vine, his own image sparkling in the setting sun, the lofty towers of the city of David, the massive walls which for so long a period resisted all the efforts of the Roman power, wept over it, and lamented that the crimes of its inhabitants should have provoked the Divine Justice not to leave one stone on another. It is, then, to encourage this sacred feeling of patriotism among the youth I now see around me, that I have been induced to take the subject of Newfoundland in this and the following lecture as most calculated to foster it. It is a great and noble country, a country of untold wealth, of wonderful and unknown resources, and the few people who now fringe its shore (for 130,000 inhabitants are but the germ of a future population of millions), sprung from the most energetic nations of modern times, English, Irish, and Scotch, possessing in themselves and intermingling the poetic and fiery imagination of the Celt, the steadiness and perseverance of the Saxon, and the enterprise and coolness of the North Britons, are destined to be the founders of a race which, I believe, will fill an important place hereafter among the hundreds of millions who will inhabit the western hemispheres in a few ages. I will, in this lecture, rather confine myself to the past of Newfoundland, reserving for another occasion the description in detail of the country and its future prospects. Every country inhabited by man has more or less a history—the more anciently civilized empires, the Assyrian, the Grecian, the Roman, have left after them imperishable records of their greatness. The last of the empires, however, the Roman, is the mother of all civilization and polity. Rome moulded all the nations of the West and the civilized people of the East, into a great empire, and from its fragments the modern nations, re-enforced by the barbaric energy of the northern tribes, have sprung. In the fourteenth, fifteenth, and sixteenth centuries, the people of Southern Europe, the Spaniards, Portuguese, and Italians, were not only the most advanced in material and mental progress, in literature, arts, and arms, but also the most enterprising, the most commercial, and the most adventurous of all other nations. In 1492, Columbus, the great Genoese navigator, after hearing Mass, and, together with his crew, receiving the Holy

Communion, in the Franciscan Church of N. S. la Bella, in Palos in Andalusia, from the hands of his friend and patron, Fr. John Peres, the guardian of the convent, unfurled the golden banner of Spain, crossed the wide waste of waters, and gave a new world to Castile and Leon. Only five years after, in 1497, Cabot, another Italian, a Venetian, discovered Newfoundland. Although these two great men are always called the discoverers of America, still it is certain that at least the northern parts of it had been visited, and perhaps partially settled by the Northmen of the Middle Ages. There always existed a dim tradition that the western shores of Europe were not the boundaries of the world. The legend of St. Brandon, the Bishop of Kerry, in the south of Ireland, sailing across the Atlantic and discovering an island of the blessed, and the Atlantis of Plato, were but the traditional embodiment of a fact. Columbus visited Iceland to seek there among the traditions of the natives some clue to the mystery of the ocean. We know not what an encouragement he may have received there, to persevere in his almost hopeless enterprise, but modern research has proved that the traditions were not without foundation. The Society of Northern Antiquaries has done much to clear away the mist which obscures that most interesting portion of history. Professor Rafn has collected and translated very many of the songs of the Scalds, or Scandinavian poets recounting the voyages of their countrymen to the western land ; many of them have been translated into English by Mr. Beamish, of Cork, and are most interesting to all early historians of America. We know for certain, that about the year 981 or 982 Eric, called the Red, a Norwegian Viking, discovered Greenland, and that a bishop's see was established in that inhospitable region about the year 1021. A list of the bishops of that remote see has been preserved down to 1406, nearly four hundred years, when all communication between it and the Mother Country ceased, and the imperfect civilization introduced perished. A few ruins of walls, or stone fences now mark the sight of the Norwegian Colony. It is quite natural to suppose that these adventurous mariners, who crossed over to Iceland and Greenland so frequently, would not content themselves without passing the few hundred miles which separated them from the Western Continent, only about five hundred from the western seaboard of Greenland. Accordingly we find accounts of voyages to, and settlements in, Helluland, Vinland, Markland, and Ireland it Mikla—Helluland is supposed to be the barren and stony land of Labrador, Vinland or Winland Newfoundland; but then as we have no wild vines, many learned men transfer the name to some more southern land in the present United States, while others again say that the Northmen looked on the abundance of the raspberry plant as entitling the country to the name of Vinland. Markland is supposed to be Nova Scotia, or Main ; and Ireland it Mickla, or great Ireland, the main Continent of America, the present United States. It is very improbable that so many accounts of voyages would be preserved, the names of the discoverers and navigators, the birth of some of their children recorded, the wreck of one of their ships on Keeler Ness, Kell Cape or Ship Cape, and the locality marked out now Keels in Bona Vista Bay, by the certain but rude way of determining the northern latitude, that is the length of the longest day in the summer solstice, if it were all a work of imagination. I have no doubt but that these sea-kings, after establishing colonies in Greenland and Iceland, visited this country and made some settlements here, but I believe the few people they brought with them either perished in their wars with the Skroelligers, or Esquimaux, or that the remnant left the country which they could not then have found very inviting. The real cause, I should imagine, of the abandonment of these lands was the invasion of more genial climes and polished nations of the Northmen. When they obtained possession of one of the finest provinces of France, now called after them Normandy, when they settled in Northumberland, and along the fertile banks of the Shannon, the estuaries of the Liffey and the Suir, in Limerick, Waterford, Cork, Dublin, Wicklow, and many other Danish towns in Ireland, and when they showed such a capacity for the remains of civilization lingering in the Roman Empire as to adopt the languages, the arts, and the sciences of the provinces they conquered, we may naturally imagine that the tide of adventurous emigration would be directed from the frightful shores of Greenland and Iceland, or the rugged and uninviting localities of Newfoundland, or Northern Continental America, to the shores of the Seine in smiling France, or the rich pastures of Ireland and England. The western land would soon be forgotten, there would be no inducement to cross a stormy ocean in ships not as large as our western boats, when they could coast along the shores of Europe, and find their countrymen settled in the maritime districts of a civilized country. It is said that a Greenland bishop, Eric, visited Winland in 1121, to endeavor to reconvert his countrymen to Christianity, which they had forgotten in those then remote and desolate regions—yet all appears buried in obscurity. We know quite enough to excite our curiosity, not to satisfy it, and it is impossible that the real history of the Northmen in America will be ever cleared up. They left no monuments after them; like all people who have abundance of wood, they would not build stone houses, and the only records we have of their existence here, are the songs of the Scalds, or the histories of Adam Bremen or others who lived ages subsequent to their settlement here, and embodied the traditions, half fact and half fable, which they found floating in the songs and the legends of the people, in the histories they compiled.

We now leave the doubtful region of romance and fable, mingled with some facts, for the sure ground of history. The wonderful discoveries of Columbus had excited, in a degree we find it difficult to comprehend, the enthusiasm of Europe—a new world appeared, not as a discovery, but almost as a new creation. Every maritime and commercial nation was aroused, and all wished to participate in the glorious inheritance acquired for Spain by the Genoese mariner. In England the Wars of the Roses were now at an end, the regal pretensions of York and Lancaster were united in the person of Henry VII., by his marriage, the ancient aristocracy of the land had almost perished, the crown, as always happens after a civil war, was strengthened, and the people, weary of bloodshed, resigned in a great measure their liberties into the hands of the Tudor sovereigns, and only looked for repose. The Italians almost monopolized the American discoveries, and two brothers of the name of Gabota, Venetians, resided in Bristol; they offered their services to Henry VII., to make discoveries in the Northern Ocean, and find, perhaps, a passage to India by that route; the offer was accepted, and on the 20th of June, 1497, Sebastian Gabota, or as his name was anglicized, Cabot, discovered Newfoundland, and gave the name of Bona Vista, happy sight, or happy view, to the cape he first sighted, which Italian appellation it retains to the present day. He returned the same year and brought with him three of the natives of the island, a race which has now been cruelly exterminated. I here pause to say a few words of the aborigines of the country. It was supposed at first that this interesting people were the descendants of the Northmen of whom I have spoken: the science of ethnology, however, proves this not to be the fact—the skulls of those people showed them to belong to the American or Mongolian race, and not to the Caucasian of which the Northmen were a branch; a semi-civilized people may become savage, but never so change the form of the cranium as to acquire the characteristics of another race, until entirely absorbed by generations of intermarriage. It may be that a little of the northern blood mixed in the aboriginal stream, but all traces of it were soon lost. We know they called themselves Beoths, that they painted themselves with red ochre, as the Britons of old did with woad, and hence, they were called by the settlers, Red Indians. They were clothed in robes of skin, their arms were the bow and arrow, and spear, like those of all uncivilized nations. They lived by hunting and preserved the flesh of the deer by bucanning. They made enormous fences, such as are used in

Ceylon to entrap elephants, sometimes extending as far as thirty miles and converging to a point where the deer in their migration were obliged to pass; thus they were enabled to kill large quantities which served them both for food and raiment. Their huts are represented as comfortable, and capable of lodging several families. Of their religion we know nothing, but something like a carved human head is said to have been found in one of their houses, which would lead us to believe that they practiced a species of idolatry. A Florentine writer, Rucellai, in 1560, in a general atlas of the world, gives a very imperfect map of Newfoundland, and a short description of the people. They, he says, are barbarous, and savage, eat large quantities of the fish called baccaloas, or codfish, raw meat, and even human flesh (which was false, for they were never known to be cannibals) and they adore the sun, the stars, or any thing that strikes their fancy. We see that there was a very erroneous opinion entertained of the Beoths at the time; the arts of civilization were never tried on them, they were a fierce people and resented the intrusion of the English on their salmon fisheries, and of the Micmac Indians on their hunting grounds. Their bows and arrows were no match for the musket of the white man and the Indian, and the government, too late, were aroused to the iniquity of leaving this interesting people to the cruelty of the Micmacs, and of the whites more cruel than the savage. The entire race, with the exception of a few individuals, had perished, and no trace of them is now to be found in Newfoundland, unless their graves and the mouldering remains of their huts and their deer fences. I have made every inquiry I possibly could among our own people, and Indians employed by the government to look out for them. Their haunts have been explored, but their graves alone remain, their fires are extinguished forever, and their fate is a disgrace to the government of those days who took no steps for their civilization or preservation. I have some slight reason to think that a remnant of these people remains in the interior of Labrador—a person told me there some time ago that a party of mountaineer Indians saw at some distance (about fifty miles from the sea-coast) a party of strange Indians, clothed in long robes or cassocks of skin, who fled from them; they lost sight of them in a little time, but on coming up to their tracks, they were surprised to see the length of their strides, which showed them to be men of a large race, and neither Micmac, Mountaineer, nor Esquimaux. I believe that these were the remains of the Beothic nation, and as they never saw either a white or red man but as enemies, it is not to be wondered at that they fled; such is the only trace I could find of the Beoths. We may wonder why England, after such a valuable discovery, did not avail herself of the acquisition; but soon after Henry VIII. commenced the Reformation, as it is called, squandered the treasures left by his parsimonious father, Henry VII.—who munificently rewarded Cabot with the sum of £10 for discovering the *New Island,* which, about this time, got the name of Newfoundland, a name so ridiculous in itself that nothing but the sanction of ages can reconcile us to it. No gold was discovered, no silver mines poured their treasures into the exhausted coffers of Henry, and so the Biscayans who are said to have fished on the Banks, and to have been aware of the existence of the island even before or as early as Cabot, the Bretons, the Spaniards, and Portuguese, enriched themselves by the inexhaustible mine of the fisheries; while Henry and his nobles were impoverishing themselves by the useless pageant of the Field of the Cloth of Gold or the wars in France, and endeavoring to repair their shattered fortunes by the plunder of the Church. An English captain wrote a letter to Henry VIII., on the 3d of August, 1527, in which he tells him that in the port of St. John's he found eleven ships from Normandy and three from Britanny engaged in the cod fishery. As all Europe was Catholic at the time of the discovery of America by Columbus, and of Newfoundland by Cabot, we find that the names imposed by the early navigators were either the names of the saints on whose days the land was discovered, or the names of some localities in their own country which it resembled, or names descriptive of some natural feature distinguishing the place—a most favorable contrast with the vulgar or trivial names given by subsequent navigators. Thus we may imagine the anxiety of Cabot, looking out for land on the western horizon, when from the lofty mast a sailor cries out, land! The Italian, perhaps often deceived by fog-banks, sees at length the cape well defined, the surges breaking on the Spillers, the dark green of the forest, gives expression to his feelings in his own musical tongue, and cries out, Bona Vista! Oh, happy sight! Gaspar de Cortereale, a valiant and religious Portuguese, especially devoted to the B. Virgin and St. Francis, discovers the great Bay of Conception, and calls it after the great mystery of the Immaculate Virgin, Conception Bay, and the cape at its entrance, C. St. Francis; he also named St.

Lewis and St. Francis Bays on the Labrador. Go round the shores of the island, and you will see the Catholic feeling which named the bays—Conception, St. Mary's, and Nôtre Dame Bay, dedicated to the B. Virgin—Trinity Bay, including the harbor of St. Bonaventure, Catalina Bay, or St. Catharine's, Catalina, like Kathleen in Irish, being the musical Spanish term for Kate or Catharine, St. Clare's Bay, now St. George's, St. John's, St. Peter's, St. Jude's, now C. Judy, Trepassey, the Bay of the Trepasses, or All Souls. Again: we have the French recollections of their own smiling land in Audierne, C. Freehel or Freels, Plaisance or Placentia, on account of its beautiful situation, the Portuguese Fermosa or Fermeuse beautiful, Renews rocky, and numberless others, a most happy contrast certainly with Bay of Despair, Fortune Bay, Gallows Harbor, Pinch Gut, Push Thro', Piper's Hole, Old Shop, Bread and Cheese, Exploits, and many others too trivial and vulgar to mention. In 1534, Jacques Cartier, the great French navigator, visited the island and named many capes and bays. In 1583, Sir Humphrey Gilbert took possession of St. John's, put up the queen's arms, Elizabeth's, and established the Book of Common Prayer as the only form of worship to be used forever in the island. The country was now about to commence a new phase of existence which, however, ended in disappointment. Sir George Calvert, subsequently Lord Baltimore, having obtained an Irish peerage, got from King James a large grant of land from Bay Bulls to Cape St. Mary's. A zealous Catholic and most enlightened philanthropist, which he proved himself to be by the universal toleration he established in his new colony of Maryland (the only part of the world in that age where, as long as Catholics held power, conscience was legally free, and no religious test was required for the enjoyment of citizenship, or office), established a colony in Ferryland, and laid the foundation of what, but for adverse circumstances, would be a great State at present. As he was thoroughly Catholic and English, he wished to perpetuate the religious memories of the English Church in his new plantation; accordingly he gave the name of Avalon to his province. It was a tradition in the early British Church, though it will not stand the test of criticism perhaps, that St. Joseph of Arimathea, after the passion of our Lord, fled from the persecution of the Jews and took refuge in Britain. He came, it is said, to Avalon, afterward called Glastonbury, in Somersetshire, and founded there a church, which was looked on subsequently by Britons, Saxons, and Normans, as the cradle of British Christianity. A splendid abbey which covered sixty acres was subsequently erected, but perished in the so-called Reformation, along with the other glories of Catholic England. There is an ancient Roman town, now called from the great abbey subsequently built there, St. Alban's, but in ancient times called Verulam. The protomartyr of Britain, St. Alban, there shed his blood for Christ, and the abbey and town afterward took his name. Calvert, wishing then to revive those Catholic glories of his country, called the province we now inhabit, Avalon, in honor of St. Joseph of Arimathea, and his own town Verulam, in honor of St. Alban. Like most of the foreign names, French or Spanish, this was corrupted into Ferulam first, and next into the modern name of Ferryland. Calvert spent over £30,000, an immense sum in those days, in the settlement, but a grant of a more favored territory on the Chesapeake, the incursions of Indians, and the attacks of the French, induced him to forsake Newfoundland, and to establish Maryland, called after Charles's queen, and the city of Baltimore, called after his Irish title. Thus Newfoundland sustained an irreparable loss which retarded its progress for two centuries. The French on the other side of the peninsula founded the town of Placentia—the environing hill, the two arms of the sea with a rapid tidal current reminding the French of the arrowy Rhone in their own land, and the almost total exemption from fog in a bay remarkable for it, induced them to call it Plaisance, a pleasant place, now Placentia. They early saw the importance of the acquisition, and provided for its security by strong fortifications. These are now in ruins—they have served as a quarry for the few buildings requiring stone or brick. The great demilune which guarded the entrance of the port is now a shapeless heap of rubbish, its vaulted brick casements have been all destroyed, and the remains of a castle on Crevecoeur Hill are slowly perishing. It is remarkable that several properties are still held in Placentia by virtue of the original French titles, and such importance did the government of Louis XIV., the grand monarch, attach to the possession of the place, that all the grants are signed by the king's own hand, and countersigned by his minister Philippeau. Nor were the French oblivious of the necessity of religion in their new settlement a convent of Franciscans, a branch of the convent of Our Lady of Angels of Quebec, was established there in 1689, on the site of the present Protestant Church and burying ground, and a few

French tombs of the date of 1680 and 1690 yet remain to mark out the place where it stood. Most of the French tombstones were taken by the English settlers after the surrender of the place by France, and applied to the ignoble purposes of hearth-stones and door-steps. Newfoundland was then under the jurisdiction of the Bishop of Quebec, and in 1689, the second bishop of that see, Monseigneur St. Vallier, made a visitation of Placentia and the neighboring parts in company with Father Giorgieu and some of the Franciscan community of Quebec. The records of the foundation of the convent and of the episcopal visitation are in the archiepiscopal archives of Quebec. Thus we see two great and powerful nations established on the shores of Newfoundland, opposed in politics, in interest, in religion, and it is easy to imagine that the progress of the country must have been, not only retarded, but absolutely impossible. A series of skirmishes, naval battles, and obscure sieges follow, until the treaty of Utrecht in 1713, when the French, exhausted by war, were obliged to resign all claim to Newfoundland, to evacuate St. John's, which they held for five years previously and were strongly fortifying, retaining only the small island of St. Pierre and Miquelon, and the right of fishing from Cape Bona Vista on the Northern to Point Riche on the western coast. England now obtained the dominion of the entire island, but had no intention of colonizing it. She wished to retain it as the French do the north and west shores at present, as a nursery for her seamen, and to make the riches of the deep in Newfoundland contribute to the strength and to the wealth of England. Freedom of Catholic worship was by treaty allowed to the French residents but with the sinister proviso, "as far as the laws of England permit." Governor Edwards, taking advantage of this, gave such annoyance to the French Catholics and their clergy that almost all of them sold their properties and left the island ; thus a body of useful citizens were lost to the colony through these bigoted proceedings, but we must in justice make allowance for the prejudices of the age. In the reign of King William III., by an extraordinary statute, a form of misrule was established tending to discourage settlement and create interminable confusion—the three first fishing captains arriving in the island each summer, took the names of admiral, vice-admiral, and rear-admiral, and without any qualification, except the priority of arrival, became magistrates, empowered to decide all Fishery rights and civil causes. We may imagine what sort of laws these men would deal out to their servants, and to the poor inhabitants whom they in general looked on as intruders. Something like a regular census of the population was taken in 1753, but ninety-seven years ago ; the inhabitants returned then were 13,112—4795 Catholics and 8317 Protestants. The fixed inhabitants, however, were estimated at only 7500, the rest being summer residents, but returning home every winter. The state of the population was miserable in the extreme ; no law, no security, the uncontrolled will of the ignorant fishing admirals being the only rule. Accordingly, Lord Vere Beauclerk, who commanded the naval force here, by his representations obtained from the Home Government the appointment of a titular governor, and in 1729, Captain Osborne was nominated as the first governor. The fishing admirals, however, and the merchants would not easily yield

up the power they possessed and misused, and though the
appointment of a local governor, even for the summer
months, was a recognition of the population of the island,
still he found himself almost powerless. The only law
known in the colony for a long series of years after was the
proclamation of the governors ; and without their sanction,
until within the recollection of many now living in St.
John's, a house could not be built or even thoroughly repaired. I should only tire your patience by recounting
the tyrannical acts of persecution embodied in the proclamations of these, perhaps honest, but bigoted men—we
therefore hasten over this dreary period, and come to the
comparatively happy epoch of 1784. On the 24th of October, that year, a proclamation was published, pursuant
to the instructions of His Majesty George III., to the
governor, justice of peace, and magistrates of the island,
whereby liberty of conscience was allowed to all persons
in Newfoundland, and the free exercise of such modes of
religious worship as are not prohibited by law, provided
people be contented with a quiet and peaceable enjoyment
of the same, without giving offense or scandal to government—thus Catholicity was permitted, and the days of open
persecution were happily at an end.

It may be interesting, especially to Catholics, to know
the state of the Church here before that time—Protestantism being the established religion, ministers were stationed
in the principal settlements, but the few priests in the
island had no fixed abode—they usually came out disguised in the fishing vessels, seldom staid long, and had no
regular missions, as the surveillance of the Local Government was too strict. In the same year of toleration,

1784, Dr. O'Donnell, the founder and father of the church of Newfoundland, landed in the island. Born in 1737, in Tipperary, he spent a large portion of his life in the Irish Franciscan Convent of Prague in Bohemia ; afterward, as superior of the Franciscans, in Waterford, and subsequently provincial of that order in Ireland. He was the first regular authorized missioner in Newfoundland after it became a purely British settlement, and no man ever had British interests more at heart—he mainly saved the island to the British crown when a mutiny broke out among the troops under the command of Col. Skerrett. By his influence among the Irish population he prevented the disaffection from spreading, and saved the colony. If such a service had been performed in those days by one of the Dominant Church, his reward would be a peerage and a pension ; to Dr. O'Donnell the British government granted, not a peerage, but the munificent pension of £75 or £50 (I am not sure which) per annum for his life ; however, they acted consistently. Catholic loyalty is an affair of conscience, and, consequently, he only gave to Cæsar what was due to Cæsar. As long, however, as rewards are given by the nation to those who do their duty, especially when that duty becomes, through extraordinary circumstances, a great public benefit, so long will the stinginess of the government of that day to Dr. O'Donnell be condemned by all right-thinking men. Dr. O'Donnell was at first only prefect apostolic, that is, a priest exercising episcopal jurisdiction, and generally having, like the Prefect Apostolic of St. Peter's, the right of giving Confirmation, which, as we see by the practice of the Greek Catholic Church, is not essentially an episcopal sacrament, if I may call it so. The importance of the population now required episcopal superintendence. The Sovereign Pontiff, to whom is committed the care of all churches, saw that Newfoundland was destined to become the home of a fixed population, not the summer residence of a floating one. Accordingly, in 1796, on the 5th of January, the great Pontiff, Pius VI., the Confessor as well as Doctor of the Faith, appointed Dr. O'Donnell Vicar Apostolic of Newfoundland, and Bishop of Thyatira in partibus, and he was consecrated in Quebec on the 21st of September the same year. Thus was the foundation of the Catholic Church solidly laid, and we hope forever. The state of morality is described at that time as very bad indeed, and this is not to be wondered at. The population was, I may say, a floating one, with no family ties and no religious ministration previous to Dr. O'Donnell's arrival, unless the casual visit of a priest from home. Money was abundant and liquor cheap; education there was none, and few even to avail themselves of it if there had been. Those who made money in the country, went to spend it elsewhere, and it is most disgraceful to reflect that, though colossal fortunes have been made in the island, not a college, an hospital, a school, an alms-house, was ever established by any one of those persons who drained the wealth of the land. Catholic or Protestant, it was all alike, as soon as a fortune was made, they went home, where it was frequently soon squandered by their children, and in the third generation no trace of it remained; but in Newfoundland they left nothing after them. It was only slowly, therefore, that population increased, and were it not for the appointment of Dr. O'Donnell, as bishop, and the certainty, therefore, that religion was permanently fixed in the island, the Irish settlers, who formed the bulk of the population of St. John's and the south of the island, would not have remained here. We have rather an interesting proof of this in a letter written by Governor Milbank to Dr. O'Donnell before his consecration as bishop, in answer to an application made by him to His Excellency for leave to build a chapel in one of the out-ports. Here is the document, and written, mark you, six years after the proclamation of freedom of religious worship: "The Governor acquaints Mr. O'Donnell that, so far from being disposed to allow of an increase of places of religious worship for the Roman Catholics of the island, he very seriously intends, next year, to lay those established already, under particular restrictions. Mr. O'Donnell must be aware that it is not the interest of Great Britain to encourage people to winter in Newfoundland, and he can not be ignorant that many of the lower order who would now stay, would, if it were not for the convenience with which they obtain absolution here, go home for it at least once in two or three years, and the governor has been misinformed if Mr. O'Donnell, instead of advising their return to Ireland, does not rather encourage them to winter in this country. On board the Salisbury, St. John's. Nov. 2, 1790." Such was the state of things exactly seventy years ago; what a contrast our governors then presented to our esteemed Sir A. Bannerman; or to the late administrator, Hon. L. O'Brien, who so far from wishing to lay restrictions on places of worship for Catholics, a Catholic himself, subscribes most liberally for their erection—witness his donation of £100 to the new church in Torbay. Thank God, those times are past, and now we have perfect civil and religious liberty ; and I may say, speaking of the Protestant population, not in the French sense, equality and fraternity. Let no one blame Newfoundland, then, for not having hitherto advanced as rapidly as other colonies. I boldly assert that never was more energy shown by any people than by the inhabitants of this island. The government that should foster them, considered them intruders, and banished them when it could. They were exposed to all the petty tyranny of ignorant fishing admirals, and of governors who proved their devotion to England by depopulating Newfoundland. They had not the liberty of the birds of the air to build or repair their nests—they had behind them the forest or the rocky soil, which they were not allowed, without license difficultly obtained, to reclaim and till. Their only resource was the stormy ocean, and they saw the wealth they won from the deep spent in other lands, leaving them only a scanty subsistence. Despite of all this they have increased twenty-fold in ninety years, have built towns and villages, erected magnificent buildings, as the cathedral in St. John's, introduced telegraphs, steam, postal, and road communications, newspapers, every thing, in fact, found in the most civilized countries, and all this on a rugged soil, in a harsh, though wholesome climate, and under every species of discouragement. We owe a great debt of gratitude to those who have gone before us, and by their energy, prepared happy homes in the stormy wilderness of Newfoundland, despite the frowns of man and nature, for the present generation. Our task is comparatively easy, we run on the smooth track, but they were the pioneers. The administration of

justice has been regarded in all communities as a matter
of the most vital importance, but, like every thing else in
Newfoundland, was most scandalously conducted by fishing admirals, arbitrary governors, magistrates without education, and surrogates, until after a great deal of opposition and delay, the Supreme Court was finally organized
in 1792, and Mr. Reeves appointed Chief Justice. Thus
another great boon was won for Newfoundland, and the
subject could always obtain a regular hearing of his cause
and legal decision. Mr. Reeves appears to have been a
gentleman well qualified for his station, and it was a Her-
culean task to clear away abuses and abolish practices
which existed for ages. In 1807, another step in advance
was made by the introduction of the press. In August that
year the first newspaper in the colony, the *Royal Gazette
and Newfoundland Advertiser*, was published, and two years
after, in 1809, a post-office was first established in St.
John's. Thus, by degrees, were improvements slowly introduced, and the English government tacitly recognized the
population of Newfoundland as having a right to live in
the land they had chosen. In the mean time, Dr. O'Donnell was laboring in his arduous mission—he had obtained
leave from the Local Government to take a piece of land
at a lease of ninety-nine years, and begun the old chapel,
which was very small at first. He made several visita-
tions to the out-ports of the island, encouraging, as far as
he could, education; we believe he was guilty of the
charge made against him by Governor Milbank, of encouraging the Irish to winter in the country, and we feel no
doubt but that he gave them absolution when they applied
for it, and even more frequently than every second or third

year, as accused by the worthy governor. During Dr. O'Donnell's episcopacy, the population was almost Irish, English, or Scotch. The Catholic district of St. John's, for it could not be called a parish, comprised the south shore of Conception Bay, and the south shore as far as La Manche toward Ferryland, and still the marriages were, on an average, only about seventeen or eighteen a year among the Catholic population—now the average of the same district gives about two hundred and sixty marriages. Both Protestants and Catholics complained at that time of the spread of infidel opinions in this country. "Paine's Age of Reason," denying all revelation, was very extensively read, trade was most flourishing, money abundant, and vice of all kinds prevalent. Protestant ministers in the principal towns, St. John's, Harbor, Grace, Trinity, and Ferryland, took charge of their own people ; priests were stationed wherever there was adequate support for them, when the bishop could procure their services. The Protestant clergy combated infidelity, principally by means of the publications of the Tract Society, but the Catholic always trusts more to the living word than to the dead letter. The mission was a laborious and rude one, and, accordingly, Dr. O'Donnell, in the seventieth year of his age, resigned his charge to younger hands, in the person of Dr. Lambert, and sought repose in his native land, where he died four years afterward, and was buried in the old parish chapel of Clonmel—he had fought the good fight in days of darkness, of danger, and of difficulty, and we hope he received the crown of justice. Having now given a rapid sketch of our scanty history from what we may call the fabulous times, until the death of the founder of the

Catholic Church in the country, I pause to make a few reflections which, in a Catholic college, and addressing a Catholic audience, the majority of whom look to Ireland with affection, as the land of their forefathers, may be interesting. History, as well as faith, teaches us that man can do nothing of himself, that human power, energy, talents, or wealth are of no avail, unless God wills that a thing should come to pass. "Unless the Lord buildeth the house, in vain do they labor," the psalmist says, "who build it." The history of the Catholic Church in Newfoundland most strikingly shows this. Twice under the most favorable auspices was the Catholic Church planted in this island—twice it failed to take root. Sir George Calvert, in Ferryland, intended this country, and particularly in this province of Avalon, to be a city of refuge to his coreligionists—what the Puritans did in New England he intended, though with more enlightened and Christian sentiments, to accomplish in Newfoundland. The Catholic glories of ancient Verulam were to be renewed here and the ancient British faith of Avalon and Glastonbury was to flourish with renewed vigor—all ended in disappointment, and the English branch of the Catholic Church never took root. The most powerful monarch of Europe, Louis XIV., justly called Louis the Grand, established, as he thought, Catholicity firmly in Placentia—founded a convent of Franciscans, the apostles of the New World, and laid, as he imagined, the foundations of our faith, broad and deep. Again a failure—the lily of France never throve on the soil, and with the departure of the last French governor the Catholic faith died away. The very churches were transferred to the professors of another creed. Well, the

Irish laborers came out to earn a subsistence by braving the dangers of the ocean ; they were not of the class of men who generally succeeded in establishing a church. Their faith, bitterly persecuted in their own country, was strictly prohibited in Newfoundland—the house where Mass was said was burned down by orders of the government—they had not wealth, nor education, nor any of those human gifts which would give them influence in the land ; still the hidden seed germinated, liberty of conscience was granted, they were grudgingly allowed to raise an humble wooden chapel here and there—the successor of St. Peter looks to this impoverished portion of his flock and gives them a pastor in the person of Dr. O'Donnell—the weakly plant, trampled on, cut down whenever it showed itself, now begins to throw out vigorous shoots, and we see at present, thank God, that it flourishes like a tree planted by the running water. This is the work of God (mind, of God alone), and it is wonderful in our eyes. Calvert failed. Louis failed, but the poor persecuted Irish fishermen succeeded, and the proud monument of his or his children's faith—the Cathedral—crowns the culminating point of the capital of the island. I fear I might tire you by continuing these dry details any longer. On this day week, please God, the present state and future development of our country will be the subject of the lecture. I thank you most cordially for the attention you have given, and if I have succeeded in making you in any way better acquainted with the by-gone times of the land we live in, and exciting in the generous young hearts I see around me an enlightened love of their native land, I am more than amply repaid. I considered it necessary to give this preparatory lecture as an introduction to the descriptive one I shall have the honor of giving this day week. As I have rapidly sketched the history of the country from the earliest records I could find down to the period within the memory of thousands in St. John's, I will principally confine myself in the next lecture to the physical description of the country, its capabilities for the support of a large population; and what I conceive to be the best means of developing them. Newfoundland has more claims on us than any other part of the world. If it is not the native country of most of you, it is the native country of your children, and I am sure that every one who has adopted the country as his home, and especially those who have brought up a family in it, loves it with a sincere, though not perhaps as tender an affection as if it were the land of his birth. If the ashes of his ancestors repose in the old land and his cradle was rocked there—his tomb will be here, and his children here will venerate and hallow his memory. Again thanking you for your attention, I remain, ladies and gentlemen, an ardent friend of the land we live in—NEWFOUNDLAND.

SECOND LECTURE.

LADIES AND GENTLEMEN,—I have, in my last introductory lecture, sketched the outlines of our scanty history as far as I could find materials, for our records are only those of an infant people, few and uninteresting to any one but ourselves and posterity. I need not recount the recent facts in the recollection of most of us, they are most important for the future historian of the country, but for us they are matters of recollection, not of record—I allude to the introduction of Representative Government first, and recently of that more perfect form of representative institutions called Responsible Government; the nomination of Dr. Lambert as successor to Dr. O'Donnell, of Dr. Scallan, whom so many of you have known, of my immediate venerated predecessor, Dr. Fleming, all three of the same institute as Dr. O'Donnell. I will not speak of the foundation of the Cathedral, of the establishment of a Protestant bishoprick in the island by Her Majesty Queen Victoria, or of a second Catholic bishoprick in Harbor Grace—all these matters are of too recent a date, and therefore I will pass at once to the physical description of the country, its climate, its capabilities, its future prospects. With politics or parties, I have nothing to do, and if I make any suggestions for what appears to me to be the improvement of the country, I hope all will esteem them as dictated solely by a love of Newfoundland and its people. The island of Newfoundland, as you may perceive by the map, is the greatest in North America, nearly four hundred miles long from Cape Ray (Raye) or Split Cape, as called by the French, from its appearance at sea, to Quirpon on the northeast, and about three hundred miles wide from Cape Race (Raze) on the east coast again to Cape Ray on the west. It contains, it is calculated, about 35,000 square miles, or 22,720,000 acres. This, however, is only an approximate calculation, as the country has not been explored, much less surveyed. It is of a triangular form, very narrow toward the north, hence called by the French "Petit Nord," very wide at the southern base, and having attached to it, as it were, the great peninsula of Avalon, separated from the great island by the Bays of Placentia and Trinity, and joined to it by an isthmus of only two or three miles, and this province is again divided by the two noble bays of St. Mary's and Conception. In no other part of the world are there more noble bays and harbors than in Newfoundland. Eighty and ninety miles the ocean penetrates by those great arms into the land, conveying to the doors of its inhabitants the treasures of the deep, and affording them a cheap means of conveying their produce to market, such as a hundred millions spent in railways could not procure. It is most providential that every thing required to carry out the great industry of the country, the Fishery, is found here better than in any other part of the world—the bays and harbors, the vicinity of the great breeding grounds, the abundance of wood adapted for boat-building, cooperage, flakes, and stages, the bracing winds and absence of a burning sun for drying, the rocky ledges the feeding ground of the cod, and above all, the hardy daring sons of the soil, men nurtured in danger, rocked in the tempest, men to whom the severest hardships are only sport, who know no danger, who tread the frozen ocean with as firm a step as their native soil, and yearly undergo without a murmur more danger than usually falls to the lot of the most daring through their entire lives. You perceive that the capital, St. John's, is placed almost in the centre of the great peninsula of Avalon, on the nearest point to Europe, with a port the most secure perhaps in the world, fortified by nature and only requiring a very moderate outlay, and a few thousand brave soldiers to make it, I may say, impregnable—the Gibraltar or Sebastopol of the North Atlantic. A fleet of war steamers stationed in St. John's, sheltered by the guns of Signal Hill and South-side batteries would give the command of the North Atlantic to Great Britain, and, with Bermuda, paralyze the commerce of the entire sea-board of the neighboring continent. I consider St. John's and Bermuda as the two great bastions of North America, but I leave the subject to be discussed by military men. It has been said that the trident of Neptune is the sceptre of the world, and unless some extraordinary change takes place in naval affairs, like the introduction of gunpowder into modern warfare, the saying has hitherto held and will hold good. See the immense importance of Newfoundland: between French, English, and Americans there are now, I suppose, from 50,000 to 70,000 men employed in the Fisheries, amid ice, fog, and storm. If the Fisheries were fully developed, as they will be in future times when the population increases and extends all along the shores and into the interior, this number will be doubled. The gulf and river of St. Lawrence depend altogether on Newfoundland—the possessor of this country holds the keys of the gulf. The Labrador, which will in time become a country like Norway, will swell the contingent of seamen. The Fisheries then will not be confined to the shores, but our mariners will each summer explore the recesses of Baffin's and Hudson's Bays, and probably follow the seal to Greenland. Now, a maritime population like this must have a great influence in the affairs of the world hereafter, and hold a place of the highest importance among the hundreds of millions who in two or three centuries hence will people those northern lands from the frontiers of Mexico to the shores of Hudson's Bay. This, ladies and gentlemen, is not a sketch of imagination, for as sure as the rivulet swells to a mighty river in its course and bears the fleets of nations, so sure, according to the laws of nature, will the wonderful development of these countries take place. Wars or pestilence may check it for a time, but nothing will stop it. The island, as you see, is trending, if I may use the expression, northeast and southwest. All our great bays, with the remarkable exception of the Bay of Islands, Bonne Bay, and Ingornachoix Bay, on the western or gulf side, follow the same direction as do the mountain ridges and the great lakes which fill up the valleys of the interior. It would appear as if the whole island was in a fluid state when the hills and mountains took this direction. The country is for the most part, geologically speaking, of primitive formation, granite, slate, old red sandstone, indeed I may describe it as a great skeleton poorly furnished with flesh. We have in the neighborhood of Conception Bay inexhaustible quarries of sienite or red granite. The front of the Presentation Convent is built of this material, and though it has not been quarried, but only taken from the bowlders on the surface, it is imperishable. In the same locality I have seen on the road and in the garden fences the most splendid blocks of Oriental porphyry, that rare material that we see in Rome alone, of green serpentine and of cipollino. The traveler is astonished at the riches of the altars in the Roman churches constructed in what the Italians call *pictra dura;* the brilliancy of the color and the high polish of the variegated material. Well, between this and Holyrood, at the head of Conception Bay, there exist materials enough to ornament all the churches and palaces of the world. It will, however, be long before these rich but intractable materials will be turned to any account. Gray granite is found in great abundance in almost every locality of the island ; slate of a superior quality in Trinity Bay, and I suppose a thousand other places, if sought for ; plastic clay and brick clay abound in our immediate neighborhood. That most useful material, lime, is most abundant in the north and northwest ; the shore about Ferroll, in the Straits of Bellisle, is almost entirely composed of it ; it is plentiful also in Canada Bay, and lately deposits have been found in many other places—I recently saw a quarry in the harbor of Burin, in the side of a cliff. Cod Roy would furnish plaster of Paris for all the purposes of building and agriculture, and one of the most beautiful sea views I know of is the painted plaster cliffs near Cod Roy. In the Bay of Exploits, remarkable for its fine timber and scenery, fine-grained red sandstone, a beautiful material for building, is found; 'tis said that good white marble is got in the Humber River; coal is said (and though I have not seen it, I have good reason to believe it) to exist in the upper part of Cod Roy River. The coarse building stone of St. John's is a fine material for rough work, and the Cathedral shows what can be done with the fine sandstone of Kelly's Island.

The mineral resources of the country have not been, as yet, turned to much account. Rich copper ore is found in many places in Conception Bay, Placentia Bay, and White Bay. If the country were explored and capital invested in mining, under judicious management, there is no doubt but that the enterprise would be a great source of wealth for centuries, perhaps as great as the Fishery is at present; but when we consider that only a small portion of the country has been hitherto explored, and only on the seacoast, that whatever mining operations have been undertaken, except at La Manche, have been of the most superficial character, merely, I may say, surface works, and that it was only very recently that any attention at all has been paid to mining, the sea being naturally considered by a maritime and fishing population as the only mine worth exploring—a mine richer, in reality, than all the silver mines of Mexico, producing millions for the last three centuries, and inexhaustible, we ought to rest satisfied with what has been done as an earnest of what will be done hereafter. I regret, indeed, that the lead mine of La Manche has been, not abandoned, but the work suspended for a time, I heard from Mr. Crocket, one of the superintendents there, two years ago, that there was then as much lead discovered as a thousand men could not remove in twenty years. To a person like myself it appeared unaccountable that such a region of lead as I saw there should be left idle, but I hope, in the spring, operations will be commenced anew and such a source of wealth not allowed to lie fallow. Silver is found in several of the lead specimens I have seen, though not in any great quantity in the La Manche ore, and I have seen minute threads of native silver in stones taken from a well dug in the neighborhood of the Hospital of St. John's. Time will tell whether, like the Lagenian Mine, sung by Moore, these indications are only spangled over the surface, but I have not the least doubt that copper and lead are most abundant, and will hereafter be an enormous source of wealth to the country. Of native gold, though the most generally distributed of all metals, I have not seen a specimen but one, with some microscopic particles glistening in the quartz; the person who had it told me he would call again and tell me the locality of his discovery, but never did so. It would be easy to try by amalgamation whether the spangles were gold or not. The gold matrix, as described by Humboldt and others, certainly exists, but the attention of the people has never been called to it. It is remarkable, that the fishermen in the lower part of Placentia Bay used to go to La Manche, take the pure galena, smelt it, and run jiggers out of it, and still the existence of the mine, though almost every pebble on the shore had specks of lead in it, was either unknown or disregarded. This shows how much we require that the country should be explored by competent persons. Since the discovery, three or four years ago, many thousand pounds of lead have been shipped off.

Once, while I was there, sixty-five tons, valued at £15 a ton, was shipped off, and another time I saw several, perhaps one hundred, tons of dressed ore in barrels, prepared for exportation; and still so little knowledge did the people possess of the treasure existing in their midst, that for generations the only use made of it was to dig out a bit to make a jigger. Before I speak of the great industry of the country, the Fisheries, and of our limited agriculture, and its future development, I have a few words to say of the climate. Climates in all countries, though principally depending on the distance from the equator, are still governed by other laws—elevation, direction of prevailing winds, but above all, by the currents of the ocean, and the proximity of the country to those marine influences. Confining myself at present to Newfoundland, we find St. John's in 47.30 north latitude; well, this same parallel intersects some of the finest wine-growing districts in France. Ireland, the Emerald Isle, is clothed with perpetual verdure, and flowing with milk and honey, while the corresponding region in Labrador is bound in the icy chains of almost perennial frost. The Gulf Stream, that great oceanic current, is the cause of the warmth of one region, and the great northern current, together with the diurnal revolution of the earth, of the cold of the other. You perceive that Cape St. Roque, on the Brazil coast, as I mark it for you, approaches so near to the African continent as to form a great basin, widening out to the north of the equator. Now, the almost vertical sun heats to an enormous degree this immense basin or cauldron of water in the Atlantic. All water heated increases in bulk, as every housewife knows who places a kettle too full on the fire; the water, when heated, begins to flow over; now the very same thing happens to the enormous cauldron of hot water between Africa and Brazil, the water so highly heated flows over toward the north; it enters into the Gulf of Mexico, heated to the highest pitch, seeks its exit through the narrow passage round Cuba and through the West India Islands, and, following the direction it gets from the set of the coast and the diurnal motion of the earth, it flows on, widening out like a fan every mile it travels, till it reaches the shores of Europe, envelops Ireland in its tepid embraces, bathes the coasts of France, passes round England, and washes the shores of Belgium, Holland, Germany, even in Norway prevents the harbors from freezing, and enables the Laplander to ripen barley under the Arctic Circle. But why does it not go directly north and bathe the shores of Newfoundland? One great cause is the diurnal movement of the earth. If it were possible to fire an Armstrong gun, for example, from the equator to the pole at the source of the Gulf Stream, the bullet would not, as we imagine, go straight, it would tend every instant to the right, describing a curve, and strike somewhere about the coast of Ireland. It is a curious fact that a railway train, going at a high velocity due north and south, always exhibits a strange tendency to fly off *at the right hand*. I beg you to remember this, for here is the secret of the climate in a great measure. The Gulf Stream, going north, curves off to the right hand, strikes the shores of Europe, rushes on to the great polar basin, the region of perpetual frost; cooled there, the great basin overflows and sends down the gelid or arctic current to fill up the place in the equatorial seas left vacant by the overflow of the Gulf Stream, which, I may remark, distributes daily as much heat in its course as would melt thousands of tons of iron if concentrated. The cold current then rushes down by Baffin's and Hudson's Bays, and, as I remarked, on account of the diurnal movement of the earth coming from the north, tends to the *right hand*, consequently hugs the American shore, bringing with it the floating ice and the cold winds of the polar basin. Thus we see the huge icebergs sailing majestically along the shores of Labrador and Newfoundland, resting on the ledges, and going forth again till they meet the Gulf Stream, and are finally melted in its tepid waters. The European coasts are, therefore, warmed by the hot water of the equatorial basin, sent to them by the Gulf Stream. Newfoundland and the North America shores are cooled by the cold water of the polar basin, coming from the north, and consequently having a continual tendency to hug the right or American shore. Let no one say, however, that Providence has not given a compensation for every thing; the abundant pastures of Ireland are compensated by rich sea pastures of Newfoundland. The codfish, the great source of our wealth, would not flourish among us if we had the hot and vapory waters of the Gulf Stream bathing our shores. The painted fishes, which inhabit the tropical and warm seas, have no flavor, can not be preserved and never would form an article of commerce like our cod, the king of all fish. The Gulf Stream gets its greatest deflection perhaps from the great submarine island, the great Bank of Newfoundland, the greatest submarine deposit on the face of the earth. Here the arctic and the equatorial currents meet and produce, by the intermingling of hot and cold water, " the fog on the banks." This great

submarine island, the great bank, is, as far as we can define
it, of an irregular oval shape, surrounded by the smaller
banks which extend many hundred miles on every side. A
great submarine island at first, it has for thousands of
years been receiving deposits from both currents, north
and south. The Gulf Stream has deposited the *infusoria*
of the tropical seas ; the deposit, as proved by the deep sea
soundings of Captain Berryman, extends all along the
course of the stream to Ireland, but from the nature of the
obstacles it meets in the southern portion of the bank, the
greatest quantity must necessarily be deposited there.
Then we have those great carriers of nature, the icebergs,
bringing from their polar home millions of tons of rock for
thousands of years, and depositing them all over the banks
when they ground. Thus nature has created and enriched
this extraordinary submarine region which forms the great
breeding and feeding ground of the cod species, and has
such an extraordinary influence on our climate and ourselves. Very beautiful specimens of coral and pebbles are
sometimes fished up by the French bankers ; for the French,
as we know, follow the bank fishery to a great extent, and
those who have been in the habit of crossing the banks, on
their voyage to Europe, must have been surprised to see
the number of French ships riding at anchor by their
hempen cables, better adapted than chains for the continual and short pitch of that sea, and the hardy fishermen
passing along in their large boats, hauling their bultows—
the most ruinous mode of fishing ever practiced. The bank
fishery, as you all know, is confined to the French and the
Americans, as we can not compete with their bounties, and
there is not a single British ship on the banks. It is a

dreary locality, the almost constant fog and drizzling rain, the doleful sound of the fog-horn or the ships' guns calling their crews, the troubled ocean, the ships rolling almost under the waves, steadied by their main or try-sails in addition to their moorings; all these make an impression on a stranger the first time he passes the banks in summer which he never after forgets. From this, also, most persons receive an erroneous idea of the climate of the island, which they imagine to be the same as that on the banks, and coming themselves from the cloudy though genial atmosphere of England or Ireland, can not believe that we are all the while enjoying a clear, bright sky, beautiful as that of Italy, and breathing an air dry and pure, never felt in the humid region of the Gulf Stream. What an awful climate, they will say, you have in Newfoundland; how can you live there without sun in a continual fog? Have you been there you ask them? No! they say; but we have crossed the Banks of Newfoundland. How surprised they are then when you tell them that, for ten months at least in the year, all the fog and damp of the banks goes over to their side and descends in rain there with the southwesterly winds, while we never have the benefit of it, unless when what we call the out-winds blow. In fact, the geography of America is very little known, even by intelligent writers at home, and the mistakes made in our leading periodicals are frequently very amusing. I received a letter from a most intelligent friend of mine some time since, in which he speaks of the hyperborean region of Newfoundland; in my reply, I dated my letter from St. John's, north latitude 47° 30″, and directed it to Mr. So and So, north latitude 52°.

The summer here is remarkable for fog, on the southern and southwestern coast especially, not on the northern or eastern side ; the reason of this is the more northerly set of the Gulf Stream in summer. During the winter months the northern or arctic current is stronger, and pushes the equatorial current to the south, consequently, as we have very little intermingling of warm water with our gelid sea, we have little or no fog. But in summer the water is not so cold ; the Gulf Stream pushes its warm current over the banks, throws a supply to the south and southwest of the island toward St. Mary's, Placentia, and Fortune Bays, and Burgeo, and the harbors on the southern shore by Ramco. St. Peter's Banks, and all the shallow seas about, begin to send off steam. The Bay of Fundy is clouded, the steamers are frequently a day waiting to grope their way into Halifax Harbor, and the dense fog, as far north as St. John's, is seen like a great wall at sea, though in general it does not penetrate far inland, as the people say, "the shore eats up the fog." The Gulf Stream, then, has to answer for the fogs of Newfoundland as well as for the humidity of Ireland, and though it does not bathe our shores, still a large portion of heat is thrown off by it, which accounts for the mildness of our climate in comparison with that of the neighboring continent. We never have the thermometer down to zero, unless once or twice a year, and then only for a few hours, and for a few degrees, three, four, or perhaps ten, while we hear of the temperature of ten and twenty below zero in Canada and New Brunswick, and this life-destroying cold continuing for days, perhaps weeks. Then see another effect of this —the Canadian and other North Americans of the same latitude are obliged to keep up hot stoves continually almost in their houses, while we have open fireplaces, or at most Franklins; our children, I may say, as lightly clad as in summer, spend a large portion of their time in the open air; and thus, while our neighbors have the sallow hue of confinement tinging their cheeks, and their children look comparatively pale and delicate, our youngsters are blooming with the rosy hue of health, developing their energies by air and exercise and preparing themselves for the battle of life hereafter, either as hardy mariners or healthy matrons—the blooming mothers of a powerful race. Thus the Gulf Stream, which clouds our skies, paints the cheek, invigorates the population, pours out to us in its return from the northern basin—the arctic current. which enriches our seas with fish, and enables us to furnish this luxurious and necessary article of food to the languid intertropical nations, for no food is so wholesome or so agreeable to the inhabitants of warm countries, whose diet is mostly vegetable, as the dried codfish of Newfoundland. I may remark, that by the climate table furnished me by Mr. Delancy, I find that the highest temperature was 96° on the 3d of July; 8° on the 3d of March, and the mean temperature of the year (1859) 44°; mean max. pres. of barometer, 29-74 inch; rain 63-920 for the year; max. quan. in twenty-four hours 2.098 inch; Wind N.N.W. and W.N.W., two hundred days; N.E. twenty-five days; W. and W.S.W. thirty-eight days; S.S.W. and S.E. one hundred and two days; rain fell on one hundred and ten days; snow fifty-four days; thunder and lightning five days. We have all the advantages of an insular climate, a mild temperature with its disadvantage, uncertain weather. I may remark, likewise, what Abbe Raynal recorded already, that the climate of Newfoundland is considered the most invigorating and salubrious in the world, and that we have no indigenous disease. It follows, naturally, that I should, in connection with our climate, speak of our limited agriculture. Besides the shallow nature of our soil in most parts of the island, we have, on account of the set of the arctic current, carrying its floating ice and icebergs along our shores, a late and uncertain spring; herbage will not, at least within the influence of the cold winds, spring up as soon as our latitude would entitle us to; we may be perhaps three weeks late, but then see the compensation we reap from those fields of ice, a crop which, I suppose, altogether realizes a million sterling in the European market; I mean the oil and skins of the seal—a crop which we do not sow, but the reaping of which encourages ship-building, rears up the hardiest mariners in the world, and throws hundreds of thousands of pounds into circulation, at a season which in all other northern countries is one of comparative idleness. The prosecution of the seal fishery does not interfere with the summer cod fishery, the winter herring fishery, or farming operations. Thus we have a great blessing bestowed on us by Divine Providence, a wonderful source of wealth coming in just at the time that, but for it, we should have nothing else to do; for this we may thank the great northern current, which retards our spring, but sends us a rich harvest, and one which no government bounty or encouragement could create elsewhere.

A doubt has been expressed by many whether the seal fishery will last—they fear that the continual destruction of both young and old seals will exterminate the breed and destroy the fishery, as was the case with the Greenland whale fishery. I can not agree with this opinion, and I will state my reasons—'Tis true the seal, *phoca cristata* or *barbata*, is one of the *mammalia*, bringing forth but one at a time and that annually—it can not multiply like the codfish with two millions of eggs. If we could get at the seals, then, I have no doubt, but that in a few years, like the Greenland whale, they would be almost all destroyed. This has happened elsewhere. In the great work of St. Bazil, the Hexameron, I find a description of seal-fishing in the Mediterranean, or perhaps in the Dardanelles or Black Sea ; the seal, he says, is speared with a harpoon to which is attached an inflated skin, so that, once struck, it can not sink, and is, therefore, easily dispatched. Now, it is remarkable that the Esquimaux and Greenlanders of the present day use the same means to kill seals. Well, the seals in the Mediterranean may be considered as exterminated, being now extremely rare ; but here, fortunately for ourselves, we can not kill the goose with the golden egg. See the great breeding and feeding ground of the seal, the polar basin, Baffin's and Hudson's Bays, the Northern Labrador—all these places are inaccessible to us ; we can not in the winter or the spring advance further than the outskirts of the great seal field—we kill hundreds of thousands, we can not reach the millions behind them ; we must wait till Providence sends us a share, for if man's cupidity had full play, he would rush at once to the arctic solitudes, kill all the seals he could find, and the North Atlantic would in a few years become like the Mediterranean—a comparative waste of barren water. To return, however, to our agricultural capabilities: first, we have the means of raising on our wild pastures, millions of that most useful animal to man—the sheep. On the southern and western shore, indeed everywhere in the island, I have seen the finest sheep walk; and what is better, the droppings of the sheep in this country induce a most luxuriant crop of white clover, and prevent the spread of bog plants. If sheep were encouraged, we should have fresh meat in abundance, and their fleece would furnish warm clothing in the winter for our people of a better quality than the stuff they now buy "half waddy and devil's dust," and which impoverishes them to procure it. Domestic manufactures would be encouraged, the people would become industrious and comfortable, and every housewife in our out-harbors would realize, in some sort, that sublime description of a valiant woman by Solomon, Prov., xxxi., " she hath put out her hands to strong things, and her fingers have taken hold of the spindle; she has sought wool and flax and hath wrought by the counsel of her hands; she shall not fear for her house in the cold of snow, for all her domestics are clothed with double garments; she hath looked well to the paths of her house and hath not eaten her bread idle; her children rose up and called her blessed; her husband had praised her." But, unfortunately, this great blessing of sheep pasture is marred by one curse, and idleness and poverty are too often the accompaniments of the poor man's fireside in the long winter —as long as a vicious herd of dogs are allowed to be kept in the country, so long will poverty be the winter portion of the poor. In no other part of the world would such an iniquity be permitted There is a law offering £5 for the destruction of a wolf, and I never have heard of £5 worth of mutton being destroyed by wolves since the days of Cabot; but why do not our legislators, if they have the interest of the people at heart (and according to their election speeches, every member is actuated by the most philanthropic and patriotic motives), pass and enforce a law against dogs, which devour every sheep they can find, and have almost exterminated the breed altogether; for no one will keep sheep while his neighbor is allowed to keep wolves. I will read you a list of certified losses, furnished to me by the Rev. M. Brown, of Bona Vista, all of which took place last year in that small locality. (Read a list of twelve milch cows, value £96 10s.; of sixty-two sheep and fifteen goats, all destroyed in Bona Vista in the year, by dogs.) I hope the government will at last see the necessity of putting a stop to this state of things, which would not be permitted by a Turkish pasha in his province; but then the pasha, perhaps, has not an eye to the next election. Nowhere can be seen a more distressing spectacle than a stalwart man yoked in with a couple of dogs drawing a load of firewood, losing his whole winter, tearing the poor clothes he is obliged to buy and which his wife ought to spin and weave (spinning and weaving are taught in the convents, but we can't get the children to learn the art), and brutalizing his children by keeping them from school, because, as the usual excuse is, they have to go to the woods. One horse would do the work of one hundred dogs and be always useful, and the man who could not keep a horse, could hire his neighbor's for a few days at an expense less than what he even wastes in boots and clothes. These observations may be unpalatable to some, but I have the interests of the people too much at heart to conceal my sentiments on a subject of such vital importance to them ; and religion, education, civilization are all suffering from this curse of dogs, worse than all the plagues of Egypt to this unfortunate country. In Canada, New Brunswick, or any of the other northern provinces, such a thing would not be allowed—but there the people have not the spring seal fishery or summer cod fishery, and are, therefore, obliged to preserve their sheep and cattle. Cattle of the best breed thrive here, and both our beef and mutton are found to be of superior flavor to those imported from the neighboring provinces. I have several times suggested the establishment of a cattle fair at Holyrood, at the head of Conception Bay, where the people of the great cattle-producing districts of the cape shore, Placentia, St. Mary's, and Salmonier, might find a market for their surplus stock, though to tell the truth, they have hitherto made very little use of their fine pastures. The populous districts of Conception Bay and St. John's would then be supplied ; farmers and victualers would know where and when to obtain stock, and an impulse would be given to cattle-breeding, at an expense of less than £10 a year to the government for printing the proclamations and paying a toll clerk, which, in a few years, would highly improve those grazing districts. Goats form a very important item in the agricultural riches of other countries ; with a large space of thin barren land like Newfoundland, they generally forage for themselves for a great part of the year ; their milk is most wholesome, and goat's cheese is not a bad addition to a poor man's meal. Kid's flesh is a delicacy, and in Rome capetto, or kid, is one of the cheapest, most abundant, and most delicious of meats while it is in season. It is a shame that, even in St. John's, we have little chance of a turkey till the Halifax steamer comes in, and the goose, the most nutritious, the most useful, and the most easily kept of all fowl in a northern country like this, is just as scarce. In the north of Europe you get goose almost every day; and a good roast goose for dinner, and a feather bed to rest on, are not to be despised; and here is the very *habitat* of the goose, the very climate of all others where the bird could be brought to the greatest perfection, and the wild goose, which breeds in enormous numbers, is the most delicate of our wild fowl, we get our geese from Nova Scotia, and our feather beds from Ireland or Hamburg. All garden vegetables, cabbages, carrots, turnips, salads, etc., are brought to the highest perfection, and the climate appears especially adapted to impart succulency to them. The potato, you all know, before the rot, was of the finest quality. It is now nearly recovered, but I regret to see in many of the out-ports the potato-field reverting to a state of nature—people prefer the hard and unwholesome Hamburg bread, American pork, and Danish butter, to the fresh and nutritious food they could raise themselves—in a great measure trusting to a supply of meal from the government, if the Fishery is short, or to the eleemosynary relief distributed in the fall under the name of road-money, instead of improving every spare hour and every leeward day in clearing and improving a plot of ground. We have not hands enough even for the Fishery, and thus we see (unless in the populous and industrious districts of Harbor Main, Brigus, and the River Head of Harbor Grace, and perhaps a few more exceptional localities), that the land brought into cultivation is rather diminishing than extending, and we are obliged even to import large quantities of hay from the States, where labor is so high and land so dear, while millions of acres are lying waste about us. Cereal crops demand a special notice—wheat will ripen very well, especially if the proper variety of seed adapted for a northern country be procured; but as long as we have the great grain country of the United States at our doors, no one will take much trouble about such an unprofitable crop. I have never seen finer barley than the growth of Newfoundland, and all persons who have bought, as I have done, Newfoundland oats, at nearly double the price of the husky grain imported here, will find that he has gained by his purchase. Hops are most luxuriant, and so are strawberries, currants, gooseberries, cherries, and many other species of fruit. The hawthorn flourishes here, when planted, and I have seen as fine hedges of it laden with haws here as in the home country; and I mention this as a proof of the comparative mildness of our climate, for I find in Russia, as far south as Moscow, it is a hot-house plant. My estimate, then, of the agricultural capabilities of Newfoundland, comparing it with what I have seen in the north of Europe, is, that if we had a large agricultural population, we could support them in comfort, and that as population increases, we must attend more to the land, and then more general wealth and comfort will be diffused a hundred-fold, than now, when our population is, I may say, wholly maritime, and we depend almost altogether on other countries for our food. My earnest advice would be, kill the dogs, introduce settlers, encourage domestic manufactures, home-made linen and home-spun cloth, and

Newfoundland will become the Paradise of the industrious man. The soil, in general, is thin, but kind, easily cleared, and besides the legitimate manure of the farm-yard, can always be enriched near the sea by scarack and fish offal; the climate is comparatively mild, and all we want are hands and industry. The Fishery, however, of Newfoundland is the great and grand industry of the country. Other lands may surpass us in every thing else, but here we are without a rival; the natural productions of one country may not only be raised in another, but even improve by transplanting, as the Peruvian potato did in Ireland, and the East India ginger in Jamaica. Tea may be cultivated out of China; but the noble codfish—this is beyond man's control, this is the gift of nature to those northern seas, and as long as the world lasts, Newfoundland will be the great fish-producing country. The codfish, the chief of the family of the *gadaceæ*, inhabits, in general, the North Atlantic, between the fortieth and sixtieth degrees of latitude on the European coast, but extends further south on the American side. In another country, the description of the capture and curing of cod would furnish materials for a very interesting lecture, but here it is superfluous to say any thing on that subject. The grand bank appears to be the great breeding ground of the species, and the finest fish are caught there. In the Lafoden Islands in Norway, under the Arctic Circle, a great cod fishery is carried on, but, as far as I could learn, the catch is under 100,000 quintals. The fishers there pay great attention to the curing; the fish is nicely packed in boxes, the fins trimmed off, and though in reality not as good fish as that of Newfoundland, brings a higher price, as a fancy fish, among the Spaniards and Cubans. I will not offer an opinion on the use or abuse of cod seines, the improvements in curing or catching, for our people know more about these matters than any other race on the face of the earth. I may remark, however, that the want of a population in many of the outports, causes a loss of a great quantity of the most nutritious and delicate food, the air-bladder, or as we call it, cod's sounds, which consists almost altogether of pure gelatine, and sells at a high rate in any market into which it has been introduced. The medicinal qualities of the fresh liver oil have been fully proved, and the manufacture of that article has brought a great increase of wealth to the country. Like all good things, however, it is easily imitated : the common cod oil, made by the putrifying process, has been refined at home by animal charcoal, filtered so as to deprive it of all bad smell, being already deprived, by putrefaction in the manufacture, of iodine and all other medicinal qualities, and pawned off by dishonest dealers as the genuine article. It would be well, therefore, for the credit of the article and the advantage of those who require to use it, if some particular seal or mark was fixed on the bottles or vessels here, which would, in some sort, serve as a guarantee of its purity in Europe. We have not only, I may say, a monopoly of the cod fishery in Newfoundland (of course, I now include the French), but we see the market every day increasing. See what a prodigious expansion the Brazil trade has taken within the last few years ; what will it be in future ages when Brazil will count its population by hundreds of millions, when Cuba will increase ten-fold ? All tropical people like codfish, and must have it ; and, therefore, if we could produce one hundred millions of quintals, we could not supply the demand in future ages. The roe of a cod contains two millions of eggs, and if all these came to maturity, one cod would fill the ocean in a few years; but though countless millions perish, we know that, if we do not violate the law of nature by destroying the mother or breeding fish, we can not lessen the species. There is another fish, however, the salmon, which requires strict legislative protection, as it comes to spawn in the river, and is therefore easily destroyed by the cupidity of man. It is the duty of the government, as the guardians of the public interest, to look to this, to appoint a committee to investigate the laws made for the preservation of salmon in Great Britain and Ireland, and to use the most stringent measures, both here and in the Labrador, to prevent any wanton destruction of the fish, or any annoyance to it in the breeding season. We know that through ignorance or carelessness, this rich fish has been almost annihilated in some of the home rivers, and it costs a series of years and the strictest precautions to nurse up the remnant and re-establish the breed once more; for by an extraordinary law of nature, this fish always returns to the place where it was spawned, and if disturbed, disappears forever. There is another delicious fish, which is now only hauled for bait and manure, for the little cured is of no consequence, but which will hereafter become a great source of wealth—this is the caplin, or, as naturalists call it, the *Salmo articus*. We see what a source of profit the sardines and anchovies are to the people of the Mediterranean. Now, I am quite sure, that if we had hands enough to cure this delicious fish, it would take rank with these delicacies, and, like the codfish, the supply of caplin is inexhaustible. I am quite sure that the habit of taking large quantities for manure from the spawning beaches, has, in some cases, chased away the fish, for instinct is so strong in all fishes, that if impeded in the operation of spawning they generally seek other localities. Indeed, I never could believe that the use of this delicious fish for manure is legitimate. If they were merely pickled and dried, a simple operation which could be performed by children, they would be worth at least a dollar a barrel, and a million of barrels would find a market, if introduced into fish-eating countries, and not sensibly lessen the quantity which every summer swarms in every bay and creek of the Island and Labrador. I have no doubt but that hereafter they will be preserved in various ways and in extraordinary quantities; but at present, coming as they do in the height of the fishing season, we have no hands to cure them at that busy time. A great mine of wealth we possess, and which is only partially worked or turned to account, is the herring fishery. In no part of the world is the herring finer, or, I believe, so abundant, and all it requires is to be properly cured. The Dutch became a great nation, it is said, principally by the herring fishery, and Amsterdam, they say, is built on a foundation of herring bones. Even at present, the Dutch herrings, though caught on the same ground as the English or Scotch, bear a higher price than any other in the world, and are eaten raw as a relish in Holland and Germany. The first barrel of new herring that is taken, is forwarded to the king at the Hague. It is carried in procession with banners and military music—the day is one of public rejoicing, and a few of the new herrings are sent as presents to the nobles of the land. I understand that the Dutch bleed each herring, use the best quality of salt, and take the greatest care in their manipulation. If they had the rich herring of Labrador, it would be worth the gold mines of Australia to them. A movement was made to procure instructors in curing, some time ago, but I know not from what cause it failed. I believe the Dutch prohibit their herring curers from engaging with foreigners, but Scotland could furnish us with many nearly as good, and thus hundreds of thousands of pounds would be yearly gained to the country, and the gifts of Providence would not be abused. One great step for the preservation of the herring on the western shore, has been made by passing Mr. Benning's bill. I have been informed, on good authority, that the waste of herring for supplying bait to the French was awful, and that one year 20,000 barrels, for which there was no sale, were cast back into the sea. No fishery then, I think, requires the watchful care of government more than this, and if properly preserved and managed, it will be nearly as great a source of wealth as the cod fishery, and more secure than the seal fishery. The whale fishery was formerly prosecuted to some extent in the Bay of Despair, but the whale, as we know, is easily exterminated, and though the fishery is yet followed to some extent, it is one we can not expect to continue—still it will be always more or less an addition to our resources. Allow me to say a few words of my experience of the people : I have found them in all parts of the island, hospitable, generous, and obliging ; Catholics and Protestants live together in the greatest harmony, and it is only in *print* we find any thing except on extraordinary occasions, like disunion among them.

I have always, in the most Protestant districts, experienced kindness and consideration—I speak not only of the agents of the mercantile houses, who are remarkable for their hospitality and attention to all visitors, or of magistrates, like Mr. Gaden, of Harbor Briton, or Mr. Peyton, of Twillingate, whose guest I was, but the Protestant fishermen were always ready to join Catholics in manning a boat when I required it, and I am happy to say that the Catholics have acted likewise to their clergymen. It is a pleasing reflection that though we are not immaculate, and rum sometimes excites to evil, still, out of a population of over 130,000, we have rarely more than eight or ten prisoners in jail, and grievous crimes, are, happily, most rare, capital offenses scarcely heard of. I will now ask you to accompany me round the coast. Leaving St. John's a few miles brings us to Bay Bull's in the southern district, a fine harbor of refuge for St. John's, along to Ferryland, the ancient but hitherto neglected capital of the district, by Cape Broyle, Fermeuse, and on to Cape Race. All this district has fine land, magnificent harbors, a great fishery, and only wants a large population. On round the cape to Trepassey with a spare population, less than 800, where thousands could find a comfortable living; on to the fine Bay of St. Mary's, with the richest fishing grounds in the island, excellent land, and the rich and beautiful arm of Salmonier, extending far up into the country, well timbered, and adapted for the seat of a rich agricultural, as well as a maritime population. I am happy to say that settlers are now coming there in numbers, and in twenty years it will be one of the finest districts in the island. The lover of scenery and field-sports could nowhere spend a pleasanter week than in Colinet. We hurry on round the Cape St. Mary's to the great Bay of Placentia, sixty miles wide, ninety miles long, rich in fisheries and minerals—copper at Mahony's Cove, lead at La Manche, studded with beautiful islands, some of them, like Merasheen, twenty miles long. It will hereafter be the most important district in Newfoundland, but as yet, the small population of the bay, including Burin, perhaps not more than 13,000, hinders its development. Fortune Bay has the most beautiful scenery, rich fisheries, and especially of herring, and several great arms—Connaigre Bay, Hermitage, and the Bay of Despair, all waiting to be filled up with a population. Between the two great bays of Fortune and Placentia we find the French colony of St. Pierres and Miquelon—the only remnant of the immense empire France once possessed in North America.

The small rocky island of St. Peter contains in the town perhaps 2000 fixed inhabitants; it is a place of great trade; the church is very handsome, though a wooden one; the great hospital, served by six Sisters of Charity, is a noble establishment. A prefect apostolic, Very Revd. Pere Le Helloco, and two assistant priests, look after the spiritual interests of the inhabitants, and Christian brothers teach the boys, as nuns do the girls. The government authorities are remarkable for their courtesy to strangers, and I never can be grateful enough for all the kindness and attention I always received from the governor and officials, the naval authorities (for there are no military stationed in the island), and the prefect apostolic and his clergy. The southern shore, from St. Peter's by the Burgeo Islands, the seat of a large fishing population, is indented with fine harbors; but the land, as far I saw it, is covered with moss and the population thin. It is the least developed district in Newfoundland. We now pass round Cape Ray into the Gulf of St. Lawrence, and enter on what is called the French Shore, which extends to Cape John on the northeast side. Cod Roy is rich in agricultural capabilities. St. George's Bay, though deficient in ports, has a fine herring fishery; and small as the population is, it consists of four races, who speak four languages: English, French, Gaelic, and Micmac Indian. The fishery in the gulf is what the French call a *nomade* fishery, they follow the cod in its migrations. We turn round Cape Norman from the dangerous Bay of Pistolet, by Quirpon, on to Croque, a fine harbor, the headquarters of the French navy, till we come to the French limits at Cape St. John. The country is very thinly inhabited all along this line, as the fixed population is, I may say, not recognized by either power. Some copper mines are opened there, which will, it is expected, turn out most valuable. Nôtre Dame Bay, the Bay of Exploits, and all the surrounding arms are rich in fine timber, good land, and productive fisheries. I may make the same remark of Bona Vista Bay, especially in the rich timbered arms. Passing the old Cape of Bona Vista, the first discovered part of Newfoundland, we enter the great Bay of Trinity, pass the fine harbor of Catalina, and soon come to the beautiful Swiss-looking town of Trinity, seated in one of the finest harbors of the world, on to Bay Bulls Arm, the terminus of the Atlantic Telegraph. We return to Baccalieu Island, so called from the Beothic name of the codfish, and enter the great Bay of Conception, with its fine town of Harbor Grace, the seat of a Catholic bishoprick; its rich population of nearly 40,000 inhabitants; its great sealing fleet; populous towns and villages, telegraphs, agriculture, in fact, every thing that a large civilized community requires. We return to Topsail or Portugal Cove where a railway to St. John's ought to convey us; and I hope that in a very few years a railway and a line of good steamers will connect the Conception Bay and St. John's trading communities, and be most highly advantageous to both. I regret that I can not take you into the unexplored interior—to the Big Pond, seventy miles long, the future seat of a great population; to Indian Pond, and the other great lakes and rivers which beautify the country. (This is only an outline of the description of the country, which, with the explanations on the map, occupied more than an hour.) The interior appears to be a country such as Britain was anciently, marshy, but easily reclaimed; there being everywhere a fall into the great lake or by the rivers to the sea. When we know what the state of the North of Europe was eighteen hundred years ago, and what a great change it has undergone since, we may reasonably hope that the climate of the interior of Newfoundland will, by cultivation, drainage, and reclamation of bog land, undergo a great change. The coast climate will always depend on the oceanic current, but the interior climate will, under those influences, be modified. I know many persons imagine that the interior will never be inhabited, but they have not studied the subject. I see the sandy and barren shores of the Baltic, with a climate and soil far worse than Newfoundland, and without any great maritime or fishery resources, as we have, the seat of a large population.

Why? Because the people of Courland, Finland, Esthonia, Prussia Proper, Mecklenburg, and all these other northern regions have no other place to go to. They can not, as of old, follow their chiefs from their forests, and carve out for themselves homes in the genial climes of Southern Europe. Suppose America to be the old country and Europe the new, and that the tide of emigration set eastward, it would naturally be directed to the banks of the Garonne, the Tagus, the Gaudalquiver, or to the shores of Italy or Sicily, not to the Elbe or the Baltic. Such is the case with us at present—the tide of European emigration sets toward the broad rich lands of the United States. But let these get filled in another couple of centuries, when land now sold at $1 an acre will be paying an annual rent of $5 or $6, and it will be as difficult to get a living there as now in the crowded countries of Europe: when taxation will be increased, perhaps large standing armies kept on foot; then the people of these northern regions, increasing and multiplying, will cultivate their now waste lands, as the Swedes, the Danes, the Russians, and Prussians have done, when there was no outlet for them, and Newfoundland will count its population, not by thousands, but by millions. The increase at present, independent of any emigration, is thirty-three per cent. *at least* every ten years. Take the present population at say 130,000, and that is a very low estimate, and see then what it will amount to in even another century—over two millions! I do not mean to say that the increase will be so constantly progressive, but it must be at least ten-fold—1,300,000. The present generation of Newfoundland then leaves a mighty inheritance to their children, and we are now form ing the character of a future nation. The development of the people is certain. Religion, education, and industry are indispensable to make them a great people. Consider what Newfoundland was fifty years ago, and then you may imagine what it will be a century hence. I hope, then, I have drawn your attention to the past and present state of the country in this and my former lecture, and excited your hopes for its future prosperity. I have merely glanced at the subjects I treated of—to take them up in detail would require many lectures longer then the present, greater abilities than I possess, and deeper research than I could afford to give to the subject. However, the man who brings only a single stone to an edifice contributes to its erection. Before I close, I consider it due to one Institute to make special mention of it—I mean that Society of Religious Ladies, the Nuns, who are now engaged in the great work of female education, in moulding the characters of generations yet unborn, instructing in religion, industry, and refinement the future mothers of the people of Newfoundland. We may look with confidence to those who come after us when such a religious foundation is laid. I thank you sincerely, ladies and gentlemen, for the attention you have shown to this long lecture, assuring you, in all sincerity, that whatever observations I made in the course of it were dictated solely by a love for our native or adopted country—NEWFOUNDLAND.

JESUITS' ESTATES

ANSWER

TO A

COMMUNICATION IN THE "MONTREAL STAR"

OF THE 19TH MAY 1888,

BY

U. E. L.

Justitia elevat gentem.

MONTREAL

1888

ERRATA.

On page	Line	Instead of	Read
11	7 }	in Father	in answer
11	8 }	(in *belongs to the line below*)	
23	22	n'y	ny
25	19	Nouillet	Noulliet
26	5	sauves-gardes	sauve-gar(
26	9	fonc,	fonc-
30	1	le	la
30	10	Aristotle	Aristote
32	last	lisence	silence
33	12	make	made
33	14	idea	ideal
34	26	in Montréal	in Montre(
46	11	Jesuits, Estates	Jesuits' E(
47	22	1756	1759
47	23	1879	1876
54	10	espace	space
54	17	murs son	murs sont
54	35	s'eperçurent	s'aperçure
56	2	only	duly
56	3	obyish	boyish
56	13	pledge	pledged
56	16	deshonest hart	dishonest
58	8	deal	deaf

And a few others of less importance which the intelligent reader will please co

INDEX.

STAR, 26th May 1888.

	Page
[Co]mmunication of the 19th May 1888.	3
[Th]e Jesuit Property. Answer to the communication.	7
[Lis]t of Mis-statements	7
[Th]e Society of Jesus, as a Mendicant Order, could and did hold property in its own right	9
[Th]e Jesuits held their property for Roman Catholic religious educational purposes.	10
[Be]auharnois, Governor-General : Hocquart, Intendant	11
[Th]e Royal Instructions of 1791, to suppress the Jesuits, are a peremptory proof of their corporate existence down to that date at least	12

STAR, June 2nd 1888.

[Th]e unjustifiable inhibition to receive new members into the Order invalidates all title through escheat for the present holders of the Jesuits' Estates	14
[Bu]t a small portion of the revenues up to the year 1831 went into the general treasury	14
[Fro]m 1831, as well as previously, the Estates should have been applied by legitimate administrators in favour of Catholic education only	16
[Th]e "Contributor" at sea	16
[A] title of conquest *in general*, according to the Laws of Nations, a conqueror has no right to the private properties of citizens or of authorized corporations.	17

STAR, 7 June 1888.

[In]dividuality and immortality : two essential properties of a body corporate	21
[Th]e Society of Jesus in Canada was a body corporate from 1678. Its right of property was protected by the Law of Nations	22
[Th]e Letters patent of the French King a solemn contract of protection with the Society. Its obligations binding on the King of England who supplants him.	24
[A] corporate body cannot be destroyed by the ruler, in virtue of his Royal prerogative alone	24
[Do]cumentary evidence of the exercise of corpora[t]e rights by the Society of Jesus down to the very year of the capitulation of Quebec	25
[A] title of the conquest of Canada, *in particular*, the right of the Jesuits to their property was unassailable	25

STAR, 8th June 1888.

[W]hat was refused with a proviso in the XXXIII Article of the Capitulation of Montreal ? Interpretation of treaty stipulations	28
[En]glish Authorities on the rights of Religious Orders in Canada to their property as secured by treaty	32

STAR, 9 June 1888.

[Pr]oof that the Crown inhibited the Jesuits from receiving new members. Consequently the title of the Province to the estates by escheat untenable	35

The Quebec Act, inasmuch as it restricts treaty stipulations, is ultra vires. It in no wise affects vested rights ; hence inapplicable to the case..........
The status of the Jesuits in France in the 16th and 17th centuries is beside the question : the Jesuits being a body corporate in Canada. The title to their property was never vested in the General.................................

(STAR, *June* 13, 1888.)

A Diversion. Second communication, June 13th...................................

(STAR, June 15, 1888.)

Side issues.—Answer to the second communication.................................
A Grantee of the Crown not protected against common law remedies...............
Jurisdiction not ownership ....
A body corporate in Canada not amenable in law for real or supposed misdeeds of body corporates elsewhere......................................
Blackstone vs. Thurlow ....
The " Contributor " again at sea..
Delegated powers expire with the instrument conferring them....................
Liability of actual possessors..
Rome, not the public, the judge in matters ecclesiastic.........................
The King by treaty may preclude himself from the exercise of certain prerogatives.—The Quebec Act once more..
English penal and common law, as such, do not hold in the Colonies.............
The Society of Jesus never totally extinct.....................................
Wrong to be righted.—Conquest the title officially alleged.....................

(STAR *June* 16th, 1888.)

Continuation of the first answer, interrupted at page 38 ....
The General's attributes in financial matters.—The non-solidarity of separate houses assailed in the Jesuits' Institute alone................................
The General incapacitated by his vow from holding property in his own right. His functions those of a Superintendent......................................
As a constituted corporation, the Society was of Canada.......................
The nationality of the General a " side issue.".................................
As years roll on youth will wane.—The Jesuits recognized at last to be what they had never ceased to be. ....
The Province amenable. (See also page 43) ....
A Document out of date..
The Bishops " ex officio " the administrators of Church property temporarily or irremediably " vacant."..
A pretext for Vandalism. Dynamite vs. Jesuit mortar...........................
They wiped out the oldest institution of learning in North America............
Good intentions, not less than malice, may work sad havoc.,....................
Albion n'est pas perfide. What would constitute perfidy........................
By whom the wrong was perpetrated..
Justice enobleth a nation..
Grateful acknowledgment to the *Star*..

(*Communication of the 19th May 1888.*)

THE JESUIT PROPERTY.

History of the Order in Quebec Province — A Mendicant Order — List of Property held in 1824—Confiscation by the Crown—Common to Roman Catholics and Protestants for Educational purposes.

Inasmuch as this question is set forth as one of the important questions which the Mercier Ministry is to legislate upon during the coming session, it may not be amiss to give a short statement of the case as it stands. The early annals of our country abound with instances of Jesuit zeal for the extension of Christianity—amongst the Indian tribes. The history of the order during these years is a long record of self-sacrifice and devotion. The Jesuits have the reputation of being the best educated of the religious orders, and are said to be exceptionally clever even in a worldly sense.

In the first Bull obtained by the Jésuits from Pius V, in 1571, the society is declared to be

A MENDICANT SOCIETY.

and cannot possess real property. living by unfailing alms, etc. The Bulls of Gregory XIII of 1576 and 1582 vested all property in the Father General. Notwithanding this provision of their constitution, it was absolutely necessary, in order that the Indians might be Christianized and converted, that the worthy fathers should have some land. On reference to a schedule of their property, made in 1787 and contained in the thirty-third volume of the Journals of the House of Assembly of the Province of Lower Canada, 5 George 4, i e., the session of 1824, the following appears as their little property :

1. Six superficial arpents on which the Quebec college and church are erected, given for the instruction of the inhabitants.
2. The two Lorettes or Seigniory of St. Gabriel.
3. The peninsula of Lavacherie.
4. Sillery, near Cap Rouge.
5. Belair.
6. Cap de la Magdelaine, near Three Rivers.
7. Batiscan.
8. The Island of St. Christophe, near Three Rivers.
9. Laprairie de la Magdelaine.
10. A piece of ground at St. Nicholas.
11. Eleven arpents of ground at Pointe Levis.
12. The Isle of Reaux, below the Island of Orleans.
13. Six arpents at Tadousac.
14. The Fief Pacherigny, near Three Rivers.
15. Another lot at the same place.
16. A remnant of ground extending to a small river near Lake St. Peter.
17. A number of lots in Quebec City, now built upon, and many used as public streets.
18. The ground used by the church and Mission House of Montreal, etc.

The whole amount of Jesuit lands was 48,000 acres in the district of Montreal; 439,000 in the district of Three Rivers; and 129,500 in the district of Quebec. The value of their property was then estimated at two to three millions of dollars. The present Government will have to make a new loan, of some magnitude, if it is decided to reimburse the present recently created Order of Jesuits.

Inasmuch as the order was a mendicant order, and could not hold any property in its own right, they held the above properties in trust for educational and religious purposes. In 1774, they were suppressed by a Royal decree and their property was confiscated, except what the surviving few might need for

A COMFOTABLE SUBSISTENCE

during their natural lives. Had they not been suppressed in 1744, their property would have become the property of the Crown at the decease of the last Jesuit in 1800. In 1789, there were only four living. As a matter of fact all the property of the Jesuits was seized by the Crown in 1800 by the Sheriff of Quebec, and the document is enrolled in the first Register of Patents and Commissions, folio 446, Quebec, March 8, 1880.

Up to the year 1831 the revenues from these estates appear to have gone into the general treasury, and portions from the year 1821 were appropriated for educational purposes. In 1831 by virtue of the Act. 1, William IV, it was provided that all the moneys arising out of the estates should be kept apart and applied exclusively to the purposes of education. The revenues from that date have been divided among the grammar schools, academies, nunneries, convents and colleges of Quebec. The fund is and has been

A COMMON FUND

for Roman Catholic and Protestant education. In as much as the Roman Catholic branch of the Council of Education consists largely of the bishops of the province, who administer the funds coming from this source, the fact of the Jesuits trying to wrest the control from the bishops is explained. By the " definitive treaty " of 1763 the King of England acquired absolute and unconditional jurisdiction over the Jesuits' estates. A vacant estate becomes the property of the Crown. By escheat of the property on the death of the last survivor in 1800 the Crown became absolute owner of the property. No ecclesiastical order has had any right or title to the property since 1774.

The Jesuits in France in the 16th and 17th centuries had no legal title to property. All the title existing was vested in the General at Rome. He being an Italian and an alien, not owing allegiance to the King of France, could hold no real property either in France in 1763 up to the conquest, and the law of England was the same at the date of or after the conquest.

The present company of Jesuits have had a legal existence in this province for only a few months. They cannot pretend to be the successors to a company which

NEVER HAD ANY LEGAL EXISTENCE.

At any rate it is quite clear that the Province of Quebec has nothing to do with the question since the forfeiture of the former so called Jesuits' property was effected by the Imperial Government. When Clement XIV suppressed the Company of Jesus in 1773, he provided that their property should return to the church for pious uses.

The following clause in a petition to the Legislature of Quebec is conclusive proof that the claim of the Jesuits was inadmissible :—

" Your petitioners humbly represent that the Order of Jesuits being extinct in this country, their natural successors are the Roman Catholic bishops of the diocese."

The petition is signed by Joseph, Bishop of Quebec, P. F. Turgeon, coadj. of Quebec, J. T. Lartigue, Bishop of Montreal.

In answer to a question of the late F. Davin, M.P.P. at the session of December 10, 1873, whether the Provincial Government in accepting from the Federal Government the Jesuits' estates, intented to indemnify the former proprietors, the then Premier of the Government replied that the Government was not bound to indemnify any corporation whatsoever. In 1876 the Jesuit barracks property was transferred by the Federal Government. In 1877 it was resolved to demolish the buildings on account of their dangerous state. In 1878 eight bishops joined in a representation to the Provincial Government claiming the property for the church at large on the ground that they were the successors and heirs to the property of the Jesuits on their suppression. The Government of the day

DECLINED TO ADMIT

any responsibility in the matter and referred the petitioners to the Federal Government. The Act 1, William IV, devoted all the proceeds from the properties in question exclusively to the purposes of education. The Speech from the Throne proposes that any compensation awarded will include a fair compensation to the Protestant minority. This is just and equitable. But the following questions remain unanswered until the project of settlement is fully submitted to the House.

Have the Governments any right to divert this fund from the educational fund in view of the fact that the claimants have no legal or equitable claim for compensation ? Will the acknowledgment of this claim be a prelude and a precedent for further claims for compensation for the balance of the property amounting to millions of dollars ? For it must be remembered that it is only the Jesuits' Barracks property which, so far as we can learn, is included in the arrangement. Is this arrangement only the insertion of the little end of the wedge, or is it final ?

THE JESUIT PROPERTY.

(STAR, 26th May 1888.)

To the Editor of the STAR :

SIR,—Under this title a communication appeared in Saturday's (May 19) STAR. The contributor premised that it would " not be amiss to give a short statement of the case as it stands." His communication however, proved to be a long mis-statement of a question of the deepest interest to the community at large. It is an easy task to heap up gratuitous assertions, but it requires time and space to refute them ; unless we have recourse to the justifiable, but to many, unsatisfactory expedient of retorting *quod gratis asseritur gratis negatur.*

We say the subject is of the deepest interest to the community ; for whether your readers be Catholic or Protestant, as fair minded men, they instinctively wish to see justice done. We have all admired the many noble qualities of the German Emperor, and to heighten that admiration the press has heralded forth in every land his chosen maxim,'*Justitia elevat gentem*," a text borrowed, or an adaptation drawn, from the 14th chapter of Proverbs. In our school days the same idea was tersely put, " Cheating never prospers." If there be any virtue in that saying once this question is fully elucidated and justice done, the finances of our province will, we trust, be of more plethoric habit. For an honest man, the first question is not what will follow if I restore ill-gotten goods, but rather have I ill-gotten goods which in justice I am bound to restore ? If so, even as the Pagans said, *Fiat justitia et ruat cælum !*

I pass over the inventory of the Jesuits' estates as of secondary importance for the present, though it be incomplete, admitting with your contributor that the valuation would foot up several millions ; but knowing at the same time that the final and definitive claim of the Jesuits will be much more modest. I come now to the many inaccuracies embodied in the communication, and shall number them off for easy reference in the order in which I find them :

List of Mis-statements.

1. Inasmuch as the order was a mendicant order it could not hold property in its own right.

2. They held the above property in trust for educational purposes.

3. In 1774 they were suppressed by a Royal decree, and their property was confiscated, except what the surviving few might need for comfortable subsistence during their natural lives.

4. Had they not been suppressed in 1744 (1774 I suppose), their property would have become the property of the Crown at the decease of the last Jesuit in 1800.

5. Up to the year 1831, the revenues from these estates appear to have gone into the general treasury, and portions from the year 1821 were appropriated for educational purposes.

6. The revenues from that date (1831) have been divided among the grammar schools, academies, nunneries, convents and colleges of Quebec.

7. Inasmuch as the Roman Catholic branch of the Council of Education consists largely of the bishops of the province, who administer the funds coming from this source, the fact of the Jesuits trying to wrest the control from the bishops is explained.

8. By the " definitive treaty " of 1763, the King of England acquired absolute and unconditional jurisdiction over the Jesuits' estates.

9. A vacant estate becomes the property of the Crown. Hence, by escheat of the property on the death of the last survivor, in 1800, the Crown became absolute owner of the property.

10. No ecclesiastical order has had any right or title to the property since 1774.

11. The Jesuits in France in the 16th and 17th centuries had no legal title to property. All the title existing was vested in the General at Rome.

12. The General being an Italian and an alien, not owing allegiance to the King of France could hold no real property either in France or its colonies. This was the law in France in 1763, up to the conquest, and the law of England was the same at the date of or after the conquest.

13. The present company of Jesuits have had a legal existence in this province for only a few months.

14. They cannot pretend to be the successors to a company which never had any legal existence.

15. At any rate it is quite clear that the Province of Quebec has nothing to do with the question, since the forfeiture of the former so called Jesuits' property was effected by the Imperial Government.

16. When Clement XIV suppressed, the Company of Jesus in 1773, he provided that their property should return to the church for pious uses.

17. The following clause in a petition to the Legislature of Quebec is conclusive proof that the claim of the Jesuits was inadmissible : " Your petitioners humbly represent that the order of the Jesuits being extinct in this country, their natural successors are the Roman Catholic bishops of the diocese."

18. In 1877 it was resolved to demolish the buildings (Quebec College) on account of their dangerous state.

The above statements are either wholly without foundation inaccurate, misleading, or foreign to the question. I shall qualify them separately as I proceed, but before doing so would observe that the list of correct statements contained in the communication would be much shorter that the foregoing.

The Society of Jesus, as a Mendicant Order, could and did hold property in its own right.

I.

In asserting at the outset that mendicant orders could not hold property in their own right, your contributor had in view a statute either of canon law or of civil law in a Catholic country. Protestant countries, in fact, ignore religious orders, and treat them as civil corporations or merely recognize their individual members as enjoying before the law equal rights with other citizens. In Catholic countries civil legislation was supposed to be enacted so as to harmonize with canon law, of which the Church was the true expounder. When, therefore, the decisions of doctors of Sorbonne, or of the advocates of the various parliamentary bodies of France are at variance with canon law, as expounded by the Church, such decisions must needs be held as not valid, not only by every Catholic, but hypothetically by every Protestant. That is, if the latter take at all into account canon law, so as to determine what a mendicant order is or is not, they must frame their definition in accordance with the declared intention of the Catholic legislator, and the sole authority in the Catholic Church who can canonically establish or suppress religious orders. The Supreme Pontiff approves their rules, declares their vows solemn or simple, modifies if needs be, according to the exigency of the times, their mode of life, and determines their relations with civil society, in contact with which they necessarily come. A professed religious, incapable of possessing property before the church, he may empower to hold real or personal estate before civil law, as, in fact, he does in all Protestant and in most Catholic countries, modernized in the sense of the French revolution.

The unqualified assestion that a mendicant order can hold no property in its own right is at variance with canon law. A mendicant order holds property and has always done so. Or to be more accurate, each separate community owns in its own right the monastery it occupies. The individual religious holds and can hold no property, save by a canonico-legal fiction before the civil law of a country which refuses to take cognizance of him otherwise than as a citizen.

Since the Revolution, jurisprudence on these matters has ceased to exist in France. Prescinding from the constitutions of the divers religious societies, constitutions which suppose or establish the non-solidarity between houses of the same order, this state of things is supported on other incontestable grounds. It was recognized by letters patent, which in sanctioning each religious establishment, college, monastery, or community imparted to each its peculiar and distinctive civil existence. These letters patent assured to each the separate and unassailable right of property over its patrimony and domains.

In virtue of similar royal enactments, each religious house enjoyed the right of making contracts through its administrator; that of sueing and being sued, of pleading and being impleaded; the right of acquiring and accepting donations, pious behests indefinitely, or with limitation, as the case might be, was equally conceded. Thus there existed as many bodies corporate as there were houses duly authorized, and the goods and chattels of the one were never confounded with those of the other.

This was the case of the Jesuits in Canada, under French rule. A glance at the Letters Patent of Louis XIV and Louis XV still preserved in the provincial archives will convince the incredulous. The Jesuits of Canada, as we intend to make good, were a body corporate before the conquest (which none will dispute), at the conquest and after the conquest, down as far even as 1791. And if they then ceased so to be, it was by an unwarrantable measure on the part of the Crown. Their civil status was known and recognized by the Supreme Pontiff, known and recognized by the Imperial Government.

The Jesuits held their property for Roman Catholic religious educational purposes,

II.

" They held their property in trust for educational purposes." This unqualified statement is also inaccurate. Of course I do not intend to quarrel with your contributor for affirming that they held it for religious purposes. Had he said they held it *in fee simple for the purposes of religious education*, I would have had no fault to find : though other objects are also mentioned in some of the deeds of donation, while again other donations were made for the objects of their institute, or with no specified object mentioned.

In the archives of the Gesu in Rome there may still be seen a letter of in Father Jerome Lalemant, dated from Quebec, 14th September, 1670, answer to the General's enquiries concerning their obligations. It says :

" The College of Quebec, according to the text of its foundation, is for succour and spiritual instruction, that is to say, catechetical instruction of the Canadians, in other words, of the Indians, to this alone are we held in justice. But gradually French children were received, as there is no other school. Whereupon we taught reading and writing, then a little latin at the request of parents, since there is no other college ; finally, the full curriculum, for otherwise, was it urged upon us, what would be the use of the start already made ? When the Bishop landed, seeing the impossibility of recruiting in France for the priesthood, he asked us to teach philosophy, together with moral and scholastic theology, since which time five or six have been educated for Holy Orders. The Bishop has gathered from 12 to 15 students for the seminary. They attend our classes as do our boarders and day scholars. Though we are not bound in justice to teach all the sciences, how can we give them up ? Should we recall our fathers from the missions ? "

As late as 1733, that is only twenty-six years previous to the capitulation of Quebec, we have another document corroborating the foregoing, it was copied by the late Father Felix Martin from the original in the Archives of the Marine, Paris :—

BEAUHARNOIS, GOVERNOR—GENERAL : HOCQUART, INTENDANT.

" The Governor and Intendant present a petition to the Minister to secure a third teacher for the college. Of the three professors, one (Father François Bertin Guesnier) teaches alternately philosophy and theology. If the students who have completed their humanities find the course of theology open they must wait two years for their philosophy. This discourages them and they give up their studies. The two teachers (regents) of the lower forms (Pierre d'Incarville and J. B. Mauriee) cannot suffice owing to the disparity of knowledge in their pupils. The classes should be subdivided. Appoint a professor at a salary say of 300 livres, and the Jesuits will appoint three professors of the lower forms at their own expense. They deserve this for the pains they take in the education of youth. They maintain a brother (Pierre Le Tellier, who gratuitously teaches the Quebec boys reading, writing and arthmetic) without there being any funds given for this object."

We are told in the obituary notice of F. Guesnier, still preserved in the archives of the Gesu, Rome, that to the last he devoted himself to catechising the boys of brother Le Tellier's class, in number over a hundred.

In the Soeiety of Jesus, according to its constitution as approved by the Holy See, professed houses held only their domiciles in fee simple, while colleges, residences, etc , held not only their respective buildings in fee simple, but their revenues likewise. Individual members of course possessed no property.

Consequently it is inaccurate to say they held their property in trust, and inaccurate moreover to add that they held their property for secular educational purposes.

The Royal Instructions of 1791, to suppress the Jesuits, are a peremptory proof of their corporate existence down to that date at least.

III.

It is historically inaccurate to say that the Jesuits were in 1774 suppressed by a Royal decree, etc.

Your contributor, however, is not the first who has fallen into this error. It occurs also on page 40 of " An account of the endowments for education in Lower Canada, London 13th June, 1838, Norman and Skeen, printers." The author's name is not given, but it is known to be the work of Mr. Andrew Stuart (then a lawyer in Quebec) and of Will. Badgley. While appealing to this fact of the civil suppression, your contributor, for reasons best known to himself, holds back the text of the document itself.

Here are my grounds for contesting the accuracy of the date given. It is a historical fact that on the 21st October, 1788, the committee of the Legislative Council, in their report to Lord Dorchester, declared that as the Jesuits had retained possession of their estates under the eye and with the sanction of the Crown an enactment became necessary, whereby the King should confirm the Pope's abolition of the order, and declare its property vested in the Crown.

In his " Institutions de l'histoire," 1855, page 340, Bibaud, jeune, alludes to this report. The date of which however, by a typographical error is given as 1785. The same report of the Legislative Council, with its correct date, is discussed in the report of Alexander Gray and

Jenkin Williams, 15th * May, 1790; now, had the civil suppression of the society of Jesus taken place in 1774, this report of the Legislative Council would lose its significance, and would have been a meaningless proceeding.

Your contributor very thoughtlessly undertakes to unravel the snarled skein of this very complicated question of the Jesuits' estates, which would require years of study for one who has not already a knowledge of the general outlines of the many contradictory and very lengthy proceedings to which it gave rise. If he would take a run up to Ottawa, he would find on the shelves of the Library of Parliament (E. No. 421) a very useful Repertory entitled " Chisholm's Papers." On page 151 there occurs this passage in the Royal Instructions of the 16th September, 1791 : " It is Our will and pleasure......... that the Society of Jesuits be suppressed and dissolved, and no longer continued as a body corporate or politic, and all their possessions and property shall be vested in Us for such purpose as We may hereafter think fit to direct and appoint ; but We think fit to declare Our Royal intention to be that the present members of the said society as established at Quebec shall be allowed sufficient stipends and provisions during their natural lives."

Were it established beyond cavil that in the year of grace 1791 an attempt at assassination was made upon the person of His Gracious Majesty George III, it would be a little more than strong presumptive evidence that His Majesty was yet alive in that year. Here we have a document emanating from the highest authority of the realm, ordering that the society of Jesuits be dissolved and suppressed, and no longer continued as a body corporate and politic. They, therefore, had continued up to that date a body corporate. The same august authority declares it to be his intention that the present members of the said society, as established at Quebec, be allowed sufficient stipends, etc. This has very much the appearence of recognizing, in a public official document, the fact that at that time there existed a society established at Quebec, and that certain of His Majesty's subjects were recognized members of that society. Would your contributor deem it too rash for me to conclude that not only before the conquest, but at the time of the capitulation of Montreal and the whole of Canada, they were a *body corporate*, as provision is made for them as a body in that document of solemn import ; and that for at least thirty-two years they continued a body corporate under English rule ? What had the Jesuits

---

* The French version of the Report of 1824, page 103, gives the 18th may as the date of this Report.

done in the meantime to justify so unwarrantable and invasion of their civil rights of holding property, etc., rights most solemnly gurranteed them at the capitulation of the country?

(STAR, *June 2nd* 1888.)

The unjustifiable inhibition to receive new members into the Order invalidates all title through escheat for the present holders of the Jesuits' Estates.

IV

" Had they not been suppressed in 1774, their property would have become the property of the Crown at the decease of the last Jesuit in 1800."

This proposition of your contributor is, to say the least, misleading by a "suppressio veri." According to civil law, and where ecclesiastical property is not protected by canon law or by treaty, such would have been the case. But as the King of England, by the law of nations and treaty stipulations, could claim as his own those rights only the King of France enjoyed, and as the latter could have no claim on vacant ecclesiastical property, the King of England very logically had none.

The suppression of truth lies in the fact that your contributor omits to say that the Imperial Government at, or shortly after the conquest, had inhibited the religious bodies in Canada from receiving novices, and thus continuing their succession. This was another unwarrantable proceeding, and as it was against natural justice and constitutional law, it would render void in any honest court the claim of the Crown to such property as vacant. No advantage should accrue to an evildoer from his misdeeds; but I shall touch upon this point under the IX heading when refuting the claim by *escheat*.

But a small portion of the revenues up to the year 1831 went into the general treasury.

V

" Up to the year 1831, the revenues from the estates appear to have gone into the general treasury, and portions, from the year 1821 were appropriated for educational purposes."

This, I also might say, appears to be a very innocent assertion.

Lord Goderich, in his despatch of the 7th July, 1831, acknowledges that the revenues ef these estates were not unreservedly set apart for what he looked upon as the object of these donations, that is to say, education : " It is to be regretted undoubtedly that any part of those funds were ever applied to any other purpose." Lord Durham, in 1838, wrote to the Home Government: " It cannot fail to be apparent that there must be great defects existing in the administration of the Jesuits' estates. Much more than half of its entire gross computed revenue is lost in arrears and expenses – in several instances the inaccuracies detected are of the grossest character—to what cause are these defects attributable? To mismanagement, corrupt or arising from mere carelessness on the part of the individuals by whom the estates are administered ?" René Joseph Kimber, for so long a time president of the standing committee on the Jesuits' estates, leaves us in no doubt as to the purposes to which the revenues were put—political intrigues, etc. But his arraignment of the Hon. John Stewart is by far too long to reproduce.

Casting a hurried glance at the accounts of the agents, or of the commissioners, covering this period, we are assured of the following expenditures : From 1812 to 1815, for purposes unknown, $24,487.36 ; from 1827 to 1831, pensions, $3,288.40 comprising an allowance to the Hon. H. W. Ryland, George Ryland and the Misses De Salabery. In 1829, 1830, $3,932.62 paid to the chaplain, the Rev. E. Sewell, as minister of the Trinity chapel, Quebec, with arrears from 1825. From 1818 to 1822, $28,372.57 to the Protestant Episcopal church, Quebec. In 1823, 1824, $1,200 to the Scotch church, Quebec. To the following Protestant churches the annexed sums were paid : In 1820, Aubigny $400 ; 1820, 1821, Sorel $1,200 ; 1821, Chambly $800 , 1824, Three Rivers $800 ; 1820, Montreal $4,000 ; 1824, Nicolet, $400 ; 1824, 1827, Hull, $2,000. Total to Protestant churches from 1818 to 1827, $39,172.57.

To the Royal Institution, from 1821 to 1831, $3,770.50. To the Royal Grammar Schools of Quebec, Montreal and Kingston, from 1817 to 1831, total, $49,481.38. These were all non-Catholic schools, and yet if there is one point transcendently clear concerning the Jesuits' estates it is that by the will of the donors they should be devoted exclusively to Roman Catholic religious purposes.

In 1802, 1803 and 1821 $4,878,20 were paid for services not specified, $259,75 going to S. Sewell, and $4,218.45 to the Hon. J. Sewell, who, accused by the Assembly, expended that sum in his voyage to England undertaken to defend himself before the Home Government.

The total of the revenue from the Jesuits' estates, from 1800 to 1831 inclusively, amounted to $198,334.85. The total of the expenses to $188,973.46, leaving a balance of $9,361.39.

I conclude consequently that it is incorrect to say that the revenues from the estates appear to have gone into the general treasury.

From 1831, as well as previously, the Estates should have been applied by legitimate administrators in favor of Catholic religious education only.

VI

I have little to say concerning this point, for the simple reason that I have not before me a detailed account of the different sums expended from 1831 to 1849. I would simply remark that it was a little late in the day to begin to dole out insignificant sums to a few Catholic educational establishments, after thirty-one years of expenditure in favor of institutions and persons unsympathetic with the Catholic religion, and that from a fund destined exclusively for Catholic religious purposes.

The "Contributor" at sea.

VII

" In as much as the Roman Catholic branch of the Council of Education consists largely of the bishops of the province, who administered the funds coming from this source, the fact of the Jesuits trying to wrest the control from the bishops is explained."

And nevertheless in my obtuseness, I candidly confess, that I require the assistance of some perspicacious interpreter to explain the riddle. The Jesuits must be an unreasonable set to find fault with the bishops controlling the Council of Education. The late Hon. Mr. Mousseau, in a public utterance, led us Catholics to believe that the bishops had very little control over the funds, or over the council at large. He gave us to understand that their Lordships were listened to with due respect, but that the superintendent and other Government officials of the Board of Education did very much as they pleased after this formality had been gone through with. The fault found with the Jesuits, outside this remarkable exception of the Province of Quebec, is generally stated to be their unbridled desire to see the bishops at the head of Catholic education and of its controlling boards. Howbeit I should like to be enlightened all the same as to the meaning of the seventh paragraph.

By title of conquest in general, according to the Laws of Nations, a conqueror has no right to the private properties of citizens or of authorized corporations.

VIII

" By the definitive treaty of 1763, the King of England acquired an unconditional jurisdiction over the Jesuits' estates." This proposition is either inaccurate or meaningless. If your contributor mean that he acquired the right of sovereignty, and consequently jurisdiction over the Jesuits' estates as over every other inch of the ceded colony, it did not require such a flourish of trumpets to announce this truism. If, on the contrary, he mean that the King owned the Jesuit's' estates in virtue of the treaty, as he owns the public lands, fortresses, and so on, which previously belonged to the King of France, and that he could dispose of them at his pleasure, the proposition is erroneous.

The opinion of all the great authorities on the Law of Nations is uniform on this point. There is not one discordant voice.

DE VATTEL. Law of Nations (Chitty) B. III, C. 13, §199. " The conqueror, who takes a town or province from his enemy cannot justly acquire over it any other rights than such as belonged to the soverign against whom he has taken up arms. War authorizes him to possess himself of what belongs to his enemy ; if he deprives him of the sovereignty of that town or province, he acquires it such as it is, with all its limitations and modifications."

§200. " One Sovereign makes war upon another sovereign, and not against unarmed citizens. The conqueror seizes on the possessions of the state, the public property, while private individuals are allowed to retain theirs. They suffer but indirectly by the war ; and the conquest only subjects them to a new master."

DE MARTENS.—Droit des gens moderne de l'Europe, Vol. II, L. 8, c. 4 § 280...... " L'action du vainqueur s'exerce directement sur les biens composant le domaine de l'Etat, indirectement sur les biens des particuliers. Le vainqueur s'empare de toutes les ressources du gouvernement vaincu, de ses domaines et de leur revenus ; il perçoit les contributions publiques, quant aux biens des particuliers, la propriété immobilière n'éprouve aucun changement dans ses conditions légales."

PINHEIRO-FERREIRA (foot note to preceding passage of de Martens). " Les contributions dont il est permis de frapper le pays conquis n'ont pas pour but d'assurer la conservation des propriétés de tout genre ; car celle du public exceptée il n'y en a pas qui ne se trouve garantie par les principes sacrés du droit des gens, que nous avons déduits précédemment."

DE MARTENS, Ibid. § 281. "On admet généralement, dans les usages modernes, que l'invasion et l'occupation militaire n'ont aucun effet sur la propriété des biens immeubles qui demeurent invariablement aux anciens détenteurs... La conquête et l'occupation d'un Etat par un souverain étranger n'autorisent pas ce souverain à disposer par donation ou autrement du domaine conquis ou occupé... Mais pour ceux qui font partie du domaine de l'Etat, si le vainqueur en a pris possession même temporaire, il peut en disposer."

TWISS. Law of Nations, ch. 4, § 66. " A victorious nation in acquiring the sovereignty *de facto* over a country, from which it has expelled its adversary, does not acquire any other rights than those which belonged to the expelled sovereign ; and to those such as they are with all their limitations and modifications, he succeeds by right of war."

" So, likewise, the landed and immovable property of private individuals is in general by the positive law of nations not liable to confiscation by a victorious enemy. A victorious nation, on the other hand, enters upon the public rights of the vanquished nation, and the national domain and the national treasure passes to the victor."

KLUBER, Part II, title 2, § 256: " According to principles now followed in Europe, the mere loss of possession by the fortunes of war does not extinquish the rights of property...... As for property and the possession of immovable estate belonging to individuals, who have not violated the laws of war, the conquest of a country brings no change according to the modern laws of war."

MANNING's (Sheldon Amos) Commentaries on the Law of Nations. (London, H. Sweet, 1875, page 116.)

" A conquering state enters upon the rights of the Sovereign of a vanquished state ; national domain and national revenues pass to the victor; but the immovable property of private individuals is, by the positive law of nations not liable to be seized by the rights of war.... it has been for many years the constant usage of European warfare, and is now firmly established as part of the European Law of Nations."

WEDDERBURNE (Solicitor-General in 1772). Wedderburne was no friend of the Jesuits. By reading the pamphlets of the times, which, to attain certain ends, were scattered profusely over the European continent, he became imbued with the most silly prejudices and had conceived the most erroneous opinions concerning the Society of Jesus. The principle, however, which he lays down in his report to the King on the Canadian question is perfectly sound. The report bears date of the 6th December, 1772, and in it he says :

" No other right can be founded on conquest but that of regulating the political and civil government of the country, leaving to the individuals the enjoyment of their property, and of all privileges not inconsistent with the security of the conquest." (Christie, vol. I, p. 29.)

It was afterwards in the application of this principle that he erred ; for evidently according to him the existence of the Jesuits in Canada " was inconsistent with the security of the conquest !"

On the 26th May, 1774, in the House of Commons, he further developed his thought : " You can preserve the acquisitions in time of peace, so as to give to the country subdued as much tranquillity, as much property, and as much enjoyment of that property, as is consistent with your own safety ; and this it is your duty to do. The principles of humanity, the principles of natural justice demand this at our hands, as a recompense for the evils of war ; and not that we should aggravate those evils by a total subversion of all those particular forms and habits, to which the conquered party have been for ages attached. Upon this principle, sir, I do maintain, that it would have been most unjust to have relapsed into the barbarity of former ages ; and this we should have done, if we had, with a rough stroke, said to the Canadians that the laws of Canada should be totally obliterated ; that the rights, civil and ecclesiastical, of that country, should be framed according to those of England, as being better for that people than their own." Cavendish — Debates of the House of Commons in 1774, pages 51, 52.

THURLOW (Attorney-General) was a different sort of man, with broad views and a well balanced mind. His principles were as sound as those of Wedderburne. Being consistent he was not afraid to face them in their logical conclusions. On the 22nd January, 1773, his report on Canadian affairs was handed in to His Majesty. In it he rehearses the different opinions of jurists and endorses the following : " They understand the right acquired by conquest, to be merely the right of empire, but not to extend beyond that, to the liberty and property of individuals, from which they draw this consequence, that no change ought to be made in the former laws beyond what shall be *fairly* thought necessary to establish and secure the sovereignty of the conqueror. This idea they think confirmed by the practice of nations and the most approved opinions." And further on : "The Canadians seem to have been strictly entitled by the *jus gentium* to their property, as they possessed it upon capitulation and treaty of peace, together with all its qualities and incidents, by tenure or otherwise; for both which they were to expect Your Majesty's gracious protection.

" It seems a necessary consequence that all those laws by which that property was created, defined, and secured must be continued to them." (Christie vol. I, pages 53 and 59.)

In his speech in the Commons on the 26th May, 1774, he clearly defines his opinion on the rights of conquest. " Now, sir, a proclamation (7 October, 1763), conceived in this general form, and applied to countries the most distant, not in situation only, but in history, character and constitution, from each other, will scarcely, I believe, be considered as a very well studied act of State, but as necessary immediately after the conquest. But, however proper that might be with respect to new parts of such acquisitions as were not peopled before, yet, if it is to be considered as creating an English constitution ; if it is to be considered as importing English laws into a country already settled, and habitually governed by other laws, I take it to be an act of the grossest and absurdest and cruellest tyranny, that a conquering nation ever practised over a conquered country. Look back, sir, to every page of history, and I defy you to produce a single instance, in which a conqueror went to take away from a conquered province, by one rough stroke, the whole of their constitution, the whole of their laws under which they lived, and to impose a new idea of right and wrong, of which they could not discern the means or the end, but would find themselves at a loss and be at an expense greater than individuals could afford, in order to inform themselves whether they were right or wrong. This was a sort of cruelty, which I believe was never practised, and never ought to be. My notion, with regard to this matter, I will venture to throw out as crude and general. To enter into the subject fully would require more discussion than the nature of such a debate as this will admit of. My notion is, that it is a change of sovereignty. You acquired a new country ; you acquired a new people ; but you do not state the right of conquest as giving you a right to goods and chattels. That would be slavery and extreme misery. In order to make the acquisition either available or secure, this seems to be the line that ought to be followed : you ought to change those laws only which relate to the French sovereignty, and in their place substitute laws which should relate to the new sovereign ; but with respect to all other laws, all other customs and institutions whatever, which are indifferent to the state of subjects and sovereign, humanity, justice and wisdom equally advise you to leave them to the people just as they were." (Debates, etc., 1774, page 29, 30.)

" If the English laws would be a prejudice to the Canadians it would be absurd tyranny and barbarity to carry over all the laws of this country, by which they would lose the comfort of their property, and in some cases the possession of it." (Debates, etc., 1774, page 32.) He had in view especially the penal laws.

Much more might be given in the same strain from these authorities, but there must be an end to all things. Now no other conclusion can possibly be arrived at, from the foregoing extracts, save that by the rights of conquest in general, that is, of any conquest not limited or qualified by treaty stipulations, the property of individuals, and the laws which create and protect it, are sacred and inviolable. That furthermore the sole measure of the extent of the conquering sovereign's rights is the extent of the rights of the conquered sovereign whom he succeeds.

What is said of the property of individuals holds good with regard to the property of bodies corporate. They exist before the law as a moral entity or person, with their rights, as to property, duely sanctioned by the sovereign.

Individuality and immortality : two essential properties of a body corporate.

(STAR, 7 *June* 1888.)

(*Continued.*)

" A corporation," says Mr. Kyd, quoted by Angell and Ames, " or body politic, or body incorporate, is a collection of many individuals united in one body under special denomination, having perpetual succession under an artificial form, and vested, by the policy of the law, with a capacity of acting, in several respects, as an individual, particularly of taking and granting property, contracting obligations, and of suing and being sued ; of enjoying privileges and immunities in common, and of exercising a variety of political rights, more or less extensive, according to the design of its institution, or the powers conferred upon it, either at the time of its creation or at any subsequent period of its existence." (Treatise on the law of private corporations aggregate by Joseph K. Angell and Samuel Ames. Introduction, § 2.)

Chief Justice Marshall, in common with other authorities, holds it to be " an artificial being, invisible, intangible and existing only in .contemplation of law. Being the mere creature of law, it possesses only those properties, which the charter of its creation confers upon it either expressly, or as identical to its very existence. These are such as are supposed best calculated to effect the object for which it is created. Among the most important are immortality, and, if the expression may be allowed, individuality ; properties by which a perpetual succession of many persons are considered as the same, and may act as a single individual......... The great object of an incorporation is to bestow the character and properties of individuality on a collective and changing body of men " (Ibid, § 3).

Kyd's definition is adopted verbatim by Chitty also. (Prerogatives of the Crown, Ch. VIII, No. 2.)

The Society of Jesus in Canada was a body corporate from 1678. Its right of property was protected by the Law of Nations.

That the Society of Jesus was a body corporate under French rule is undeniable. We have alluded to the Royal Letters Patent, still extant at Quebec, as establishing this fact. Chitty in his " Prerogatives of the Crown, &c." (Ch. VIII, edit. London, 1820 pg. 122), assures us that " The exclusive right of the Crown to institute corporations and the necessity for its express or implied consent to their existence is undoubted...... The King's consent to the formation of a corporation is expressly given in the case of his granting a charter. This need not be done by any particular form of words ..... a gift of land from the King to the burgesses, citizens or commonalty, of such a place, was conceived to be sufficient to incorporate them under such collective name*....... Nor is it necessary that the charter should expresly confer those powers, without which a collective body of men cannot be a corporation, such as the power of suing and being sued, and to take and grant property ; though such powers are in general expressly given, etc., etc."

The following is an extract of the Diploma or Letters patent of Louis XIV, of May 12, 1678 :

" Louis, par la Grâce de Dieu, Roy de France et de Navarre. A tous ceux quis ces présentes lettres verront, salut.

" Nos chers et bien aimez *les Religieux de la Compagnie de Jésus résidant en nostre pays de la Nouvelle France*, nous ont fait remonstrer qu'en considération du zèle qu'ils ont tesmoigné pour la conversion.

Confr. Ibid. pg. 124.

des sauvages, nos vice-roys, lieutenants généraux et gouverneurs du dit pays, ensemble les compagnies establies pour le commerce, leur ont donné en differents temps plusieurs terres dont ils ont jouy, et sur partie desquelles ils ont fait construire les bastiments nécessaires pour leur collège, esglise, et communauté, dans la ville de Québec, les dites terres consistantes, scavoir : (here follows the enumeration of Seigneuries, etc.) Et d'autant que les dites terres, lieux, et bastiments n'ont pas été amortis, les exposants craignent d'estre troublez en la jouissance d'iceux, nous ont très humblement fait supplier qu'il nous plust les amortir, et leur permettre de les tenir en main morte et exempts de nos droits.

" A ces causes, voulant favorablement traiter les exposant, contribuer autant qu'il nous sera possible à la plus grande gloire de Dieu, et a l'établissement de la religion catholique, apostolique et romaine, dans le dit pays de Canada, et les obliger à continuer leurs prières pour notre prospérité, et santé et la conservation de cet Estat, de nostre grâce spéciale, pleine puissance, et autorité royale, nous avons agrée confirmé et amorty, agréons, confirmons et amortissons par ces présentes signées par nostre main toutes ces terres et concessions cy-dessus déclarées......... ensemble les bastiments construits sur les dites terres, sans que les supplians puissent jamais être contraints de les mettre hors de leurs mains, n'y qu'ils soient tenus pour ces dits héritages, lieux et droits, nous payer anciens devoirs et droits, donner homme vivant et mourant, faire foi et hommage, payer indemnités ou droits de francs fiefs et nouveaux acquests à nous et à nos successeurs Roys, dont nous les avons quittés et exemptés, quittons et exemptons, &c., &." ·

This instrument alone, without its being necessary for me to hunt up other documents, constituted the Society of Jesus a body corporate, and by granting the privilege of holding their property *in mortmain* constituted them a corporation for ever.

Therefore, as by the right of conquest in general, as laid down in the Law of Nations, the rights of property of private individuals are secured, so also are the rights of the corporation of the Society of Jesus, to these intents and purposes, holding property as an individual

The Letters patent of the French King a solemn contract of protection with the Society. Its obligations binding on the King of England who supplants him.

I go further, and say that even were the laws of nations silent on the point of the inviolabillity of private property, establishing as they do the principle that, at the conquest, the King of England succeeded the King of France, in the sovereignty of these provinces, he succeeded him not only in all his prerogatives but also in all his obligations. The letters patent are a solemn contract, guaranteeing protection to the Society of Jesus. The King of England is equally bound by them. He accepted the sovereignty of Canada with all its limitations and modifications such as it was.

A corporate body cannot be destroyed by the ruler, in virtue of his Royal prerogative alone.

Nor was the King of France, in virtue of his Royal prerogative alone empowered to destroy a corporation he had once sanctioned, and to deprive it of its franchise.

Here are the principles accepted by jurists who treat of this matter.

" In its more extensive sense the term 'franchise' signifies every description of political right which a freeman may enjoy and exercise. Being derived from the Crown, these franchises can in general only arise and be claimed by royal grant or by prescription which supposes it. They may be vested either in natural persons or bodies politic, in one man or in many. But the same identical franchise that has been before granted to one cannot be granted to another, for that would prejudice the former grant. It is a clear principle that the King cannot by his mere prerogative diminish or destroy immunities once conferred and vested in a subject by royal grant." (Chitty, on the Prerogatives of the Crown, Ch. VIII, No. 1, pg. 119).

" It is admitted on all hands, that the charter by which a body is incorporated must be accepted as it is offered...... that they may reject a new charter *in toto* is indubitable ; because the King cannot take away, abridge or alter any liberties or privileges granted by him or his predecessor, without the consent of the individuals holding them." (Ibid. No. 2, pg. 125).

" It is a principle in law that the King is bound by his own or his ancestors' grants, and cannot therefore, by his mere prerogative take away vested immunities and privileges. But a corporation may be dissolved by surrendering its franchise into the hands of the King, though legal dissolution is not occasioned thereby, and the charter operates till the surrender be enrolled, because the king can take nothing but by matter of record without enrolment. (Ibid, pg. 132).

Documentary evidence of the exercise of corporate rights by the Society of Jesus down to the very year of the capitulation of Quebec.

I may be asked if, in point of fact, the Jesuits exercised their franchise as a corporation down to the very period of the conquest? In answer I may state : Quebec capitulated on the 18th September, 1759, and I have lying before me at the present writting an original document dated the 30th March, of that same year. It bears the signature of the Superior of the Society in Canada, that of his procurator and the seal of the corporation. This instrument appoints the Sieur Mathieu Hianveu as assistant notary for their Seigneuries of Notre Dame des Anges, St. Gabriel, Sillery and Bélair, and enjoins on Paul Antoine François La Nouillet, *juge prévot*, to see that Sieur Hianveu be duly qualified and sworn into office. Therefore, down to the conquest they remained a corporate body, which the King of England, neither by his own prerogative, nor by that of the King of France was empowered to destroy.

By title of the conquest of Canada in particular the right of the Jesuits to their property was unassailable.

If the case in favor of the Jesuits be already so strong, supported by the laws of nations, defining the rights of conquest in general, it gains a hundred fold when we come to deal with the inviolability of their property as guaranteed by the capitulations and treaty.

I shall quote here mainly from English authorities, as the question, if not a domestic one, is one I would not like to have settled by the opinion of foreigners, lest they be deemed partial.

Let me first set before the eyes of your readers extracts from the capitulations and the treaty which have some bearing on the question. I have not at hand the English version of the Capitulation of Quebec, so I am obliged to quote from the French.

CAPITULATION DE QUÉBEC (18 Sept. 1759) : Art II. Que les habitants soient conservés dans la possession de leurs maisons, biens, effets et privilèges.—Accordé en mettant bas les armes.

Art. VI. Que l'exercise de la Religion Catholique, Apostolique et Romaine, sera conservé, que l'on donnera des sauves-gardes aux maisons ecclésiastiques et religieuses, particulièrement à Monseigneur l'Evêque de Québec, etc., etc.—Libre exercise à la Relígion romaine-sauves-gardes à toutes personnes, religieuses, ainsi qu'à Monseigneur l'Evêque, qui pourra venir exercer librement et avec décence, les fonc‚ tions de son état, lorsqu'il le jugera à propos, jusqu'à ce que la possession du Canada ait été décidée entre Sa Majesté Britannique et Sa Majesté Très-Chrétienne.

CAPITULATION OF MONTREAL (and of the whole province, 8th Sept. 1766). " Art. XXVII. The free exercise of the Catholic, Apostolic and Roman religion shall subsist entire, etc., etc.

Answer.—"Granted as to the free exercise of their religion. The obligation of paying tithes to the priests will depend on the King's pleasure.

" Art XXXII. The communities of nuns shall be preserved in their constitution and privileges. They shall be exempted from lodging any military, and it shall be forbid to trouble them in their religious exercises, or to enter their monasteries ; safe-guards shall even be given them if they desire them.

" Answer.—Granted.

" Art. XXXIII. The preceding article shall likewise be executed with regard to the communities of Jesuits and Recollets, and to the house of the priests of St. Sulpice at Montreal. This last, and the Jesuits, shall preserve their right to nominate to certain curacies and missions, as heretofore.

" Answer.—Refused till the King's pleasure be known.

" Art. XXXIV. All the communities, and all the priests shall preserve their movables, the property and revenues of the Signiories and other estates which they possess in the colony of what nature soever they be, and the same estates shall be preserved in their privileges, rights, honors and exemptions.

" Answer.—Granted.

" Art. XXXV. If the canons, priests missionaries, the priests of the Seminary of the foreign missions, and of St. Sulpice, as well as the Jesuits and the Recollets, choose to go to France, passage shall be granted them in his Britannic Majesty's ships, and they shall all have leave to sell, in whole or in part, the estates and movables which they possess in the colonies, either to the French or to the English, without the least hindrance or obstacle from the British Government.

(STAR, 8*th June* 1888.)

(*Continued.*)

" They may take with or send to France the produce of what nature soever it be of the said goods sold, paying the freight as mentioned in the 26th article. And such of the said priests who choose to go this year shall be victualled during the passage at the expense of His Britannic Majesty, and shall take with them their baggage.

" Answer—They shall be masters to dispose of their estates, and to send the produce thereof, as well as their persons and all that belongs to them, to France.

" Art. XXXVII. Lords of manors (les seigneurs de terre), military and civil officers, etc., etc., shall preserve the entire peaceable property and possession of their goods, movable and immovable, merchandize, etc., shall keep and sell them as well to the French as English ; to take away produce of them...... whenever they shall judge proper to go to France, paying freight as in the 26th article.

" Answer—Granted, as in the 26th article.

" Art. XLVI. Inhabitants and merchants to enjoy all the privileges granted to subjects of His Britannic Majesty.

" Answer—Granted.

" Art. L. The present capitulation shall be inviolably executed in all its articles, and bona fide on both sides, notwithstanding any infraction and any other pretext, with regard to preceding capitulations, and without power to make reprisals.

" Answer—Granted."

TREATY OF PEACE.—" His Britannic Majesty, on his side, agrees to grant the liberty of the Catholic religion to the inhabitants of Canada. He will consequently give the most effectual order, that his new Roman Catholic subjects may profess the worship of their religion according to the rights of the Roman Church, as far as the laws of Great Britain permit."

" His Britannic Majesty also agrees, that the French inhabitants, or others, who had been the subjects of the most Christian King in Canada, may retire with all safety and freedom, wherever they shall think proper, and may sell their estates, provided it be to subjects of His Britannic Majesty, and bring away their effects as well as their persons, without being restrained in their emigration, under any pretence whatsoever, except that of debts or of criminal prosecution ; the term limited for this emigration shall be fixed to the space of eighteen months, to be computed from the day of the exchange of the ratification of the present treaty."

I shall be as concise as the subject will allow in reasoning on the text of the foregoing documents.

In the 2nd Art. of the capitulation of Quebec " The inhabitants (no exception whatever being made detrimental to the rights of the Jesuits to their property) are to be preserved in possession of their houses, goods, effects and privileges."

In the 32nd, 33rd and 34th Art. of the capitulation of Montreal, and of the whole province, communities are mentioned three times. In the two foremost articles, certain privileges are granted and refused to certain specified communities. In the last mentioned article certain privileges are secured to all the communities alike, in contradistinction to what was refused and granted in the two preceding articles. In other words, all communities and all the priests shall preserve their movables, the property and revenues of the Seigniories, and other estates which they possess in the colony of what nature soever they be, etc. The Jesuits forming a community and being priests, and not being *de facto* formally excluded (which they could not be *de jure* according to the laws of nations), are entitled to the full benefit of this article.

What was refused with a proviso in the XXXIII Article of the Capitulation of Montreal ? Interpretation of treaty stipulations.

Your contributor will no doubt say that Art. 33 refuses them certain privileges till the king's pleasure be known. I shall not ask here, after what I have already said, what right Amherst had to refuse any one of the points mentioned. But I maintain that the refusal, with its proviso, falls upon the latter part of the 33rd article.

That the refusal fell upon the last clause is certain. For Burton, the Lt.-Governor of Three Rivers, wrote to Amherst, but two months after the capitulation, the 19th of November, to complain that F. de Glapion had ordered Roubaud, who had disgraced himself with the Indians of St. François, to make room for a more worthy successor, " without," Amherst says, " having given the least notice. As soon as I heard of it I put a stop to it, looking on it as a breach of the 33rd and 40th Art. of capitulation" (See Canadian Archives (Ottawa) B, 21—1 p. 33.)

The XL Art. closes thus :... " The actual vicars-general, and the bishop, when the Episcopal See shall be filled, shall have leave to send them (the Indians) new missionaries when they shall judge it necessary."

" Answer—Granted, except the last article which has been already refused."

The refusal did not fall upon the first part of Art. 33, if it must be distorted so as to mean that the Jesuits could not continue to hold their estates (which interpretation would be indeed overstrained) for the reason that after the 34th Art. Amherst simply wrote "Granted," whilst if the above interpretation is to be maintained he should have written : " Granted, except for the Jesuit community, holding their estates, which was already refused in the 33rd Act."

Now putting the thing *at its worst*, what, according to the canons laid down for the interpretation of treaties, was refused with a proviso in the 33rd art. ?

Grotius gives this canon : "Voici encore une règle qui est fréquemment d'usage dans l'interprétation des Traités de Paix. Toutes les fois qu'on se rapporte sur certains articles, à quelque article précédent, ou à quelque ancien Traité, auquel on renvoie, toutes les qualités ou les conditions exprimées dans l'article précédent ou dans l'ancien Traité, sont censées répétées comme devant avoir lieu dans celui dont il s'agit " (*Grotius*, livre II, ch. XX, § XXIV, No. 1.) We have simply to repeat the Art. 32 adapting it to the Jesuits, etc. " The communities of Jesuits, Recollets and Sulpicians shall not be preserved in their constitution and privileges (*the holding of property is a right*). They shall not continue to observe their rules. They shall not be exempted from lodging any military, and it shall not be forbid to trouble them in their religious exercises, or to enter their monasteries ; safeguards shall not be given them when they desire it. The Sulpicians and the Jesuits shall not preserve their right to nominate to certain curacies and missions as hetofore." Though the whole of this in its complex is palpably absurd, as the refusal may fall on one clause only, no mention is made in it of their not being preserved in the peaceable possession of their estates.

I said, taking the thing at its worst, which the conquered are certainly not obliged nor the conqueror allowed to do.

" Lorsqu'il y a quelque chose de douteux et d'ambigu dans une clause l'interprétation doit se faire plutôt au préjudice qu'à l'avantage de celui qui a lui-même prescrit les conditions du Traite. (Note) C'est le maxime que posait autrefois Hannibal : Est quidem ejus qui dat, non qui petit, conditiones dicere pacis. C'est-à dire, pour l'ordinaire, du plus puissant, de même que les articles d'un contrat de vente s'expliquent au préjudice du vendeur. (Note) Cela est décidé par le Droit Romain : Veteribus placet, pactionem obscuram, vel ambiguam venditori et qui locavit, nocere ; in quorum fuit potestate legem apertius conscribere. En effet il pouvait l'expliquer plus clairement, s'il ne l'a pas fait, tant pis pour lui. L'autre était en droit d'interpréter à son avantage des termes et des expressions susceptibles de plusieurs sens. On peut rapporter ici ce que dit Aristotle : Qu'en matière d'amitiés contractées par un principe d'intérêt, l'utilité de celui qui reçoit est la mesure de ce qui est dû." (Grotius, Liv, II, ch. XX, § 26).

De Vattel, is equally emphatic in the rule he gives : " In case-of doubt, the interpretation goes against him who prescribed the terms of the treaty, for as it was in some measure dictated by him, it was his own fault if he neglected to express himself more clearly, and by extending or restricting the signification of the expressions to that meaning which is least favorable to him, we either do him no injury, or we only do him that to which he has wilfully exposed himself ; whereas, by adopting a contrary mode of interpretation, we would incur the risk of converting vague or ambiguous terms into so many snares to entrap the weaker party in the contract, who has been obliged to subscribe to what the stronger had dictated." (Chitty's *de Vattel*, Law of Nations, B. IV. Ch. III, § 32.)

" Articles of a treaty stand sometimes in need of interpretation ; in which case the rule we have already given elsewhere must be first observed To wit, the more favourable the thing is the more should the meaning of the terms be extended ; on the contrary the less favourable the more should the sense be restricted. Considering mere Natural Law, there is nothing more favourable than that which tends to secure to each one his own, or what he has a right to. Thus ambiguous clauses should be explained after this fashion : that he whose cause is just, should lose nothing, etc." (Grotius B. II, ch. XX. § 11. N. 1, 2.)

Of course I do not expect that there will be any quibbling concerning the term treaty in the foregoing quotations, as we are here discussing a capitulation. They are certainly not identical in every case, but are so taken in the matter under consideration. It is evident from the following :

" It is very certain, that, in order to discover the true meaning of the contract, attention ought principally to be paid to the words of the promising party. For he voluntarily binds himself by his words ; and we take for true against him what he has sufficiently declared. This question seems to have originated from the manner in which conventions are sometimes made : the one party offers the conditions, and the other accepts them ; that is to say, the former proposes and he requires that the other shall oblige himself to perform, and the latter declares the obligation into which he really enters. If the words of him who accepts the conditions bear relation to the words of him who offers them, it is certainly true that we ought to lay our principal stress on the expressions of the latter, but this is because the person promising is considered as merely repeating them in order to form his promise. The capitulations of besieged towns may here serve us for an example. The besieged party proposes the conditions on which he is willing to surrender the place ; the besieger accepts them, the expressions of the former lay no obligation on the latter, unless so far as he adopts them. He who accepts the conditions is in reality the promising party ; and it is in his words that we ought to seek for the true meaning of the articles, whether he has himself chosen and formed his expressions, or adopted those of the other party, by referring to them in his promise. But we still must bear in mind the maxim above laid down, viz., that what he has sufficiently declared is to be taken as true against him." (Chitty's de Vattel, B. II. ch. XVII, § 267.)

This shows that what I have said is applicable indiscriminately to treaties and to capitulations, and, moreover, further confirms my point ; for what the beseiger has sufficiently, nay very distinctly declared in the 34th art., I take to be true against him, viz., that with all other communities the Jesuits were to preserve the property and revenues of the Seigniories and other estates, etc., and we conclude with de Vattel that : " We ought to interpret his obscure or equivocal expressions in such a manner that they may agree with those clear and unequivocal terms which he has elsewhere used, either in the same deed or on some other similar occasion." (Ibid. B. II. ch. XVII,§ 284)

To my mind the meaning has always been perfectly clear, and if I have gone into these considerations it is rather out of deference for a preconceived notion, that as the estates were taken by the Government, the capitulations or treaty must in some way have sanctioned the seizure.

I would say that Amherst, a blunt soldier, knew and cared very little about the constitution and rules of the Jesuits, nor was he man to wish uselessly to molest them in their religious exercises. But he needed barracks for his troops, and he with others, fondly entertained the hope, which events proved to be delusive, of seeing the realization of a pet plan of the Government, that of supplanting the bishops or other ecclesiastical authorities in the appointment to benefices. This was all he wished to secure in his conditional refusal of the 33rd article.

English Authorities on the rights of Religious Orders in Canada to their property as secured by treaty.

These are my own personal conclusions from the canons concerning the interpretation of treaties ; but I promised to quote our own English authorities on what was and what was not stipulated in the same capitulations and subsequent definitive treaty. And in this I want my purpose to be clearly understood, for I maintain *that even had the King of England the power, by his mere prerogative, on the occasion of the Conquest, to confiscate the Jesuits' estate*, which he had not, *he clearly yeilded that power through is general and plenipotentiary.*

THURLOW.—(Report to His Majesty, 22 January, 1773.) " On the eighth of September, 1760, the country capitulated in terms which gave to Your Majesty all that belonged to the French King ; and preserved all their property, real, and personal, in the fullest extent, not only to private individuals, but to the corporation of the West India Company, and to the missionaries, priests, canons, convents, etc., with liberty to dispose of it by sale if they should want to leave the country. The free exercise of their religion by the laity, and of their function by their clergy, was also reserved."

(*To be Continued*)

(STAR, 9 *June* 1888.)

(*Continuea.*)

" The whole of these terms were stipulated on the 10th of February, 1763, in the definitive of peace, etc." (Christie, Vol. I. pg. 48).

Again : "......and if this general title" (rights of conquest as determined by the Law of Nations) to such moderation could be doubted, they " (the jurists whose opinion he endorsed) " look upon it to be a necessary consequence of the capitulation and treaty alluded to before, by which a large grant was made to them of their property and personal liberty, which seem to draw after them the laws by which they were created, defined and protected, and which contain all the idea they have of either." (Ibid. pg. 53).

Though I am fully alive to the fact that this communication is already voluminous and the quotations copious, I cannot pass over in lisence the closing passage of his report :

" Although the foregoing observations should be thought just, as a general idea, yet circumstances may be supposed, under which it would admit some exceptions and qualifications. The conqueror succeeded to the sovereignty in a title at least as full and as strong, as the conquered can set up to their private rights and ancient usages.

" Hence would follow every change in the form of Government which the conqueror should think *essentially necessary* to establish his sovereign authority and assure the obedience of his subjects. This might possibly produce some alteration in the laws, especially those which relate to crimes against the state, religion, revenue and other articles of police, and in the form of magistracy.

" But it would also follow that such a change should not be make without some actual and urgent necessity, which real wisdom could not overlook or neglect; not that idea necessity which ingenious speculation may always create by possible supposition, remote inference and forced argument : not that necessity of assimilating a conquered country, in the article of laws and Government to the metropolitan state, or to the older provinces which other accidents attached to the empire, for the sake of creating a harmony and uniformity in the several parts of the empire, unattainable and, as I think, useless if it could be attained ; not the necessity of stripping from the lawyer's argument all ressort to the learned decisions of the Parliament of Paris, for fear of keeping up the historical idea of the origin of their laws : not the necessity of gratifying the unprincipled and impracticable expectations of those few among your Majesty's subjects who may accidentally resort thither, and expect, to find all the different laws of the different places from which they come ; nor according to my simple judgment, any species of necessity which I have heard urged for abolishing the laws and government of Canada." (Ibid. pg. 61.)

Here are the broad views and sound principles of the man, whose erudition and manliness raised him later on to the peerage. In June 1778, he succeeded Lord Apsley as lord high chancellor of England.

His report is the outcome of reflection and research. In it the warmth of his expressions is tempered by the thought that he is addressing his Sovereign. But if we wish to measure the depth of his convictions, we must listen to him on the floor of the House, endeavouring to safeguard the honour of England and the inviolability of treaty stipulations.

" When it (Canada) was taken, gentlemen will be so good as to recollect upon what terms it was taken. Not only all the French who resided there had eighteen months to remove with a'l their moveable effects, and such as they could not remove they were enabled to sell, but it was expressly stipulated that every Canadian should have the full enjoyment of all his property, *particularly the religious orders of the Canadians*, and that the free exercise of the Roman Catholic religion should be continued. And the definitive treaty of peace, if you examine it as far as it relates to Canada, by the cession of the late King of France to the Crown of Great Britain, was made in favour of property; made in favour of religion; *made in favour of the several religious orders.*" (Cavendish—Debates, etc., 1774, pgs. 27, 28.)

There is a true ring of conviction in these words, and no room for doubt or hesitancy; yet in them is embodied the legal opinion of the highest authority on these matters in England at the time in which they were uttered. And how can he speak so positively of the treaty, as confirmatory of the capitulation, since the divers articles of the latter are not rehearsed in full, and the good pleasure of the King has apparently not been made known as to several of the articles? The King's silence is rightly interpreted to mean that he can take no exception to one who signed, in his name, without overstepping his powers, articles of capitulation which become then inviolable. Things remain as they were, if in provisions, as to his assent, he remains silent; in which case, the general maxim finds its application : *melior est conditio possidentis.*

However, this right of possession is indirectly confirmed by the treaty, when for the Jesuits and others, it was made facultative or optional to sell their estates. They were not of course obliged to do so, but *de facto* the Society of Jesus, on the 5th May 1764, sold 172 arpents, a large portion of St. Lawrence Ward in Montréal, to Sieur Plessis Belair (See *Terrier des Seigneurs de Montréal*, at that date), and this sale was effected with due authorization. "Vente par le Supérieur des Jésuites de la mission de Montréal, autorisée par acte de justice à Charles Plessis Belair 1º d'une terre, etc." (See Canadian Archives, Ottawa, Series Q. Vol. 50 A. pg. 188).

Another contract of donation was passed by the Jesuits in favour of the Ursulines of Quebec as late as the 24th April, 1788. (See report 1824, page 123.)

In the report of two commissioners of the nine appointed to ascertain, among other points, what portion of the Jesuits' estates the King might in justice grant to Lord Amherst, and as rehearsed in the report of Alexander Gray and J. Williams, it is said : " Ils (les commissaires) observent aussi qu'il est de notoriété publique que par différents jugements des cours de justice en cette Province ils (les Jésuites) ont été maintenus dans leurs droits, et qu'à leur connaissance ils continuent à posséder toutes les dites terres, à l'exception d'une partie du Collège

— 35 —

de Québec, maintenant occupé comme magasin des provisions du Roi, et comme casernes pour une partie de la garnison." (Rap. 1824, p. 93.)

Nor can your contributor derive much consolation from the clause in the treaty, even if it would affect the matter in hand, and which provides for the execution of the terms of the treaty " as far as the laws of Great Britain permit."

Lord North, the then premier, effectually disposed of that objection in his speech in the. House of Commons on the 26th May, 1774 : " It has been the opinion of very many able lawyers, that the best way to establish the happiness of the inhabitants is to give them their own laws, as far as relates to their own possessions. Their possessions were marked out to them at the time of the treaty ; to give them those possessions without giving them laws to maintain those possessions would not be very wise.........As to the free exercise of their religion, it likewise is no more than what is confirmed to them by treaty, as far as the laws of Great Britain can confirm it. Now, there is no doubt that the laws of Great Britain do permit the very full and free exercise of any religion, different from that of the Church of England, in any of the colonies ; therefore, I apprehend, that we ought not to extend them to Canada." (See Debates 1774, pg. 11 and 12. Confr. also page 63.)

As final conclusion of this point we repeat that it would be inaccurate to say, putting it very mildly, that by the "definitive treaty" of 1763 the King of England acquired absolute and unconditional jurisdiction over the Jesuits' estates otherwise understood than that he acquired sovereignty.

Proof that the Crown inhibited the Jesuits from receiving new members. Consequently the title of the Province to the estates by escheat untenable.

IX

" A vacant estate becomes the property of the Crown. Hence by escheat of the property on the death of the last survivor, in 1800, the Crown became absolute owner of the property."

As we have already made good, on the best legal authority, that it is not within the mere prerogative of the Crown to diminish or destroy immunities once conferred on corporations, nor take away, abridge, nor alter any liberties or privileges granted by him or his predecessors (Jos. Chitty, Prerogatives of the Crown, ch. 8. Edit. Lond., 1820, p.

119, 125, 132) ; and as the Society of Jesus was a recognized body corporate, as previously proven, the action of the Imperial authorities in preventing the accession of new members was ultra vires and wholly unwarrantable. Any subsequent advantage accruing to the Crown from such and illegal proceeding is invalid in law.

It remains simply to show that such was the case. As a matter of fact, it is a historical certainty that after the conquest no new members were received into the Society of Jesus. That this was the result of an inhibition on the part of the Crown is proven by the two following documents.

On the 15th Nov. 1772, Mgr. Briand, bishop of Quebec, in reference to the Jesuits, thus wrote to Cardinal Castelli : " The English have not molested them (the Jesuits) in Canada and together with the Recollets, they here serve the church with great edification. But neither the former nor the latter have leave to receive new subjects. I have asked that permission of the King of Great Britain, in an address signed by the clergy and the people. I fear much that I shall not obtain it, for two years have already gone by and I have received no answer." (Archives de L'Archevêché, Québec.) The prohibition was renewed later on in 1791.

In the Royal Instructions of the 16th Sept. of that year the following passage occurs : " It is also Our will and pleasure that all other religious seminaires and communities (that of the Jesuits only excepted) do for the present and until we can be more fully informed of the true state of them, and how far they are or are not essential to the free exercise of the religion of the Church of Rome, as allowed within our said province. remain upon their present establishments. *But you are not to allow the admission of any new members* into any of the said societies (the religious communities of women only excepted) without our express orders, for that purpose. (Chisholm's Papers p. 150—Lib. of Parliament, E. No. 421.) The Crown in consequence did not in right, through *escheat*, become owner of the property at the death of Père Casot.

The Quebec Act, inasmuch as it restricts treaty stipulaions, is ultra vires. It in no wise affects vested rights ; hence inapplicable to the case.

X.

" No ecclesiastical order has any right or title to the property since 1774."

A right may be either legal or legitimate. Laws may be framed which invade the rights of a private citizen or corporation so as forcibly to dispossess them of their rightful property, and may be carried into effect in spite of all remonstrance. His or its title ceases to be *legal*, as it is ignored by the unjust law, but it does not cease to be *legitimate*, as it is based on justice.

The act 14 George III, ch. 83, otherwise the "Quebec act," is a striking instance of this. It was passed in 1774, and in its Art. VIII it decrees : " It is also established by the authority aforesaid that all the Canadian subjects of His Majesty in the said Province of Quebec (religious orders and communities alone excepted) may also preserve their properties and possessions, etc., etc."

But as I have clearly proven that the Jesuits by the laws of nations, by the capitulations and by the treaty, had a full right in justice to their property and estates, the 8th article of this act is frustrated by its third, which I give in French, as I have not at hand the English version :

" Pourvu aussi, et il est établi, que rien de ce qui est contenu dans cet acte ne s'étendra, ou s'entendra s'étendre à annuler, changer ou altérer aucuns droits, titres ou possessions, résultans de quelque concession, actes de cession, ou d'autres que ce soit, d'aucunes terres dans la dite province, ou provinces y joignantes, et que les dits titres resteront en force, et auront le même effect, comme si cet acte n'eut jamais été fait."

So that, as far as concerns the rights of the Jesuits, we are authorized to look upon this act as if it never existed, or at least as *inapplicable*.

But it is morever *ultra vires*, if it mean that the Jesuits are not to be preserved in their property ; for a statute cannot annul a treaty. Chief Justice Jay, a most eminent jurist, in the celebrated case of Henfield, tried in the city of Richmond, on the 22nd May, 1793, observed : " Treaties between independent nations are contracts or bargains which derive all their force and obligations from mutual consent and agreement and consequently, when once fairly made and properly concluded, cannot be altered or annulled by one of the parties without the consent and concurrence of the other. Wide is the difference between *treaties* and *statutes*—we may negotiate and make contracts with other nations, but we can neither legislate for them nor they for us to vacate or modify treaties at discretion; Treaties, therefore, necessarily become the *supreme law of the land.* The peace, prosperity and reputation of the United States will always greatly depend on their fidelity to their engagements, and every virtuous citizen (for every citizen is a party to them) will concur in observing and executing them with honor and good faith, and that whether they be made with nations, respectable and important, or with nations weak and inconsiderable, our obligation to keep our faith results from our having pledged it and not from the character or description of the state or people to whom neither impunity nor the right of retaliation can sanctify perfidy, for although perfidy may deserve chastisement, yet it can never merit imitation."

If, therefore, the act of Quebec is to be read as a step towards the gradual absorption to the Jesuits' estates, it is a clear case of infringement of treaty stipulations, and as De Vattel said : " The following rule is better calculated...... at once to cut short all chicanery. If he who could and ought to have explained himself clearly and fully has not done it, it is the worse for him. He cannot be allowed to introduce *subsequent restrictions* which he has not expressed...... The equity of this rule is glaringly obvious, and its necessity is not less evident." (Chitty's *De Vattel.* B. II. ch. XVII., § 264.)

In answering this assertion, No. 10, I prescind entirely from the known maxims of Canon Law, with regard to the church property.

The status of the Jesuits in France in the 16th and 17th centuries is beside the question : the Jesuits being a body corporate in Canada. The title to their property was never vested in the General.

XI

" The Jesuits in France, in the 16th and 17th centuries, had no legal title to property. All the title existing was vested in the General at Rome."

The first part of this article I have shown to be fallacious. The second is a thread-bare objection. It is based on a copy of an " Arrêt du Parlement de Paris," which latter was annexed to a letter addressed to the Attorney and Sollicitor-General, Norton and DeGrey. The letter bears date May 12th 1765, and was written by the famous (?) James Marriot, a man as bitter in his blind hostility to the Society of Jesus as he was friendly to Voltaire.

Both documents are to be found in the report of the Committee of the House of Assembly of Lower Canada concerning education, dated the 25th February, 1824. In the French version they are reproduced at pages 205 and 211 respectively. It lies with you, Mr. Editor, to determine whether you can spare sufficient space in your paper for a disquisition on them. I am ready to undertake it, as I court enquiry, and shall evade no objection proposed.

A DIVERSION.

(STAR, *June* 13, 1888.)

THE JESUIT PROPERTY.

In reply to the courteous and ingenious arguments of U. E. L., we consider it useless to discuss side issues, which are totally irrelevant. U. E. L. admits that the property in question was confiscated by the Imperial Government. This disposes of the question of the liability of the Provincial Government. He argues however that the Provincial Treasurer is bound to restore "ill gotten gains." If this principle is to be admitted, all the revenue derived from licenses to sell liquor ought to be applied to relieving the families impoverished by inebriety.

That the Company of Jesuits was an illegal organization, U. E. L. can easily satisfy himself by a reference to his Blackstone under the title "Mortmain" or the memorial of Mariott in favor of Lord Amherst's pretensions in 1787. In case U. E. L. is dissatisfied with or does not admit the British Law, let him refer to *Guyot, Répertoire de Jurisprudence, Vbo. Jésuites.* He will find that in France the Jesuits were allowed (in 1561) letters patént "*à la charge que l'évêque diocésain aurait sur eux toute surintendance, juridiction et correction :*" We infer from this that when the order was suppressed the property reverted to the bishops.

In 1761 the celebrated Père Lavallette became a bankrupt. The creditors sued the Society of Jesus. The Jesuits defended the action. The Parliament of Paris, struck with the immense commercial enterprises of the Society, under the assumed name of Father Lavallette, took this opportunity of examining the constitutions of the order. Their examination resulted in the celebrated *arrêt* of 6th August, 1762.

This *arrêt* declares this religious order inadmissible by its nature in any civilized community ("*tout état policé*"), as contrary to natural law, menacing (*attentatoire*) all authority spiritual and temporal, and tending to introduce into church and state a political body, the essence of which consists in a continual activity to become by every means, first to secure absolute independence, and eventually to usurp all authority.

The *arret* further goes on to say that there are abuses in the vows and oaths, and declares them null, and orders that all the members of the said society who are 33 years of age cannot claim any rights of succession ; enjoins all the members of the society to abandon their colleges, and prohibits them in the future from observing the rules of the order and its constitutions, enjoins them also to take the oath of allegiance to the Gallican Church, and to abandon all correspondence with the General of the order. The Parliament of Rouen in November, 1764, had passed a similar order. In the month of November, 1764, an edict was passed and enregistered in all the "Parlements," dissolving completely the order of Jesuits in France. The greater number of the states of Europe imitated this example. The King of France by an edict of May, 1777, provides, Art. 2, that they (the Jesuits) "shall never live together in company, under any pretext soever." Article 7 restores the Jesuits under 33 years of age to complete civil rights, thereby cancelling their religious vow. Under this edict the Jesuit disappears completely as an order, and merges into the religious orders authorized by law, after pledging themselves to maintain and profess the liberties of the Gallican church. The Company of Jesuits was now completely dead and extinct as a legal order in France.

The following extract from the "Encyclopedia Britannica" 9th edition verbo Jesuits is also interesting :

"On July 21st, 1773, the famous Brief *Dominus ac Redemptor* appeared, suppressing the Society of Jesus. This remarkable document opens by citing a long series of precedents for the suppression of orders by the Holy See, amongst which occurs the ill-omened instance of the Templars. It then briefly sketches the objects and history of the Jesuits themselves. It speaks of their defiance of their own constitution expressly revived by Paul V, forbidding them from meddling in politics ; of the great ruin to souls, caused by their quarrels with local ordinaries and the other religious orders, their conformity to heathen usages in the east and the disturbances, resulting in persecutions of the Church, which they had stirred up even in Catholic countries, so that several Popes had been obliged to punish them. Seeing then that Catholic Sovereigns had been forced to expel them, that many bishops demand their extinction, etc." The Pope concludes by suppressing and extinguishing the order of Jesuits forever.

In 1814 the Pope restored the society to corporate existence. Napoleon compelled the Jesuits to quit France in 1804. They reappeared in France in 1814, obtained a formal license in 1822, were dispersed in 1830, and finally expelled under the Ferry laws of 1880. In 1874 while the bishops were agitating at Quebec the subject of a restitution of the Jesuits' estates, a memorial edited by " A Jesuit " was circulated amongst the members. At page 96 of this little book the following clause occurs: " The Jesuits in 1773 having been suppressed, the government acquired no right to their property, etc." The writer goes on to say that the bishops of that day should have claimed the property, which they did not. He maintains that under the cannon law the property of the suppressed order reverted to the church at large. There is no claim put forth for the Jesuits. Nor is it pretended that the confiscation of their estates was illegal. If U. E. L. will refer to a petition of the Roman Catholic Bishops to the Legislature under the date January, 1845, he will find that they recognised the fact that these funds were to be devoted to the purposes of superior education, inasmuch as they offered to bind themselves, if the funds were restored to them, to found one or more establishments for superior education. This petition was signed by the bishops and coadjutors of Quebec, Kingston and Montreal, and the bishops of Toronto.

There is also on record a letter dated 17th Oct., 1878, signed by F. G. Marchand, Provincial Secretary, and ordered to be sent to the Archbishop of Quebec, in which the following sentence occurs :

" They (the advisers of the Lieut.-Gov.) have informed His Honor that the land of the Jesuits' College was ceded to the province by the Dominion Government, who received it from the Imperial Government, and they have concluded that it was to the latter government the protest of the bishops was addressed. They therefore have advised His Honor to transmit the letter of the bishops to the Federal Government for communication to the Imperial Government."

Our statement of facts was written with the intention of showing that there was no legal claim of the Company of Jesuits to this fund. If any such claim existed, it could only be in favor of the bishops as frequently demonstrated in their petitions on this subject. U. E. L. admits that the property of the Company of Jesuits amounts in value to millions. He also adds that they will be satisfied with a modest sum. Besides, the recognition of a part of their claim in as good as a recognition of the whole, and as soon as they want more money we fear that they will forget their present modesty and file a claim for the whole.

It is reasonnable to suppose that this is only the insertion of the little end of the wedge. U. E. L. will find on reference to 19 or 20 Vic., Chap. 54, Sec. 2, that the whole of the revenue arising from the Jesuits Estate Fund is specially devoted to the Superior Education Fund. U. E. L. quotes the articles of capitulation 8th September, 1766, in support of his pretensions. He must know that the Quebec

Act of 1774 superseded this. If he will consult article 5 of the Quebec Act, he will discover that in strict law the funds proceeding from the Jesuits' estates must be entirely devoted to Protestant education, because the section provides that the Church of Rome in Canada shall be subject to the supremacy of the king according to the Act 1 Elizabeth, which was in reality a manifest injustice and contrary to the articles of capitulation : *Dura lex sed lex.*

A *resumé* of the foregoing facts results as follows : The Jesuits were suppressed throughout the world in 1773 by Papal brief. They were restored to corporate existence by the same authority in 1804. They were suppressed in France in 1764. It is certain that the order was completely extinct from 1773 to 1804. The Imperial Government knew this, and they were quite justified in assuming the vacant estate. The Canadian bishops, whose authority in ecclesiastical matters and the rights of the church and the status of its members is undoubted, have ever maintained that the property in question reverted to the Roman Catholic Church on the extinction of the order. The Quebec Act settled the question forever. The Province of Quebec owes the order of Jesuits nothing. If any claim exists in equity, for no legal claim exists, it is the Bishop of Quebec who is entitled to restitution and the Imperial authority is the power from whom restitution is due. The Quebec Government of 1874 and their successors have very properly taken this view of the case. The Company of Jesus, from the date of its suppression in 1773 until the year 1887, has had no legal or corporate existence. The Company of Jesus was duly incorporated by the Quebec Parliament during the session of 1887. The Company of Jesus suppressed and extinguished by edict of the French King in 1764, and suppressed by papal brief in 1773, has not had a legal existence in Canada until 1887.

(STAR, *June* 15, 1888.)

THE JESUIT ESTATES.

Side issues.

To the Editor of the STAR :

SIR,—No one would be more pleased than your correspondent to have all " side issues " ruled out of the present controversy, and I regret that your contributor after so praiseworthy a resolve, formally taken, at the opening of his reply, has not adhered to a rule which would cut short much useless discussion.

A Grantee of the Crown not protected against common law remedies.

He exonerates, on grounds too slender, the Provincial Government of all liability in the matter. You have not yet found space, Mr. Editor, for the remainder of my communication, but when it appears I would refer your contributor to the XV heading.

I would state, in the mean time, that the weightiest authority on such matters, Joseph Chitty, in his Prerogatives of the Crown, ch. XVI, sec. IV, does not seem to bear out your contributor in his inference. He says :

" In the case of lands the grantee does not, by taking them from the Crown, acquire any particular privileges. He is not thereby protected against the common law remedies and rights which others may possess in respect of the property, however such remedies and rights might be impeded whilst the King held it."

Jurisdiction not ownership.

Your worthy contributor persists in confounding jurisdiction with ownership. The fact that the bishops in France may or may not have had over the Jesuits "*toute surintendance, juridiction et correction,*" would lead no jurist to infer that "therefore when suppressed the property reverted to the bishops." The bishop of Montreal exercises absolutely the same control over the various convents of nuns in the diocese, and nevertheless were they suppressed to-morrow their property would not, in virtue of their suppression, revert to His Lordship.

A body corporate in Canada not amenable in law for real or supposed misdeeds of body corporates elsewhere.

However well it might suit your contributor to draw me after him in the discussion of "side issues," I must, for the present at least, refuse to follow. The question of the *arrêts* of French parliaments, or the case of Lavalette, is indeed "irrelevant." The corporation of Jesuits, recognized as then existing civilly in Canada, can in no wise be held responsible for what has falsely been ascribed to the Jesuits of France.

For those of your readers who wish to be informed on these different points, they will find the whole question lucidly put, with documents given and authorities quoted, in V vol., *Histoire de la Compagnie de Jésus*, by Crétineau-Joly, chap. IV., V. The author completely vindicates the Society of Jesuits.

Blackstone vs. Thurlow.

To the several dates given by your contributor, I shall add one of two more. Blackstone published the first volume of his commentaries in 1765. Thurlow, who was created Lord High Chancellor of England in June 1778, presented his report to the King on the 22nd of January, 1773, and delivered his speech in the House of Commons in 1774. He was throughly conversant with the doings and decrees of the parliaments and courts in question, and was probably more familiar with Blackstone's utterances than are your contributor and myself; and nevertheless he emphatically declares that the capitulations and treaty are binding on the King. And in what sense? " That every Canadian should have the full enjoyment of all his property, particularly the religious orders of the Canadians." That the treaty "was made in favour of religion, made in favour of the several religious orders."

The "Contributor" again at sea.

" Nor is it pretended in the pamphlet (of 1874) that the confiscation was illegal," says your contributor. His memory is short ; but a few lines above he thus quotes from the pamphlet : " The Jesuits in 1773 having been suppressed the Government acquired no right to the property." If the Government seized it, when they had no right to it, the confiscation, to the mind of the writer, was illegal. What is more remarkable, on the very page he quotes from is a heading of a section : " *L'usurpation des biens des Jésuites.*" From this page 96 to 104 " the Jesuit " denounces the gradual encroachments of the administration as " usurpations " and " spoliations."

Delegated powers expire with the instrument conferring them.

The writer on page 96 speaks indeed of the powers conferred on the bishop by the decree of suppression, but which he maintains, on page 77, was never promulgated in Canada, and intimates as much on page 96. These special powers were long since revoked by the bull restoring the Society of Jesuits throughout the world. So that were the estates placed in the hands of the bishops to-morrow, they could put them to no use without previously obtaining the sanction of the Holy See.

Liability of actual possessors.

" There is also on record a letter dated 17th Oct., 1878." Yes, and another, I must add, of the 27th April, 1885, emanating from the most august ecclesiastical authority in Canada, which, in answer to a similar objection, says : " But there still remains the eternal question of justice ! May he who retains the goods of another transfer it to other hands, and thus free himself, or the new possessor, of the obligation of making restitution ? *Res clamat domino,* says a familiar maxim. The actual detainer is always the first bound to restore."

Rome, not the public, the judge in matters ecclesiastic.

For any further answer on the score of the prior claims of the venerable body of the Episcopacy of the province, I refer your readers to the XVII heading of my former communication, which I trust will soon find place in your columns. Let your contributor, meanwhile, keep an even mind ; for neither will our venerable Bishops nor the Jesuits find fault with the decision of the Holy See.

I am sorry that the " little end of the wedge " is again preventing your contributor from being perfectly happy. But when a debtor pays but five cents on the dollar, though the sum be, I admit, ridiculously small, still the legal discharge he receives, sufficiently protects him from further molestation on the part of the creditor.

The King by treaty may preclude himself from the exercise of certain prerogatives. – The Quebec Act once more.

Your contributor, moreover, assures me that " I know that the Quebec Act of 1774 superseded this (the capitulation)." No, I scarcely dare say that I know it. What I have said under the X heading, pg. 36, (see STAR 9th June) even shows clearly that I do not. It is a comfort however, even in the matter of ignorance, to be in good company. Chitty himself did not know it. See Prerogatives, etc., ch. III, pg. 20, edit. London, 1820 : " Nor can the King legally disregard or violate the articles on which the country is surrendered or ceded ; but such articles are sacred and inviolable according to their true intent and meaning." Page 30: " The King may preclude himself from the exercise of his prerogative legislative authority in the first instance over a conquered or ceded country, by promising to vest in it an assembly of the inhabitants, and a governor, or by any measure of a similar nature, etc." Therefore *a fortiori* he may preclude himself from conficating private property, even had he a right otherwise to do so. This he did, through his general, at the capitulation of Canada.

But I moreover have proved (X heading) that the Quebec Act, by its own wording, cannot be applied to the case of the Jesuits. Again, if the 5th Art. of the Quebec Act appropriates the Jesuits, Estates (of which there is not even mention made in said article) for Protestant education, the gentlemen of St. Sulpice, the Quebec seminary, the Catholic clergy at large, must forfeit their property. Much more, every loyal Canadian Catholic, who has laid down his life for his Queen, or those who are ready to do so when duty calls, never had any right to their possessions, since not one ever recognized the spiritual supremacy of the Sovereign. Your contributor's assertion becomes incomprehensible when we are clearly told in the 5th Article : " Que le clergé de la dite Église (de Rome) peut tenir, recevoir et jouir de ses dûs et droits accoutumés, eu égard seulement aux personnes qui professent la dite religion."

English penal and common law as such do not hold in the Colonies.

The penal laws had no existence whatever in Canada—see opinion of Lord North (VIII heading, pg. 35 ; STAR 9th June). Chitty goes still further : " Hence it is clear that, generally speaking, the common law of England does not, as such, hold in the British colonies." (Prerogat, ch. III., pg. 32). Therefore it does not follow that because the Jesuits were an illegal society in England they were illegal also in Canada.

The Society of Jesus never totally extinct.

I must disagree on another point with your contributor. The Jesuits were never completely extinct. They continued in Russia, even after 1773, what they had been before. The *Oracula vivae vocis* of Pius VI, on the 24th July, 1785, recognized their status in that empire. They elected their General as usual and were authorized to receive novices. The brief " *Catholicae Fidei*" of Pius VII, 7th March, 1801, reinstated them there in all their rights. The brief "*Per alias*" extended these rights to the Two Sicilies, and finally the Bull "*Solicitudo Omnium,*" rehabilitated them throughout the world. They never ceased to exist canonically in Canada as the brief "*Dominus ac Redemptor*" was never published here.

Wrong to be righted.—Conquest the title officially alleged.

From what I have said in this and the former communication it follows: That the Jesuits, as a body corporate, were guaranteed their possessions at the capitulations and treaty. That they were illegally inhibited from receiving new members. That they remained a body corporate at least until 1791, the date of the Royal Instructions for their civil suppression. Were these ever promulgated? That before the law, it is a mere "side issue," what their status was in France, as their headquarters as a corporation were in Canada.

That at the death of the last Jesuit, in 1800, the estates were illegally vested in the Crown by a seizin. This was done, not by title through escheat, but by title of conquest. (See Writ to Ja. Sheppard, Sheriff, dated March 8, 1800. Registered—Qnebec, 1 Reg., folio 446.) When the property was conveyed to the Provincial Government, the same title was given: " the tenure of which is stated to be the conquest of 1756 and the Provincial Act, 17 Vic., ch. 11." Signed, Edw. Blake—Ottawa, May 10, 1879. And as no statute can render void a treaty, it follows that a gross injustice was perpetrated, for which the public conscience demands redress.

June 14, 1888.   U. E. L.

The General's attributes in financial matters. The non solidarity of seperate houses assailed in the Jesuits' Institute alone.

(STAR, *June* 16, 1888.)

(XI. *Continued from page* 38).

In the meantime, I most formally and emphatically deny the truth of the assertion that the title to the property of the Jesuits is vested in the General of the Jesuits at Rome. Like the president, or avowed head, of any civil corporation, whose field of action may extend to more than one country (let us take the G. T. R. for instance, whose lines extend into the neighboring States), the General of the Jesuits exercises a certain control over the movable and immovable property of the order. He is not the owner. Let your contributor recall what I have already said under the 1st heading concerning the non-solidarity of the different houses of the society. He cannot take from one house to give to another. His office is to administer, through himself or others, the estates belonging to these separate houses, and may pass contracts only to the advantage and for the utility of these houses, (Constitut. P. IX, C. IV.; Examen gen., C. I., No. 4; Bulla, Greg. XIII, 1582). If the annual income of the colleges, destined, in virtue of the intention of founders or of the provisions of the institute, for the sustenance and clothing of the Jesuits who are their inmates, exceed the outlay, the surplus in each house is to be employed, not in new establishments, but in liquidating outstanding debts or increasing the revenues (Inst. pro admin., tit. pro rect, No. 6). Both Church and State had recognized this right of non-solidarity. For when one house was in penury, its revenues being insufficient, both powers, without taking into consideration the comparative prosperity of other houses, assisted the poorer house with their endowments. They recognized thus their non-solidarity.

In France down to 1760 no one ever though of questioning this non-solidarity which all religious orders enjoyed in common with the Jesuits. Subsequently it was never assailed in other institutes, it was attacked only in that of Loyola. It was alleged that the general of the society held despotic sway, that he was absolute master of persons and things, and consequently universal proprietor of all the worldly goods of the order. According to the terms of their constitution, this assertion was groundless, but under the influence of certain bitter hatreds it assumed the proportions of a principle.

The General incapacitated by his vow from holding property in his own right. His functions those of a Superintendent.

The legislation of the Institute is nevertheless clear on this point. The General is ranked in the same category as his brethren ; if they cannot hold property, in their own right, for having vowed perpetual poverty, neither can be, for the same identical reason. In religious societies it is not the individuals nor the superior who possesses, but the various establishments, as bodies corporate, legally recognized as such before both civil and ecclesiastical law. The text of Loyola's constitutions exhibits every where the General as the administrator and not the proprietor of the Society's possessions. In his administration, which the constitutions (P. IV. c. 11) term superintendence, as it is he who names the other superiors, who must give him an account of their administration, the General is subject, on all essential points, to the control of general congregations. Without their assent, he can neither alienate nor suppress a college or other establishment, and the breach of this law would be for him a case of deposition, or even expulsion from the society, provided for in the constitutions (P. IX. c. 4). He is empowered to accept property or donations for the Society ; he may, when the intention of the donor is not determined, allot them to this or that house ; but once they are allotted, it is beyond his powers to divert what accrues, or to collect a percentage on the revenues either for his own use or for strangers.

As a constituted corporation, the Society was of Canada.

But had it even been the case, as far as France was concerned, at the time of the conquest and after, it certainly was not the General who held possession of the Jesuits' estates in Canada. The merest tyro in jurisprudence is able to appreciate the meaning of the letters patent and of the Royal Instructions. Louis XIV styles the Jesuits : " Nos chers et bien aimez les religieux de la compagnie de Jésus *résidant en nostre pays de la nouvelle France*," and the Royal Instructions of the 16th September, 1791 : " the present members of the said society (*i. e.*, society of Jesuits already mentioned) *as established at Quebec*." There is no question here of a sole but of an aggregate corporation ; no question of the General of the Society, but of the body established at Quebec. To all intents and purposes, for a Canadian court, the

·General was a legal nonentity. It was this all important point that Marriot in his bitter hatred feigned to overlook, and that your contributor, taking him at his word, has so thoughtlessly ignored.

Hence all the title to property existing was not vested in the General at Rome.

The nationality of the General, a " side issue."

XII

" The General being an Italian and an alien, not owing allegiance to the King of France, could hold no real property either in France or in its colonies. This was the law in France in 1763, up to the conquest, and the law of England was the same at the date of or after the ·conquest."

For once, Mr. Editor, to your great relief, not less than to my own, I may be short.

I shall not enquire at what particular date the disability of foreigners to hold property in France ceased. The thing is also entirely foreign to the subject, and its inability of proving anything against the Jesuits' claims equally manifest. Who ever told your contributor that foreigners, at that period, could hold property in France or England? Certainly no Jesuit ever maintained it. I shall not begrudge your contributor all the comfort he can derive from this harmless assertion.

As years roll on youth will wane. The Jesuits recognised at last to be what they had never ceased to be.

XIII

" The present Company of Jesuits have had a legal existence in this province for only a few months."

I acknowledged already that they were a very unreasonable lot. Only a few months! They have scarely begun to enjoy civil life, when, in downright earnest, they, like their other civil fellow-beings, seem alive to the fact that their civil existence entails certain civil obligations, but at the same time also certain civil rights. The Apostle of the Gentiles was given to the same little weakness.

A certain man was ejected from his homestead under pretence that he held it for a foreigner. For it was known that his mother-in-law was a Pennsylvania Dutch woman, and she ruled the household. The country he lived in was, legislatively speaking, a little backward, so that a foreigner could not hold property. The man protested that he held it in his own name ; but through the stupidity of his lawyer, or perhaps there was boodle in the case, his titles were not thought to be in order. He reluctantly went west, to the land of the blizzard ; but was frozen out of Dakota and returned a few years later. The land meanwhile had been sold for a mere song to an honest citizen. Our friend, this time, engaged an Ontario lawyer, who, to make certainty doubly sure, told him to take out his naturalization papers. Only a few months later, the case came into court. The lawyer proved the titles clear. The honest man gave up the farm, and the last that was heard of him was that he was looking for the boodler.

Moral – Never allow many months to go by, after you qualify, without claiming what belongs to you.

XIV

" They cannot pretend to be the successors to a company which never had any legal existence."

If we are to believe what is oftentimes said of them, they scarcely could. Only I remind your contributor that the society had de facto down to 1791 a very distinctly defined legal existence ; and that consequently de jure have never ceased to have a legitimate existence. For wrong is to be redressed when and wheresoever it is detected. Time can never legitimate injustice. There is no room for prescription when there is mala fides at the inception.

The Province amenable. (See also page 43).

XV

" At any rate it is quite clear that the Province of Quebec has nothing to do with the question since the forfeiture of the former so called Jesuits property was effected by the Imperial Government."

This is a new principle in law. The detainer of ill-gotten goods must not be molested by the rightful owner. We recommend it to the commission for the codification of our laws.

At any rate, it does not fairly convey the same meaning as that conveyed by the written communication of a very high ecclesiastical dignitary to the head of a late cabinet, on the 27th April, 1880 :—

" But the eternal question of justice still remains ! May the one who holds the goods of another transfer them to other hands and thus free himself or free the new possessor of the obligation to restore? " Res claniat Domino," says a well known axiom. The detainer is always the first bound to make restitution." These are the words of wisdom and of sound ethics. Nor shall I presume to dilate on them.

A Document out of date.

XVI.

" When Clement XIV suppressed the Company of Jesus in 1773, he provided that their property should return to the Church for pious uses."

That is, wherever the Society of Jesus was canonically suppressed, the bishop, acting as minister in the execution of the decree was to take possession of their goods, etc., and hold them for such uses as the Holy See should designate: " Bonorum, etc., possessionem nomine Sanctae Sedis apprehendat et retineat pro usibus a Sanctissimo designandis."

Now it is a historical fact that Lord Dorchester intervened and deterred Mgr Briand from sequestrating the estates, so as they were not taken they could not be held for purposes to be determined by the Holy See. The commission delivered to the bishops, to act thus in the name of the Holy See, lasted just so long as the brief of suppression was in force. It was annulled by the bull *Sollicitudo Ominum* of Pius VII, in 1814, which allowed the Jesuits, who had never ceased to exist in Russia, to reorganize the Society once more throughout the world. So it is rather late in the day to invoke the documents emanating from the Holy See, at the time of the suppression, as sanctioning any action that might at present be taken. After the re-establishment of the Society throughout the world, the Holy See, very naturally, restored to the Society what had been taken in those places *where it was canonically suppressed*. Pius VII and Leo XII were foremost in this work, and their example was followed by several Christian monarchs.

The Bishops " ex officio " the administrators of Church property temporarily or irremediably " vacant."

XVII.

" The following clause in a petition to the Legislature of Quebec is conclusive proof that the claim of the Jesuits was inadmissible : Your petitioners humbly represent that the order of Jesuits being extinct in this country, their naturel successors are the Roman Catholic bishops of the diocese."

It is a conclusive proof of no such thing. It is a pity your contributor has such a short memory. But a few phrases above he gravely told us that the Jesuits could not pretend to be the successors to a company which never had any legal existence, and now he supposes that the bishops were capable of so silly an act. This is scarcely respectful, coming from the quarter from which the communication of Saturday, 19th May, proceeds. Their Lordships were at least shrewd enough to perceive, that if they claimed to be the natural successors to a company which never had any legal existence, they would stand a very poor chance of being listened to. I shall not do them so grievous a wrong, but shall say they therefore acknowledged that the Jesuits were the real proprietors, and that it was only because the Order was extinct in this country that they claimed control over the estates.

Canon law, in fact, imposes on them the obligation ex officio of seeing that no pious foundation be diverted from the purpose for which it was made. They acted, consequently, in this matter wisely, and in accordance with the dictates of their conscience. Had the province listened to them and placed the estates in their hands, the property would have remained in their keeping, in trust, either until the return of the Jesuits, or until the Holy See had given directions as to its application.

Allow me here, Mr. Editor, in reference to the venerable body of rhe Episcopate of this Province and to the Jesuit fathers, to make one point clear. The Papal indult placed in the hands of the Procurator of the Jesuits, was given them, because they alone could given a legal discharge, or receipt in full to the Province, and so ease the public conscience. The Society of Jesus, once it has received the sum the Government proposes to give, is not empowered to appropriate to its own use one single farthing, until the Holy See has determined whether or not a division is to be made, and what portion of the sum is to be placed at its disposal. Therefore there is no conflict, as your contributor would have us believe, between the venerable body of the Episcopate and the Society of Jesus.

A pretext for Vandalism. Dynamite vs. Jesuit mortar.

XVIII.

" In 1877 it was resolved to demolish the buildings (the old College in Quebec) on account of their dangerous state."
It would be here the place for every lover of our common country to exclaim : " Infandum, regina, jubes renovare dolorem ! " The old college was the cradle of classical learning in North America. It was founded in 1635, one year before Harvard University.

I shall not attempt to give the particulars of its demolition, it was a piece of vandalism ; and it would take more espace than you could afford me to lay bare the numerous intrigues which resulted in its demolition. The true motives were held back, and the vain pretext, that it threatened ruin, was put forward.

In June 1877, M. Baillarge, the engineer of the corporation of Quebec, affirmed in a written document : "La couverture est encore excellente et meilleure que beaucoup de couvertures dernièrement faites à Québec...... Les murs son parfaitement bons, saufs dans le voisinage du sol, quelques écoinçons en partie degradés.... Il y a à réparer presque tous les planchers, toutes les croisées et portes extérieures et intérieures, les plafonds, cloisons, etc., en un mot tout l'intérieur qui a beaucoup souffert dernièrement de la part des incendiés du quartier Montcalm, qui se sont servis de la charpente et menuiserie de l'intérieur pour se chauffer en hiver."

M. Faucher de St-Maurice, in his " Relation de ce qui s'est passé. etc., Québec, 1879," and who was an eye-witness to the whole proceeding, makes the following observations at page 22 :

" Pendant quelques années, les murs silencieux du vieux collège des Jésuites semblèrent se recueillir, jusqu'au jour où la charité revenant frapper à la porte des cellules des Pères, celles-ci se rouvrirent pour donner l'hospitalité à une partie de la population du quartier Montcalm, qu'un incendie venait de chasser de leurs demeures.

Erigé pour venir en aide aux souffrances humaines, le collège des Jésuites finissait comme il avait commencé. Il redevenait l'asile des malheureux, et les pauvres y trouvèrent un abri, jusqu'à ce que certains philanthropes s'rperçurent que ses murailles étaient dilapidées et dirent qu'elles menaçaient la vie des passants. Il fallut alors en finir au plus vite. La bande noire s'abattit sur cette relique de notre passé. Mais, chose étrange ! Ces pierres branlantes, condamnées comme étant dangereuses, résistèrent à la sape et à la mine. Le bélier,.

la poudre à canon mordirent à peine dans ces assises, où le mortier avait la consistance du granit. On employa les plus forts explosibles connus pour avoir raison de ces murs, et encore la maçonnerie du frère LeFaulconier, la charpente du frère Ambroise Cauvet, ne semblèrent s'écrouler qu'à regret, mettant à découvert des ossements que des rapprochements de faits et des coïncidences historiques semblent identifier avec ceux du frère Jean Liégeois, le grand architecte qui avait eu ' la surintendance du tout,' et à qui, pendant 214 ans, son œuvre aurait ainsi servi de tombeau.

They wiped out the oldest institution of learning in North America.

Dans quelques jours, il ne restera plus rien de ce qui fut, pendant cent quatorze ans, l'Alma Mater de l'instruction dans l'Amérique du Nord. Plus vieux d'une année que le collège de Harvard, près de Boston, celui des Jésuites de Québec n'existera plus maintenant que dans les souvenirs de ceux qui ont la fierté de leur passé."

Good intentions, not less than malice, may work sad havoc.

Mr. Editor, I leave you, and the public in general, to judge whether I have been justified or not in asserting that the communication, with which I find fault, is a long misstatement of the case. I have not insisted on one of the opening phrases, in which your contributor styles the Society of Jesus a recently created order. For I would fain suppose that on these as on other points, he has simply been misinformed, and had no intention of doing a grievous injury to a Society whose history is interwoven with the whole history of the colony, our now common country. I take therefore his words as implying nothing more than that on the supposition that the Society never having before in his judgment been a body corporate, it, at the moment of its incorporation, became in a legal sense a newly created order.

Albion n'est pas perfide. What would constitute perfidy.

Is it necessary, Mr. Editor, that I should explain the reason of my trespassing so ruthlessly on your limited space? Brought up in the admiration of England and of every thing English, my first impressions of her chequered history were that never had she, nor never was she capable of violating her sacred promises once only pledged. My obyish ideas, as those, no doubt, of the young generation rising around us, though not formulated with all the preciseness of a DeVattel, might, however, be rendered in his words: " Let us simply observe, that an evidently false interpretation is the grossest imaginable violation of the faith of treaties. He that resorts to such an expedient, either impudently sports with that sacred faith, or evinces his inward conviction of the degree of moral turpitude annexed to the violation of it : he wishes to act a deshonest hart, and yet preserve the character of an honest man ; he is a puritanical impostor, who aggravates his crime by the addition of a detestable hypocrisy........"

" Our faith may be tacitly pledge as well as expressly ; it is sufficient that it be pledged, in order to become obligatory ; the manner can make no difference in the case, the tacit pledging of faith is founded on a tacit consent ; and a tacit consent is that which is, by fair deduction, inferred from our actions. Thus, as Grotius observes (L. III c. 24 : § 1), whatever is included in the nature of certain acts which are agreed upon is tacitly comprehended in the agreement, or in other words, everything which is indispensably necessary to give effect to the articles agreed on is tacitly granted." (Chitty's DeVattel—Law of Nations, B. II, ch. 15. § 233).

What England owes to the descendants of the heroic handful, headed by de Montcalm and de Levis, who, abandoned by their own mother country, hoped against hope, and defended to the last their hearthstones and their altars, must be defined not by the Treaty, taken alone, but by Treaty and capitulations taken in the complex. For the latter are as sacred as the former.

" Since the general of an army and the governor of a town must be naturally invested with all the powers necessary for the exerci-e of their respective functions, we have a right to presume that they possess those powers ; and that of concluding a capitulation is certainly one of the number, especially when they cannot wait for the Sovereign's order. A treaty made by them on that subject is therefore valid and binds the sovereigns in whose names and by whose authority the respective commanders have acted." (Chitty's De Vattel, B. III ; c. XVI, § 261).

Their articles are not cancelled by a definitive treaty, unless it be clearly so stated and agreed upon. " In things favorable (in interpreting treaties) it is better to pass beyond that point, than not to reach it ; in things odious, it is better not to reach it, than to pass beyond it. (Ibid. B. II ; c. 17 ; § 300).

" Whatever tends to change the present state of things is also to be ranked in the class of odious things ; for the proprietor cannot be deprived of his right, except so far, precisely, as he relinquishes it on his part; and, in case of doubt, the presumption is in favor of the possessor. It is less repugnant to equity to withhold from the owner a possession which he has lost through his own neglect, than to strip the just possessor of what lawfully belongs to him. In the interpretation, therefore, we ought rather to hazard the former inconvenience than the latter. Here also may be applied, in many cases, the rule we have mentioned in § 301, that the party who endeavors to avoid a loss has a better cause to support than he who aims at obtaining an advantage." (Ibid. § 305).

By whom the wrong was perpetrated.

These, Mr. Editor, are no doubt your sentiments also, and those of the honest public. And if any of us were called upon to act as arbiters in a case in which we have no interest at stake, our natural sense of equity would supply our deficiency in technical training, and prompt us to adjudicate according to these notions.

And no doubt we all thought that no reproach could be laid, on that score, at the doors of our own Mother Country. At least it was my own settled conviction, until, in studying more closely the history of this colony, I was rudely startled by the fact that an injustice had been done by some one in her name. It was not done by the law officers in England, who for thirty years refused to legalize the proposed spoliation, avowing that they could not determine over what properties of the Order of Jesuits His Majesty might claim full control, and which he could consequently legally grant to Lord Amherst's heirs. The iniquity was consummated on the advice and with the concurrence of a handful of men within the limits of this province, men who had not at heart the true interests of their sovereign nor of their country.

Justice enobleth a nation.

If the Hon. Mr. Mercier succeeds in effacing this blemish from our nation's history, of easing the public conscience, for I suppose there must be such a thing, he will deserve the gratitude of generations to come.

There is, however, one shoal on which this great project may come to grief, and which he must shun at all hazards, it is this : That while aiming at reducing to a minimum, for the advantage of the province, the sacrifice to be made, it is just possible that a fresh injury may be inflicted, by forcing the Jesuits to accept, as a final settlement, a compensation wholly out of proportion to their immense possessions so unjustly confiscated. For not taking into account that but a portion of that sum may eventually go into their hands, it leaves no chance for redress. That he may have the courage to turn a deaf ear to the clamours of a few prejudiced politicians, it will be well for him to bear in mind that *Justitia elevat gentem.*

May, 26th, 1888.

U. E. L.

Grateful acknowledgment to the "Star."

(STAR, *June* 19).

THE JESUITS ESTATES.

To the Editor of the STAR :

SIR,—In reading over the last instalment of my all but interminable correspondence, I notice that a mistake of some consequence has crept in, *suadente diabolo*, I mean the printer's. The intelligent reader will kindly save me the trouble of correcting other slips of minor importance. I refer to a phrase under the XV heading, which would make sense if read as follows :

" At any rate, it does *not* fairly convey the same meaning as that conveyed by the written communication, etc."

I take this occasion, Mr. Editor, to thank you for having so hospitably opened your columns to a stranger, whose only title to much kindness on your part was that spirit of Anglo-Saxon fairness, with which he rightly supposed you to be animated.

Yours, etc.,

U. E. L.

Second Edition.

Order and Chaos;

A LECTURE,

DELIVERED AT

Loyola College, Baltimore, in July, 1869,

BY T. W. M. MARSHALL, Esq.,

AUTHOR OF "CHRISTIAN MISSIONS."

BALTIMORE:
PUBLISHED BY JOHN MURPHY & CO.
182 BALTIMORE STREET.
NEW YORK... CATHOLIC PUBLICATION SOCIETY.
BOSTON... P. DONOHOE
1875.

Entered, according to the Act of Congress, in the year 1869, by
JOHN MURPHY,
In the Clerk's Office of the District Court of Maryland.

PRINTED BY
JOHN MURPHY & CO.
BALTIMORE.

TO

The Catholics of Baltimore,

WHO

To an Ardent Zeal for the Faith,

UNITE

The Virtues which that Faith Inspires,

This Lecture is Dedicated,

In Grateful Memory,

OF

Pleasant Hours Spent among them.

ORDER AND CHAOS.

Ladies and Gentlemen:

There is in our world a certain creation of human art, which some Christians are able to contemplate with sympathy and satisfaction; others, only with repugnance and disgust. You are all familiar with it, yet I do not flatter myself that I can describe it to you in a single sentence. It is too eccentric in its outward form, as well as too irregular in its internal structure, to be defined in a few words. No two fragments of this composite fabric, of which I am going to speak to you to-night, have the same shape, nor even belong to the same material. Perhaps the truest description of it would resemble that which the prophet gave of the "*great statue*" which the King of Babylon saw in his dream. Like that, it has "feet of clay," but it has also a head of wood, and a face of brass. All the wide regions of Chaos seem to have been searched, that they might contribute something towards its heterogeneous mass. Innumerable quarries have been opened, with a perverse industry, only to borrow from each a solitary specimen of its contents, so that nothing might be wanting to its perfection as a symbol of Disorder. With the materials thus derived, men built up, about three centuries ago, a new Tower of Babel. More successful than their ancestors in the plain of Sennaar, they were allowed to complete it. It has changed its original form many times since then, and is now almost without shape. It has fallen in here, and bulged out there, but though rent and torn in every direction, and only sustained by props and buttresses as decrepit as itself, it still stands, to the great astonishment even of its admirers, who predict every day that the final catastrophe is at hand. Around this falling Tower, you may see on certain days a confused multitude, who appear to meet together for a common purpose, but of whom it is to be noted that each individual speaks a different language, which no one can interpret, not even himself. The ear is wounded and bruised with the uproar of contending voices, which fill the air with ceaseless clamor, as if each strove to prevail over every other. The president of this tumultuous assembly is the Angel of Discord, and the building round which it is gathered is the Temple of Chaos. Yet there are men of excellent natural gifts, some even of great natural virtues, who have persuaded themselves to believe, and really do believe, that the architect of this monstrous fabric is the Most High God. They even imagine, so strong is their delusion, that the incoherent sounds which are heard in this temple constitute a species of worship peculiarly acceptable to Him, and much superior to anything of that kind hitherto invented by His creatures. But this curious fact need not surprise you, when you call to mind that the noblest intellects of antiquity — a Plato, a Socrates, or a Cicero — were able to accept as realities even the picturesque fictions of Pagan mythology; that an Alexander the Great, could seriously invoke Mercury, and a Julius Cæsar offer sacrifice to Minerva. Man is the same in every age, when left to himself, or to teachers like himself. In that lamentable condition, he can believe *anything* — except the truth. You know, ladies and gentlemen, what name has been given in every land to this Temple of Chaos. It has the same name in America as in Europe. Men call it Protestantism.

There is also in our world another creation, *not* of human art, nor imitable by human skill. All the pretended spiritual architects who ever lived, from Confucius to Calvin, could not have fashioned *this* building, nor any part of it. They could not even have imagined it. From its foundation stone, which shall never be moved, to its topmost pinnacles, which are reared so high above the clouds that they are bathed day and night in the pure light of Heaven, all is the work of God. Man could no more make such a fabric as this than he could make a world. It is the last and most perfect conception of Omnipotent wisdom. It is the mirror in which the Uncreated Beauty is most clearly reflected. Within its walls only *one* language is spoken and all can interpret it. It is the home of tranquil peace, unbroken unity, and the largest liberty which the creature can ever know. Long ages ago, the prophets of Judah saw, in a vision, the building of which I am now speaking, and even that far-off contemplation of its glories filled them with rapture. "*Go round about her*," said one of them in a spirit of inspiration, "*mark well her towers; set your hearts on her strength.*" "*I will lay thy foundations with sapphires,*" cried another in the same spirit, "*and I will make thy bulwarks of jaspar, and thy gates of graven stones, ... and great shall be the peace of thy children.*" And lest men should suppose that it was a thing of purely material beauty, which they were invited only to *admire*, and not a Living Power, which they were commanded to *obey*, on pain of eternal death, the great prophet of Redemption uttered this final warning: "*The nation and kingdom that will not serve thee shall perish, . . . No weapon that is formed against thee shall prosper, and every tongue that resisteth thee in judgment thou shalt condemn.*" And when at last the hour arrived, more than eighteen centuries ago, when this "City of the Great King" was to be set up on earth, that its courts might be filled with human guests; when the same Omnipotent Voice which had once said, "*Let there be light*," now pronounced the new decree, "*Upon this rock I will build My church;*" it sprang at once into being, so perfect in its supernatural loveliness that even its Creator was enamoured of it, and called it His *Bride*. Never since He began to create had He given such a name to any thing which He had made. Never had He deigned to unite to Himself by such a tie any of His works. And as if all the magnificent promises which had gone before too feebly shadowed forth the glory to which this Bride was destined, He now added, no longer by the mouth of angel or prophet, but with His own lips, these astonishing words: "*The gates of hell shall not prevail against thee;*" and He confirmed the new promise by this transporting assurance: "*Behold, I am with thee all days, even to the consummation of the world.*" Other works which He had made might be defaced or come to an end, but not this, for He would keep it always in the hollow of His hand. Like the Temple of Chaos, of which I spoke just now, this building has also a name, a name known in heaven and on earth, and which, to us who dwell within its walls, is as music in the ear. Men call it the Catholic Church.

I presume to invite you this evening to visit these two buildings—the one human, and betraying in every stone its human origin; the other divine, and reflecting everywhere the beauty and majesty of Him who made it; the one, the Temple of Confusion and Chaos, and the prolific source of the worst evils which afflict human society; the other, the sole fountain of supernatural Order, both in the spiritual and the social sphere. But before we enter either of these temples, I ask your permission to make a single preliminary observation, which is necessary to prepare the way for the argument which I am going to address to you. It is this:

If there be in this lower world any authority which represents God, and speaks in His name—as all Christian communities, though with hesitating and stammering lips, profess to do, in some sense or other—that authority or institution, whatever it be, must reflect, as far as the creature can, the mind and the attributes of God. Otherwise it is convicted of imposture. For whatever in our world does *not* reflect God, in its own measure and proportion, is either a delusion or an abomination. Generally it is both at once. The whole argument which I am going to submit to your patient attention is based on this simple proposition. And now, keeping carefully in mind that whatever professes to belong to God must faithfully reflect Him, we may ask, without further preface, the question which this lecture is designed to answer: Is it in Protestantism, or in the Catholic Church, that the Divine presence and attributes are reflected?

I commence the reply to this question as follows. If we have any sure and rational conviction about God, it is this, that He is eternal *harmony*, essential *unity*, inviolable *order*, and ineffable *repose*. Even reason can find out thus much, as St. Paul reminded the heathen to their condemnation, by simply contemplating the visible universe. Is it, then, once more, in Protestantism, or in the Catholic Church, that harmony, unity, order, and repose are found? Let us visit the temple in which each dwells, and as courtesy requires us to give our first attention to strangers, let us begin with the Temple of Chaos. Our visit, I hasten to assure you, will be a brief one, and we may hope, in spite of its precarious condition, that it will not fall down whilst we are within it.

Well, I suppose that we have passed the portal of this singular temple, and are fairly inside. What do we see? Our first impression, which will be corrected presently, is, that we have found our way into an empty sepulchre. How chill and gloomy it is! It reminds one of nothing so much as one of those Egyptian tombs, monuments of the inanity of human pride, which people visit listlessly, as they visit other historical buildings, only to remark how perfectly useless they have become. They note the broken tomb, or examine the empty sarcophagus, but hardly care to ask whose dust it once contained. What is it to them? But a greater surprise awaits us in this building. It is supposed to be devoted to some kind of religious worship, yet you cannot find in it, however long you may remain, the faintest trace of God! Before we go any further, let me offer you an explanation of His absence. The founders of this structure, half-temple and half-tomb, were in such a hurry to banish God from it, in order to enthrone man in His place, that they did not even pause to say, "Depart from us, O Lord!" They were bringing in a new worship, in which, as the event has proved, *man* was to be everything. Henceforth, the highest conception of religion was to be — a group of men listening to a *man*. Yes, they had brought Christianity to that. Every mystery was now rejected. Mysteries, of which science could give no account, might be tolerated in everything else, because they could not get rid of them. There might be mysteries all around them, and in their own persons, but at all events there should be none in religion. And so they made short work of them. St. Paul had said, *habemus altare,— we have an altar;* but the first act of these new builders was to cry out: "*We* have neither altar, nor priest, nor sacrifice." The next was to cast the Christian altar to the ground. The tabernacle, in which God had dwelt for fifteen centuries, was broken to atoms. By these prompt and energetic proceedings they had already reduced the sacrifice of Mount Calvary to the dimensions of an historical event, of which henceforth no daily commemoration need be made. And the sequel was in harmony with this beginning. So eager were they to root out the very memory of the "*Daily Sacrifice*," which had been the chief rite and central mystery of the Christian religion, from the hearts of the people, and to substitute for it what the prophet Daniel, who foresaw this sacrilege, called "*the abomination of desolation*," i. e. the unprofitable talk of human teachers, that their leaders commanded the very altar stones to be placed in the porch, that all who came in might trample them under foot. This horrible iniquity, feebly imitated in later times by the Pagans of China and Japan, was actually enjoined by the English Ridley and his fellows, the founders of the Anglican church, and diligently accomplished throughout the realm of England. Can you wonder if from that hour God deserted the place? How should He dwell *there*, when they had taken His altars away? There was no longer any throne for Him. And so the place became, as His prophet foretold, "the abomination of desolation." The preacher is there, but not God. Man has taken His place.

But we are still only at the threshold of this deserted temple. As you stand there, it seems to you not only dark but empty. Yet you will find, as your eyes become accustomed to the feeble light, that it is not so. Advance a little into the interior, and you will see a curious scene. The whole place is filled with different groups, more than the eye can count, and in the midst of each is a man, who is addressing those around him.

If your ear could take in simultaneously what each speaker says, you would find that they are all talking about the same thing, and all giving a different account of it. Every man is flatly contradicting in his own group what is being confidently asserted in the group next to him. And many of the hearers constantly pass to and fro from one to the other, and seem to be equally pleased with the affirmation and the contradiction. Some have not made up their minds which to prefer. But as it is impossible to hear them all at once, and would be intolerable to hear them all in succession, I propose to you that we should select one of the groups at random, and join ourselves to it. There is a man in the middle of it, as in all the others. He occupies a sort of pulpit, and seems to be preaching. But he is not. He is praying, only he does it after a fashion of his own, with which you are not familiar. I must attempt to describe it to you. He knows very well that the people there are listening to him, and that he is expected to be what they call "impressive;" so he proceeds to satisfy the expectation to the best of his ability. You may often read in certain newspapers, having a large circulation in the regions of Chaos, of certain religious ceremonies, in which one of the officiating personages is invariably reported to have offered "an impressive prayer." I have read such an announcement a hundred times. You will ask, perhaps, how in the world can a man on his knees before the dread majesty of God contrive to be "impressive?" The notion of trying to produce a *sensation* under such circumstances seems to you as wildly extravagant as if a man should undertake to sing a comic song at his own funeral. But you are not acquainted with the resources of a ministerial artist in the Temple of Chaos. He can do things quite as difficult as this. Of course, he can only do it in one way,—by forgetting all about God, and thinking only of himself, and the poor creatures around him. In this way, he can be, after a certain fashion, very impressive indeed—at least in his own judgment and theirs. But the misfortune is that his hearers, who also forget all about God, are tempted to worship the preacher instead, who has not much objection to their doing so, and is still more irresistibly tempted to worship himself. You and I only know of two kinds of prayer, one offered in heaven, the other on earth, and neither of them in the least resembles the style of prayer which is known in the Temple of Chaos. In heaven, the mightiest angels, at the bare sight of whom the strongest among ourselves would faint away with fear, cover their faces with their wings, and hardly dare to look up: on earth, they who will one day consort with angels, also hide their faces, smite their breasts, and say, "God be merciful to me a sinner." They both see a Vision before them which takes away all ambition of being "impressive." *They* are not thinking of themselves, but of Him in whose presence they stand. How should they turn away their eyes to any meaner object? We are told indeed of a certain Pharisee, who "prayed *within himself*," a phrase of which you have often appreciated the significance,— and he too, I doubt not, was very impressive to those who happened to be looking at him. But you remember what our Lord, who was also looking at him, said of his prayer.

In spite of this formidable judgment, I venture to predict that, if you are in the habit of looking at the public journals, you will read, before a week has elapsed, of somebody offering somewhere, an "impressive" prayer. There is a class of teachers with whom it is a professional necessity to do so. They are paid to be impressive, and cannot escape the miserable obligation. It is a melancholy fact that, in too many cases, their prayers are offered, not to God, who does not require them to be impressive, but to *man* who insists upon their being so, and would consider himself defrauded, if they were not. This is one of the fatal consequences of putting man in the place of God. In the sight of God, we are only impressive when we forget *ourselves;* in the sight of man, we have most claim to admiration when we forget *Him*. And thus it comes to pass that, in the Temple of Chaos, what professes to be a supplication to God, is really a discourse to men, and what might have been a good prayer, is converted into a bad sermon.

However, the gentleman with whom we are immediately concerned, has finished his eloquent prayer, and is now beginning to preach. Let us hear what he has got to say. We have come into his temple at a fortunate moment, for he is preaching about heaven. But as you listen, you will find that it is not the heaven to which *you* aspire—the heaven of saints and martyrs. He has nothing to tell us about that, probably because he knows nothing about it. He is immensely affecting about what he calls "the recognition of departed friends," and "the reunion of husbands and wives,"— as if the chief employment in heaven was to be the perpetual celebration of nuptial rites,—and he draws such a ravishing picture of these human delights, he is so steeped and saturated in earthly anticipations, that we are almost tempted to think the man must be a Mahometan. His hearers, who are evidently enchanted, do not seem to care much whether he is or not, and the earthly view of heaven which he advocates with so much pathos seems to be sufficiently attractive to them. They do not appear to notice, as you and I do, that in his enumeration of future joys, he does not make the slightest allusion to God, and perhaps they think, if they think about it at all, that it is quite consistent, after banishing Him from *their* temple on earth, that they should expel Him from His own temple in heaven. With their peculiar views of celestial felicity, which is simply the perpetuation of familiar joys and the society of sympathising friends, heaven would probably be a much more agreeable residence without Him. I fear it must be said that the Beatific Vision, if they had ever heard of it, would rather repel than attract them. They consider too that heaven belongs to them,—one does not exactly understand by what title,—and as they fortunately possess the power to admit all their friends, without whom it might be a little dull and monotonous, it is natural that they should be generous, and to borrow a phrase of this world, "keep open house." Perhaps, they sometimes abuse the privilege. I have heard since I came here of a book, which I have not seen, but which is described, by those who have, as a meritorious attempt to be witty, without the smallest success. It is called, I am told, "the Comedy of Canonization." I can say nothing about its contents, of which I am wholly ignorant, but I very much approve its title. It *is* a transparent Comedy, that people who belong to the same school as the writer of this book, and who disdain the slow and cautious judicial proceedings of the Roman courts, should canonize all *their* friends, whatever may have been the nature of their life or opinions, and without a syllable of enquiry, as soon as the breath is out of their bodies. I agree with the Baltimore clergyman that this *is* a very comic proceeding indeed, only I am not quite sure that these jubilant decrees of canonization pronounced in the Temple of Chaos are always ratified in the

Temple of God. But we are forgetting our preacher, who by this time has almost got to the end of his sermon. I confess to a suspicion, begotten in my mind while listening to him, that the only rapturous feeling with which *he* anticipates Paradise, is inspired by the delightful expectation that he will there find a congregation who will never go to sleep, and to whom he may preach for all eternity. This, I suspect, is his private notion of celestial bliss. Let us hope, for the sake of his congregation, that he will be disappointed. It is dreary enough, judging by this specimen, to listen to one such sermon: who can conceive a more terrible fate than to have to listen to it for ever? An official of the great University of Oxford, once observed to a visitor, to whom he was showing the beauties of that ancient city; "I have heard all the sermons preached in the University pulpit for forty years, and thank God, Sir, I am still able to believe in the truth of christianity." I suppose that most persons whose hard fate it has been to hear such sermons, in which the vanity of one man makes such an exorbitant demand upon the patience of many, would confess that they rarely come to the close of life without a feeling of bitter resentment against those who had inflicted so heavy a trial upon them. I conceive too that if the epitaph of most of the preachers in the Temple of Chaos were composed, not by the heirs of their worldly goods, who can afford to offer them a parting compliment which costs nothing, but by their more dispassionate hearers, it would be apt to resemble that which was suggested for the tomb of a well known architect, who had covered the earth with many a pile, not of words but of bricks, and over whose body it was proposed to inscribe these vindictive lines:

> "Lie heavy on him, Earth, for he
> Laid many a heavy load on thee."

But it is the peculiar misfortune of all the worshipers in the Temple of Chaos that, let the preacher be ever so flat, stale and unprofitable, let his dull conceit impel him to handle subjects ever so far above his comprehension, *they* have no alternative but patience—unless they prefer slumber. One shudders to think of the sufferings inflicted, especially upon innocent women and children, by the insatiable vanity of human preachers, "these earthly god-fathers of heaven's lights," as Shakspeare calls them. The late Sydney Smith, who could say bitter things, as some of you know, about those who offended him, and who said very bitter things indeed about certain people in Pennsylvania, once suggested, I suppose after being irritated by a tedious sermon, that it would be a righteous retribution if the man himself could be " preached to death by wild curates." The famous Canon of St. Paul's must have been very angry when he uttered this intemperate wish, for only the extremest ferocity of malice could desire to condemn a fellow-creature to such a fate. It may be, however, that a better day is in store for these poor sufferers, who begin to find that they have not gained much by putting God out of their temples, and substituting man in his place. Man-worship has proved to be a dreary as well as an unprofitable amusement. Already, murmurs deep and loud are heard. English newspapers and reviews—I do not know how it is in this country—are full of indignant protestations against the prosy incapacity or feeble sensationalism of self-complacent preachers, and perhaps their reign is drawing to a close. I once heard the sorrowful indignation of their victims expressed in such ingenious terms, that I will venture to relate the anecdote to you. " How hard it is," said a Protestant, whom I knew and loved, " that we can never go to Church without being forced to listen to a bad essay, in which there is nothing amusing except the vanity of the preacher." " Every age," responded another, whose name is known to you if I were at liberty to mention it, "has its own peculiar trials. Thus, the primitive Christians suffered martyrdom, and *we* suffer—sermons." I am happy to add that both these gentlemen have since become Catholics, and are now acquainted with an order of preachers who speak only of divine things, and who are too much absorbed in striving to promote the glory of God, to have much leisure to think about their own.

And now, ladies and gentlemen, as we shall certainly gain nothing by prolonging our visit, we will quit the Temple of Chaos. I know not whether you have remarked it, but to me it seems there is a smell of earth in it which after a few minutes becomes overpowering. However long we staid there, we should find always the same dismal entertainment—a man talking to men. That is the beginning and end of it. The human can only beget the human. Let us go out into the pure air, where we can breathe more freely, and where we can make certain reflections which our visit suggests. But before we do so, let us enter for a moment that other temple with which we are more familiar, and where a different scene awaits us.

Do not fear that I am going to describe to you what you all know so well. I will ask you to notice only a single point of contrast in the two buildings. In the one which we have just quitted, man is the sole object of attraction; in that which we now enter, man is nothing, and God everything. There are indeed human ministers in this temple also, to whom we give our love, our gratitude, and our respect, and none know better than you how well they deserve them ; but they will be the first to approve my words when I say, that it is not *their* presence which attracts us. We go as gladly, drawn by the same irresistible power, when they are absent, as when they are present. I will not say we can do without them, which would be senseless ingratitude, for they are "the stewards of the mysteries of God," and have been endowed with special gifts for our sake; but this I will say, and you will confirm it, that even when they stand before the altar, neither do they think of us, nor we of them, except to recommend each other to the same Master, whose Presence makes both them and us forget every other. This is the essential difference between the two temples, of which, the one is all human, the other all Divine. It has often been admitted, at least in part, even by those who could discern the contrast without deriving any lesson from it. The present Duke of Argyle, who is a sort of Presbyterian, has confessed, in one of his writings, probably because he thought it useless to deny it, that within the precincts of the Temple of Chaos, man is everything, and that people only go to church for the sake of the preacher. I will only add that the two modes of worship display in every other detail all the difference which might be expected between what is human and what is Divine. Consider if this be not so. There is in the whole Book of Revelation only one description of the worship in heaven. What is it? It is such an exact description of the worship which you may see any day in any Catholic Church of this city, that only inveterate and judicial blindness can hinder men from seeing that the one is a mirror in which the other is reflected. See how exactly the rites correspond. In heaven, we are told, by one who saw what he describes, there is an "altar," and upon the altar "a lamb that was slain," and on their knees before this altar worshipping spirits, who offer "incense" from "golden censers," and make intercession for their brethren on earth. That is St. John's description. Who does not see that nothing which is done on earth resembles it except the Holy Mass? You know, on the other hand, what sort of worship they offer in the Temple of Chaos. We looked in just now for a moment to see it. There was a man talking, but there was neither altar, nor victim, nor silent adorers, nor golden censers, nor the sweet perfume of incense, nor the intercession of saints. There was literally *nothing* of what the apostle describes. Compare this naked human scene, repulsive in its earthliness, with what takes place in the Sanctuary which *you* frequent, and say, which seems to you the truest resemblance of the worship which St. John saw in heaven?

If, then, in considering the question whether God and His attributes are most clearly reflected in the Temple of Chaos or in the Catholic Church, we limit our enquiry to the two buildings, and to what goes on within them, the decision cannot be doubtful. We may even say, that if it were possible to regard the skeleton ritual of the human sects — in which the only pretence of *unity* consists in a common resolve to suppress the truth, the only attempt at *variety* in the multitude of errors substituted for it — as a counterpart, however remote, of heaven, men would no longer expect the future life with eager desire, but with unutterable dismay. No one, in truth, not even, I suppose, our Protestant friends, would desire to dwell in *such* a heaven. The angels would abandon it with horror. Yet there is not one of *you* who does not know, by a most blissful experience, that the worship in every *Catholic* church is a true and real reflection of that which is offered round the throne of God; that the joy with which it inspires you is the same in kind, though not in degree, as that which you will hereafter derive from the Beatific Vision; and finally, that it is no exaggeration, but the simple truth, to say, that whenever you assist at the sublime mystery of the Christian altar, in which God offers Himself to God,* and take part in that august worship which alone is equal in worth and majesty to Him who is worshipped; for *you* the true life of Paradise has already begun, and *you* can aspire to the joy which God has prepared for you in the Church in heaven, because you have already tasted that kindred joy which He gives you in the Church on earth.

Thus far we have noticed only a single point of the contrast between the kingdoms of Order and of Chaos. We have insisted, not without reason, that a religion which reflects nothing in heaven can only be the product of earth—unless you trace its origin to a still lower region. We may now advance a step in our argument, and proceed to prove, if indeed it needs to be proved, that a religious system which is the most complete negation to be found among men of all the prime attributes of God, and especially of the Divine *Order* and *Unity*, cannot have God for its author, because God cannot contradict Himself.

I suppose I may venture to assert, without fear of contradiction from any quarter, that if there is anything absolutely repugnant to the nature of God, it is Confusion and Disorder. Sin itself is not more abhorrent to Him than the Disorder which is but the fruit and evidence of sin. Examine the material creation, and find, if you can, a single department of it which is not under the inexorable reign of *Law*. From the stately march of the planets in their orbit to the insect in the narrow home in which every want of its ephe-

---

* *Ipse offerens, Ipse et oblatio.*—St. Augustine.

moral life is provided, in every corner of the Universe, and in every form of matter, animate or inanimate, Law and Order assert their despotic and uncontested dominion. Even the king of poets understates the truth, when he says:

"There is nothing, situate under heaven's eye,
But hath his bound, in earth, and sea, and sky."

I am not going to weary you with many examples, but you will permit me to notice one or two, which will render any further illustration of this point superfluous. If you find, as you certainly will, that even where Order is least apparent — nay, that even in the very phenomena which seem to be the direct result of its absence — an energetic and invariable law is actively working; you will feel that this part of our case is superabundantly proved. I will give you only three examples, to which I solicit your patient attention,— one in the far-off regions of space, one on the earth, and one in the clouds which are its curtain and canopy.

1. When the great Kepler strove to penetrate the mystery of our planetary system, and to correct the astronomical errors of the Egyptian Ptolemy, he was startled by this discovery. He found that the various planets which revolve in that system appeared, at a first glance, to have been formed and projected into space, without order or method. They all varied in dimension, in density, in velocity, and in their distance from the sun. In the smaller planets, or asteroids, as Vesta and Pallas, a man could spring into the air sixty feet, and return to the ground without a shock; while in other planets his own weight would crush him to atoms, so great is the force of attraction. In a word, they differed in every point, and seemed to have no mutual relation. Here, then, was a singular apparent

absence of law and order. When Kepler saw this, inspired partly by his genius and partly by a profound religious sentiment, he said to himself: "That is not so! There *is* a law, if I could only find it, for God is never at variance with Himself." And then, after many a patient toil and vigil, he made that splendid discovery which astronomers call the Third Law of Kepler. Not only did he find a law even in this apparent confusion, but a law which could be expressed with mathematical precision, which bound together in a magnificent symmetry every planet in our system, and which disclosed to him and to us this truth—that the squares of their periodic times are proportioned to the cubes of their mean distances from the sun. It was then that the illustrious student, full of gratitude to Him from whom all knowledge comes, cried out, with a rapture which was more religious than scientific: "I have stolen the golden vases of the Egyptians, to build up a tabernacle for my God."

2. The second example which I will briefly notice is not less remarkable. The late Alexander Von Humboldt, who probably possessed as much human and as little divine knowledge as any man who ever lived, used to say that if the philosophers of an earlier generation had carefully observed the phenomena of terrestial magnetism, discoveries of the most momentous kind might have rewarded their labour. He probably did not know that, more than a century before any one else had paid much attention to the subject, the missionaries of the Society of Jesus, as great in human as in divine science, had been in the habit of constantly registering during their innumerable apostolic journeys, the variations of the magnetic currents. All honor to this noble Society, to which we all owe so much. But what I wish you to notice is a fact which later investigations

in this science have revealed, that even the most apparently eccentric movements of that subtle and mysterious agent to which I am alluding, and which heretofore were supposed to be due to purely accidental causes, are now known to be the result of an invariable *law;* so that in this department of creation also, and generally even in what are called the "disturbing forces" of nature, the idea of confusion is finally eliminated, and we learn once more that, in all the works of God, from the least to the greatest, when you rashly deem that you are face to face with Chaos, one ray of light dispels the mists which produced the deception, and Order stands unveiled before your astonished gaze.

3. One more illustration, and then I will endeavor to complete my argument, and release you from the attention which I am so little able to recompense. If there be anything in nature, anything of which man's senses can take cognizance, which appears to belong undeniably to the realm of Chaos, it is surely the tempest, which, on sea or land, bears ruin on its wings, leaves ruin in its track, and seems to have the same relation to Order, which Madness has to Reason. But we have learned by this time to distrust appearances, especially when we are talking about the works of the Creator. And what is the fact? Your own Maury has shown in this country, and Colonel Reid in England, that even the hurricane and the cyclone, in all their might and fury, are as docile to the reign of *law* as the humblest machine constructed by human ingenuity is submissive to the hand that made it, and the English writer referred to has actually given to his book this significant title, "The *Law* of Storms."

And now to apply these facts, and show how they bear upon our argument. You are asked to believe, by those who prefer the Temple of Chaos to the Sanctuary of God, this monstrous proposition; — that although Disorder is inexorably banished, as we have seen, from every other part of His dominions, as a thing abhorrent to the Divine Architect, it finds its true home and congenial refuge precisely in that spiritual kingdom of which He is at once the Law Giver and the Life. Brute matter knows nothing of it; earth, and sea, and sky, refuse to give it a place; the very beasts of the field obey a law which regulates all the conditions of their existence; but Confusion and Chaos, which can find a home nowhere else, reign, and ought to reign, in the Christian Church, and in the kingdom of souls! That is the proposition which is deliberately maintained, at this hour, and in this land, by men whose profession it is to teach others eternal truth. They gravely assert that Religion—which, when it is Divine, is a bond of union stronger than adamant, and when it is human, is the most active dissolvent, the most powerful disintegrating agent which divides and devastates modern society—*gains* by ceasing to be one, and that Christianity derives its chief vitality from the very divisions which make it contemptible in the sight of unbelievers, and have often provoked the scorn and derision even of the pagan world. As this statement may seem to you impossible, even in this nineteenth century, which is tolerant of all absurdities in the sphere of religion, I will quote to you the very words of one of the most conspicuous preachers of this land, who holds a high position in the Hierarchy of Chaos. I take them from one of your own local journals, of the second of this month, (June.) You know that of late years many Protestants, weary of their ceaseless conflicts and ashamed of their unending divisions, have begun at last to sigh for the unity which they have lost, and that in England they have even formed a society, with the express object of bringing together what they ignorantly call "the different branches of the Church." We are told, however, by the journal to which I allude, that the Reverend Henry Ward Beecher, vehemently rejecting every such project, lately "preached against the schemes of church union, whether planned by Pope, Protestant, or Pagan,"—pray understand that these are not my words,—and added this characteristic dissuasive from unity. "The strength of the Christian religion lies," he said,—in what do you suppose? in its truth, its holiness, or its peace? no, but—"*in the number of the existing denominations.*" The hands fall down in reading such words. "I pray," said He who will judge the world, "that they may all be *one*, as Thou, Father, art in Me, and I in Thee." I sincerely trust, replies Mr. Beecher, that they never will be one. "Be perfect," said St. Paul, "in the *same mind* and the *same judgment.*" It is much more important, rejoins Mr. Beecher, that you should maintain your divisions and perpetuate your differences, for in *them* lies the strength of Christianity. "Sects," observed the same Apostle, "are the work of the flesh." Mr. Beecher judges them more leniently, and warns his hearers, as you see, against the mistake of St. Paul. Yes, these human teachers have come at last to this. They know so well that supernatural Unity is beyond *their* reach, that they have come to hate it, and to call it an evil! Yet even they will not deny that it was the Unity of the first Christians which conquered the heathen world; and when the victory was accomplished, and the surviving pagans had only strength enough left to beat themselves against the ground where they had fallen, *they* also cried out in their impotent rage: "*Execranda est ista consensio*—cursed be this Unity of the Christians."

They had found it to be invincible, but did not know that it was Divine. Mr. Beecher dares not say openly, "Cursed be the Unity for which Christ prayed," for even his disciples, though they can bear a good deal, could not bear *that;* but he is not afraid to say: "Blessed be Chaos!" "Confusion, thou art my choice!" "Disorder, be thou mine inheritance!" Let us wish him a happier lot, both in this world and the next.

The truth is that our separated friends do not and cannot understand the sacred mystery of Unity, because they are so exclusively occupied about man, that the secrets of God are hidden from them. What is Unity? It is in essence purely Divine, and in its perfection exists only in the Adorable and Incomprehensible Trinity. But for this very reason, whenever you find Unity in created things, you may be sure that you are looking upon an image and reflection of God. Now there is in this world one society, and one only, in which that Unity has never been interrupted. That society is at once the most numerous and the most ancient of all Christian communities. It is found in all Kingdoms and States, it reaches from pole to pole, and embraces all orders and degrees of men. Yet, in spite of the infinite diversity of their character and temperament, of their education, modes of thought, habits of life, sympathies, prejudicies, language, and of whatsoever else distinguishes man from man; this vast multitude, speaking all the dialects of the world, and differing from each other, often with unnecessary vehemence, about all else, are as indissolubly *one* in all which relates to supernatural truth,—to God, their own souls, and the relations between them,—as if they had only one heart and one mind. And they are *one*, not only in faith, but even in discipline and government. In the whole history of the human race there is no record of any such miracle as this. If all the dead should come to life again at the same hour, and crowd our streets and thoroughfares, it would not be a greater. The men of this generation, like the Jews of old, "*desire a sign*," in order that they may believe. Here is one more luminous than the noonday sun. The lightning does not shine out of heaven with a more dazzling brightness. The essential character of God is *Unity*, and whatever professes to belong to Him, whether in the kingdom of nature or of grace, must reflect that Unity. If it does not, it is not His work. Now, not only do the sects know nothing of it, but their very existence is a perpetual protest against it. Yet in the Church, though her children are, by nature, frail and mutable, like all the children of Adam, there is a Unity and a Repose like the Unity and the Repose of God. Who has wrought this marvel? Consider over what an array of countless impossibilities this miraculous Unity of the Church has triumphed. The supple Italian, keen of wit and of ardent imagination; the stolid Englishman, who moves slowly to attain his ends, but only to pursue them with a more unwearied tenacity; the brilliant Frenchman, who unites restless vivacity with exquisite common sense, and is not more fertile in inventing paradox than merciless in exposing it; the thoughtful German, who numbers all the truths in his possession like objects in a museum, and knows exactly the place which he has assigned to each; the stately Spaniard, who is almost oriental in his immobility, and in whom we discern a gravity of mind which gives even to the mendicant the dignity of a king; the impulsive Irishman, who has more wit than the English, more enthusiasm than the German, and, wherever he finds fair play and just laws, more industry than either of them; the acute American, whose boast it is that no difficulty can baffle his enterprise nor any counterfeit escape his detection; all these, and twenty other races whom I do not stay to enumerate, contrasting violently with each other in every natural gift and habit, while retaining all their distinctive peculiarities as men and citizens, become absolutely *one*, as if all fashioned in the same mould, and moved by the same spirit, as Christians and Catholics. And this astonishing unity of elements so various and contradictory is perpetuated from age to age, in a world where all else is in a state of chronic flux and solution, silently, peacefully, without effort, and without constraint. Nay, so irresistible is the mysterious power which works this miracle, that even the convert of yesterday, whether in the centres of European civilization or amid the semi-barbarous populations of China or Hindostan, though admitted but a few hours ago into the family of God, has already the sweet spell upon him, and finds, to his own exceeding astonishment, that his heart beats in unison with the great heart of the Church, as if he had been suckled at her breasts, and had lain in her bosom from infancy.

On the other hand, in the human communities which owe their existence to earthly founders, though there is much virtue, much acuteness, much learning, it has ever been found impossible to keep even the members of the same sect — I will not say in one country, or in one town, or in one village, but alas! in one family —from perpetual disputes even about the sublimest truths of revealed religion. Never since the Fall has the enemy, whose mission it is to scatter and divide, obtained so great a triumph over any portion of our race—a triumph so complete, that even the same individual at different epochs of his life, is often in flagrant contradiction with himself, avows to-day opinions which yesterday he abhorred, and which to-morrow he will exchange once more for new ones, and after belonging successively to various religious denominations, frequently ends by professing equal contempt for them all. And thus it has come to pass that in the world of Chaos,—in that dismal region which lies outside the Church of God,—two modes of thought now prevail to the gradual exclusion of all others: the first, that truth is what every man thinks it to be; the second, which is the logical equivalent of the first, that truth has no existence.

In presence of this immense contrast, which the least observant of mankind can detect, between the indefectible unity of the Church and the hopeless disorder of the sects, the members of the latter have felt the urgent necessity of attempting some explanation. They have comprehended, in spite of the inactivity of their spiritual apprehension, that since Unity is an infallible indication of the presence of God, *because God alone can produce it*, it follows that it is only in the Catholic Church that He resides. The conclusion is peremptory, and they feel it to be so. For this reason, while some have ventured in their anger to revile Unity, which is to blaspheme God, and to sing the praises of Disorder, which is to chant a hymn to Satan; others have sought to *account* for the Unity which they despair of attaining on purely human grounds. It is, they say, the subtle organization, the persevering arts, and the inexplicable skill of the Roman Church which binds all her members together with that adamantine chain which neither the world nor the devil can break asunder. They do not seem to perceive that the answer is suicidal, like that which the serpent makes when he turns his fangs against himself, and dies of his own sting. Catholic Unity the result of human art! Why the same men tell us every day, with the touching humility and self-abasement which, as you know, is the chief characteristic of Protestantism, that sagacity, enlightenment, penetration, knowledge of the human heart, skilful diagnosis, and generally every mental and spiritual pre-eminence, are their own peculiar heritage; while *we* are so slenderly equipped with both moral and intellectual gifts, that our continued success in attracting the pure, the wise, and the learned of all ages and countries is the most incomprehensible of the triumphs of the Catholic Church. If, then, Catholic Unity be the result of *human* art, will these spiritual and intellectual giants tell us how it is that *they* are totally unable to imitate it? What! so much more ingenious and spiritual than we are, and yet always ignominiously baffled in doing what the Church always accomplishes without effort? There is evidently nothing serious in such an explanation as this. It means nothing, and was not intended to mean anything. What, then, is this Power which is given to us, and denied to them? If it be human, let them define and localize it. But this they will never do. They cannot say *where* nor *what* it is, because its source is concealed in a far-off region to which *they* have no access. The earth says, It is not in me. The sea murmurs, It is not in me. Hell confesses, It is not in me. If, then, by the testimony of all mankind, there is one Power, and one only, which works this miracle, and unites all hearts in a mysterious and supernatural unity, in spite of human frailty and caprice, and if that Power can be found neither on the earth nor under the earth, where shall we look for it but in heaven?

We are sometimes told that good men abide contentedly in some earthly sect because, in spite of honest intentions, they are really unable to recognize the true

Church. It may be so, though such involuntary ignorance seems to us only a bare possibility. For if St. Paul could say, as he did, to the heathen world, "you might have found out the true God by His *works*, if you had cared to do so;" surely the God of St. Paul may say to the children of Chaos in the great Day, "you might have known the true Church by her *Unity*, if you had not closed your eyes."

Without presuming to anticipate the judgments of God, which we have neither the power nor the inclination to do, there is one conclusion which even we mortals can draw, without the risk of error, from the considerations which I have now submitted to you. We have seen that in the kingdom of souls, as in the kingdom of matter, it is the will of the Most High that His own essential Unity should be reflected. It follows, that religious sects, which are the perpetual negation of that Unity, can only be agreeable to Him on this supposition,— either that He has changed His nature, or that, having failed to suppress what is in irreconcileable opposition with Himself, He ceased to take any further interest in the affairs of men, and consented, as far as they were concerned, that Order should be replaced by Chaos.

It is to be noted of the argument which I have just employed, that while the most powerful intellect can suggest no reply to it, a little child can use it with full appreciation of its force. Permit me to give you a proof of this.

Some years ago, I was present officially at the examination of an English primary school, in which the children displayed such unusual accuracy and intelligence as long as the questions turned only upon secular subjects, that I was anxious to ascertain whether they could reason as well about the truths of the Catechism, as they could about those of Grammar and Arithmetic. I communicated my desire to their clergyman, who kindly permitted me to have recourse to a test which I had employed on other occasions. I requested him to interrogate them on the Notes of the Church, and when they had explained in the usual manner the meaning of the word Catholic, I took up the examination, with the consent of the Priest, and addressed the following question to the class: "You say the Church is Catholic because she is everywhere. Now, I have visited many countries, in all parts of the world, and I never came to one in which I did not find heresy. If, then, the Church is Catholic because she is everywhere, why is not heresy Catholic, since heresy is everywhere also?" "If you please, sir," answered a little girl about twelve years of age, "the Church is everywhere, and everywhere the *same;* heresy may be everywhere too, as you say, but it is everywhere *different.*"

I related this incident not long after, as a proof that faith is an intellectual power, to one of the greatest lawyers in England, a man accustomed to appraise all the products of the human intellect. He declared to me his opinion that it was the most astonishing answer ever made by a child. He was wrong. I have myself heard similar answers a hundred times. And you, Ladies and Gentlemen, will certainly not share the surprise of this eminent lawyer, because you know that a little Catholic child, who has learned the Catechism, and nothing else, is a truer and deeper philosopher, in the sight of God and the angels, than all the Pagan sages of the past, or all the Protestant doctors of the present.

As I have strayed once more into the region of anecdote, perhaps you will allow me to linger there for a moment. It may relieve the tediousness of a discussion which I fear has exhausted your patience, if I add two or three which will be found to possess at least this merit, that they all confirm, in various ways, the argument which I have had the honour to address to you this evening.

A young English lady, with whom I became subsequently acquainted, and from whose lips I heard the tale, informed her parents that she felt constrained to embrace the Catholic faith. Hereupon arose much agitation in the parental councils, and a reluctant promise was extorted from the daughter that she would not communicate with any Catholic priest till she had first listened to the convincing arguments with which certain clerical friends of the family would easily dissipate her unreasonable doubts. These ministers were three in number, and we will call them Messrs. A, B, and C. The appointed day arrived for the solemn discussion, which one of the ministers was about to commence, when the young lady opened it abruptly with the following remark: "I am too young and uninstructed to dispute with gentlemen of your age and experience, but perhaps you will allow me to ask you a few questions?" Anticipating an easy triumph over the poor girl, the three ministers acceded with encouraging smiles to her request. "Then I will ask you," she said to Mr. A., "whether regeneration always accompanies the Sacrament of Baptism?" "Undoubtedly," was the prompt reply, "that is the plain doctrine of our Church." "And you, Mr. B.," she continued, "Do you teach that doctrine?" "God forbid, my young friend," was his indignant answer, "that I should teach such soul-destroying error. Baptism is a formal rite, which," &c., &c. "And you, Mr. C.," she asked the third, "what is your opinion?" "I regret," he replied with a bland voice, for he began to suspect they were making a mess of it, "that my reverend friends should have expressed themselves a little incautiously. The true doctrine lies between these extremes"—and he was going to develop it, when the young lady, rising from her chair, said: "I thank you, gentlemen, you have taught me all that I expected to learn from you. You are all ministers of the same Church, yet you each contradict the other even upon a doctrine which St. Paul calls one of the *foundations* of Christianity. You have only confirmed me in my resolution to enter a Church whose ministers all teach the same thing." And then they went out of the room one by one, and probably continued their battle in the street. But the parents of the young lady turned her out of doors the next day, to get her bread as she could. They sometimes do that sort of thing in England.

Another friend of mine, also a lady, and one of the most intelligent of her sex, was for several years the disciple of the distinguished minister who has given a name to a certain religious school in England. Becoming disaffected towards the Episcopalian Church, which appeared to her more redolent of earth in proportion as she aspired more ardently towards heaven, she was persuaded to assist at a certain Ritualistic festival, which it was hoped would have a soothing effect upon her mind. A new church was to be opened, and the ceremonies were to be prolonged through an entire week. All the Ritualistic celebrities of the day were expected to be present. Her lodging was judiciously provided in a house in which were five of the most transcendental members of the High Church party. It was hoped that they would speedily convince her of their apostolic unity, but unfortunately, they only succeeded in proving to her that no two of them were of the same mind. One recommended her privately to pray to the Blessed Virgin, which another condemned as, at best, a poetical superstition. One told her that the Pope was by Divine appointment the head of the Universal Church; another, that he was a usurper and a schismatic. One maintained that the "Reformers" were profane scoundrels and apostates; another, that they had at all events good intentions. But I need not trouble you with an account of their various creeds. Painfully affected by this diversity, where she had been taught to expect complete uniformity, her doubts were naturally confirmed. During the week she was invited to take a walk with the eminent person whom she had hitherto regarded as a trustworthy teacher. To him she revealed her growing disquietude, and presumed to lament the conflict of opinions which she had lately witnessed, but only to be rewarded by a stern rebuke; for it is a singular fact that men who are prepared at any moment to judge all the Saints and Doctors, will not tolerate any judgment which reflects upon themselves. It was midwinter, and the lady's companion, pointing to the leafless trees by the roadside, said, with appropriate solemnity of voice and manner: "They are stripped of their foliage now, but wait for the spring, and you will see them once more wake to life. So shall it be with the Church of England, which now seems to you dead." "It may be so," she replied, "but what sort of a spring can we expect, *after a winter which has lasted three hundred years?*" You will not be surprised to hear that this lady soon after became a member of a Church which knows nothing of winter, but within whose peaceful borders reigns eternal spring.

My next anecdote, you will be glad to hear that it is the last, shall be borrowed from your own country. A few weeks ago, the heads of one of the largest religious denominations of this land assembled in council. Their body had been split into two sections, and they desired to heal the schism. "It is *impossible* to do so," observed one of them, who appears to have had some dim conception of the nature of Christian truth, "for we differ on the gravest points of doctrine." But the majority promptly overruled this trivial objection. What was mere unity of doctrine compared with the advantage of presenting an apparently united front to the public eye? And so the objectors were silenced, as such objectors generally are in the Temple of Chaos. One gentleman, a Doctor of Divinity,—of what sort of Divinity you will see in a moment,—clenched the whole matter with this decisive argument: "We do not differ," he said, "about doctrine, but only about the philosophy of doctrine." From which ingenious distinction you clearly perceive, that when one man teaches the Atonement, and another denies it; or, when one believes in the Incarnation, and the other rejects it; they still remain in perfect harmony as Christians, and merely differ a little in opinion as philosophers. It is possible, according to this remarkable theory, to err to any extent in philosophy, but not possible to err at all in religion. One would have been glad to ask this Doctor of Divinity, since that is his title, just for the sake of information, how a false philosophy can possibly be a true religion? But it is probable that he would have declined to answer the question. A celebrated person once said: "O Liberty, how many crimes are committed in thy name." Perhaps, we may say in our turn: "O Philosophy, how much nonsense is talked in thine."

I have detained you too long, though I have said but little, and said that little imperfectly. Yet we have seen, perhaps with sufficient evidence, this essential distinction between the kingdoms of Order and Chaos, between the Church and the Sects; that in the one everything reflects the presence and the attributes of God, while in the other, man has usurped His place, and reigns alone, surrounded by all the customary emblems of human feebleness, vanity, and imperfection. I must not conclude without calling your attention to this correlative fact, that in the Church, which is God's realm, effectual provision has been made for the remedy of all transient disorders, and the prompt repair of all waste and loss; while in the Sects, where man is the sole lord, and must do his own work because there is none to help him, no sign of any such provision exists. This also is just the distinction which we might have expected to find between what is human and what is Divine.

Every student of nature has noted with admiration the astonishing *faculty of recuperation* which it displays in all its departments. The same phenomenon exists in the kingdom of grace. In both a machinery has been created, and is constantly in active operation, by which wounded and enfeebled organisms are able to attain a new vitality. I ask your permission to dwell for an instant on this analogy. It was worthy of our God so to arrange the order of the universe, and assure its stability, that no fatal shock, no irreparable disaster, should be permitted to disturb its equilibrium. The sun may not quit its allotted place, nor the planets wander from their appointed sphere. In like manner, though her habitual lot is trial and suffering, the Church remains for ever unmoved on her eternal foundations. But if God has thus limited the field beyond which no serious derangement of His work shall be allowed, either in the world of nature or of grace, till the end of time, His Providence has not excluded the possibility of disorders on a smaller scale. Yet even in tolerating these apparent defects, He only gives a new proof of His omnipotence. Both in the material and the spiritual creation, there resides a marvellous power of correcting momentary disorders, of applying a remedy to transient corruptions. With respect to the first, you know that there is no more elementary truth in physics than that life is actually begotten of death. You see this every day in the vegetable world, and even in the animal economy, you are not ignorant by what process the daily waste of tissues and other parts is incessantly supplied, and that even the most formidable ravages of disease in the human frame can be repaired by that astonishing growth of matter which is called the granulation of new flesh. I wish you to observe, without attempting to multiply such examples, that these phenomena of reproduction, which you notice with so much admiration in the kingdom of matter, are incomparably more beautiful and surprising in the kingdom of grace, and that they exist, as I said, only in the Catholic Church.

In the kingdom of souls there are two possible evils, — corruption of doctrine, and corruption of morals. For both, God has provided remedies so divinely efficacious, that nothing which occurs in the material universe can be fitly compared with them, except by way of analogy. Thus, in the sphere of morals, there resides in the Church a power of healing so mighty, that only the direct co-operation of God can explain its action. No depravity, however inveterate, can resist it. I need only remind you that St. Mary Magdalen and St. Mary of Egypt, are both canonized Saints, whom the Church has raised upon her altars as models of humanity. Tens of thousands since their day, who have fallen as they fell, have been *created anew* as they were, by the omnipotence of the same remedial Sacraments. It would not become me to attempt to describe them. Such a theme is too high for me. I leave it to those who speak with consecrated lips. But I ask, and you have already anticipated the question, what similar provision for sick souls exists outside the Church of God?

My personal experience, as one whose misfortune it was to be during seven years a teacher in the Temple of Chaos, compels me to affirm that there is *none*. According to my observation, the common case of those who sin mortally outside the Church is this, that when the hour of awakening arrives,—for many it never comes at all, or only comes too late,—they either embrace some new heresy still more monstrous than any which they had previously professed, or fall into deadly presumption. I remember being called, during the melancholy period of my life to which I have alluded, to the death-bed of a woman in whom it was impossible to detect a single feature of the Christian character. Yet she replied to my exhortation, with the sneer of pride on her dying lips: "You need not trouble yourself about me, Sir, I was saved long ago." In this case, as in many like it, I was reminded of the malediction pronounced upon those "whose last state is worse than the first." Nor was it more consoling to witness other deaths, in which counterfeit rites and spurious sacraments strove to hide the mortal wound of the soul without being able to heal it, and copied the external forms of the Christian ritual only to disguise the ruin which they were powerless to avert. But I pass from this sorrowful subject to the corruption of doctrine.

To record all that the Church has done from the beginning to preserve the faith from corruption would be to write her history. You know how in every age, she alone has baffled all the arts of the wicked one, and preserved the deposit entrusted to her keeping. I will not remind you of her victories over every heresy in ages gone by, but will ask you to notice only a single example in our own time. It will amply suffice as an illustration of the point which we are considering. It so happens that during the present generation four of the most eminent of her priests, conspicuous by the splendour of their intellectual gifts, have merited the admonition or provoked the censures of the Church. We need not hesitate to recall the fact, for it will be found only to add new lustre to her imperishable glory. De Lamennais and Gioberti, Rosmini and Ventura,— of whom the two last have been imitators of the lowly Fénelon, the two first of the arrogant Tertullian,—are examples in our own day of the ceaseless vigilance of the successors of St. Peter, in rebuking and destroying error. The two first resisted him, and withered away like a tree blasted by lightning; the two last obeyed his paternal remonstrance, and by their humility acquired fresh titles to the love and respects of Christians, to whom they have bequeathed so excellent an example. Such is the sleepless fidelity of God's Vicar, and such are the fruits of his Divine mission to preserve the children entrusted to him in the purity and simplicity of our most holy faith. Before his presence error hides her face, and the spirits of darkness, despairing of success, return to the abyss from which they came out.

And how is it with the Sects? Far from warring against religious error, they exist only to maintain and defend its sovereign rights! They claim to *believe* whatever their own diseased imagination may persuade them to accept, and to *teach* whatever the "itching ears" of others may induce them to hear. What is feebly repudiated by one sect is cordially welcomed by another, and even in the same sect every conflicting interpretation of revealed truth has exactly the same title to respect, because it has its origin in the same right of private judgment, and appeals to the same personal infallibility in those to whom it is addressed. The Church of England, the most powerful of all Protestant communities, by reason of her vast endowments and connection with the State, differs from the other sects mainly in this, that within her fold are taught at the same time *all* the errors maintained in every other, in addition to those which have been invented by herself. And they are all taught with equal authority, and with the same absolute immunity from remonstrance or correction. How should one man remonstrate with another for doing what he claims the right to do himself, or correct in his neighbour the aberrations which he may adopt as his own whenever he feels inclined to do so? And thus the eternal confusion of the Kingdom of Chaos is renewed from generation to generation, as one wave follows another in a stormy and tumultuous sea, and while the Church reflects in every age the unbroken Unity of God, the Sects represent only the strife and disorder which is the eternal portion of the fallen spirits in their own home, and which they have succeeded too well in introducing into ours, wherever they are not confronted by those invincible allies, the Mother of God and the Vicar of Christ.

It is a satisfaction to me, and will be at least an equal satisfaction to you, that I have now arrived at the last point upon which I think it necessary to trouble you with a few words. We have compared the Temples of Order and Chaos, as carefully as the time at our disposal permitted, in some of their most conspicuous features. It remains only to determine, as far as we have the means of doing so, what will be the relative position of the worshippers in each, when both temples shall have ceased to exist in their present form. Without this final enquiry, all that we have already said would be incomplete.

With respect to Catholics, it is evident that, in passing from the Church on earth to the Church in heaven, no change need come upon *them*, except that which is implied in passing from the state of grace to the state of glory. They will be *one* there, as they have been one here. For *them* the miracle of supernatural Unity is already worked. That mark of God's Hand is already upon them. That sign of God's election is already graven upon their foreheads. Faith indeed will be replaced by sight, but this will be no real change, because what they *see* in the next world will be what they have *believed* in this. The same *Sacramental King*, to borrow an expression of Father Faber, whom here they have worshipped upon the Altar, will there be their everlasting portion. The same gracious Madonna, who has so often consoled them in the trials of this life, will introduce her own children to the glories of the next. They will not in that hour have to "buy oil" for *their* lamps, for they are already kindled at the lamp of the sanctuary. No wedding-robe will have to be provided for *them*, for they received it long ago at the baptismal font, and have washed away its stains in the tribunal of penance. The faces of the Saints and Angels will not be strange to *them*, for have they not been familiar with them from infancy as friends, companions, and benefactors? And being thus, even in this world, of the household of faith, and the family of God, not only no shadow of change need pass upon *them*, but to vary in one iota from what they now believe and practice would simply cut them off from the Communion of Saints, and be the most overwhelming disaster which could befal them.

It is evident, on the other hand, that if the children of Chaos are to enter heaven,—a lot which we earnestly desire for them,—*they* can only do so after undergoing a radical and fundamental change. This, I say, is evident, for this reason among others, because *they* are *not one*, and nothing is more indisputably certain than this, that there can be no division in heaven. "God is not the God of dissension," says St. Paul, "but of peace," and if He has not suffered any interruption of Unity even in the Church Militant, the most disordered imagination cannot suppose that He will tolerate it in the Church Triumphant. How should disunion exist in the very presence of God? It would not be more monstrous to suppose that sin could sit on His right hand, throned and crowned. It follows, that if the members of the rival sects, which make up in their aggregate the great army of Chaos, are to enter heaven, whatever else they may take in with them, they must leave their differences at the door. Heaven is not a debating society, in which the disputes and contradictions of the children of error are to be eternally perpetuated. They have had *their* reign on earth, but must not expect to continue it in heaven. *There* dwells absolute and eternal Unity, the Unity of the Undivided Godhead, the same Unity which in the Catholic Church has already triumphed even over the frailties of men, and which, as far as *Catholics* are concerned, will only be renewed and perfected in the company of the elect.

If, indeed, it were possible,—and with this observation I conclude,—that the children of the Sects should enter heaven in their present state, each with his own personal creed, his own particular corruption of Christianity, have you ever considered what must be the inevitable result? We are told that there are in heaven, besides Angels and Archangels, Thrones, Dominions, Principalities, and Powers. Imagine, then, if you can, an Episcopalian Archangel leaning over the battlements of heaven in hot dispute with a Methodist Seraph, or an angry Presbyterian Throne flinging texts of Scripture in the face of a Baptist Principality. What a heaven it would be! Who can conceive the consternation of the Angels in having such a company thrust upon them? Farewell, for ever, the peace which they have known from the first hour of their creation. Chaos has mounted up into heaven, and Order unfolds her wings to fly from an abode where she has no longer a home. I do not affirm that no Episcopalian, Methodist, or Presbyterian will enter heaven, but only that before they do so, since God will certainly remain what *He* is, *they* must cease to be what they are, and become something which now they are not. From this dilemma they can escape only by supposing,—and perhaps we shall some day see a new sect of which this will be the distinctive tenet,—that each denomination will have a heaven to itself, and that the inhabitants of one heaven will not be permitted to visit those of another, for fear they should renew in the next world the quarrels which were their chief employment in this. Well, this arrangement has perhaps the merit of simplicity, but it wants something to make it complete. Will the children of Chaos tell us, if they can, in which of these earth-begotten heavens where neither Saint nor Angel would stoop to dwell, will the Holy and Undivided One establish His throne?

www.ingramcontent.com/pod-product-compliance
Lightning Source LLC
Chambersburg PA
CBHW031327230426
43670CB00006B/266